World Food

MALAYSIA & SINGAPORE

Su-Lyn Tan
Mark Tay

WORLD FOOD Malaysia & Singapore
1st edition – February 2003

Published by Lonely Planet Publications Pty Ltd ABN 36 005 607 983

Lonely Planet Offices
Australia Locked Bag 1, Footscray, Victoria 3011
USA 150 Linden Street, Oakland CA 94607
UK 10a Spring Place, London NW5 3BH
France 1 rue du Dahomey, 75011 Paris

Publishing manager Peter D'Onghia
Commissioning editors Martin Heng & Lyndal Hall
Project manager Bridget Blair
Series design & layout Brendan Dempsey
Editors Joanne Newell, Kyla Gillzan, Patrick Witton
Mapping Natasha Velleley
Photography Aun Koh, except images listed on page 276

Photography
Many of the photographs in this book are available for licensing from
Lonely Planet Images: www.lonelyplanetimages.com

Front cover – Mee rubus & mee siam, two very typical Malay dishes, Singapore
Back cover – A waitress at Hua Ting restaurant, Singapore

ISBN 1 74059 370 7

text & maps © Lonely Planet Publications Pty Ltd, 2002
photos © photographers as indicated 2002

Printed by Printed through Colorcraft Ltd, Hong Kong
Printed in China

10 9 8 7 6 5 4 3 2 1

MAP KEY

Place to Eat & Drink	Primary Road	Ruins
Building	Secondary Road	Buddhist Temple
Mall	Tertiary Road	Fort
Plaza Square	Tunnel	Church
Campus	Railway, Station	Hindu Temple
Cemetery	International Border	Mosque
Park, Garden	Regional Border	Museum
Sports Ground	National Capital	Stately Home
Freeway	Regional Capital	Taoist Temple
	Town	Mountain

About the Authors

Main author: Su-Lyn Tan. Su-Lyn started her career as an entertainment writer for *8 Days* magazine, the best-selling weekly English entertainment magazine in Singapore, and soon became the magazine's primary food reviewer, writing weekly restaurant reviews, interviewing chefs and developing food features that would be of interest to a broad-based readership. As a freelance food writer, she has written for *The Asian Wall Street Journal, Travel + Leisure* and *The Four Seasons Hotel Magazine*, among other publications. She has recently taken up a permanent position as Managing Editor at *Wine & Dine* magazine, the best-established food publication in the region. Su-Lyn is also currently putting the final touches to a doctoral thesis examining the celebrity chef phenomenon. Her food obsession of the moment centres on competing at the annual *La Foire aux Fromages* in Livarot where contestants have to eat their way through two Livarot cheeses (each weighing 900g) in under 15 minutes.

Su-Lyn & Aun Koh wish to thank Mr Mohd Hafiz Hashim & Mr Viji of Tourism Malaysia; Christine Khor of the Singapore Tourism Board; Mrs Kee Gim See & Ms Tong Ee Ling, Penang, for welcoming us into their homes, feeding us and introducing us to their friends; Mr Wong Chee Keong & family, Penang, for driving us all the way to Balek Pulau for homemade *belacan,* amazing durian and the best Penang laksa in town; Joann K, Penang; Albert of Zealand Bah Kut Teh & Seafood Restaurant on Gurney Drive, Penang; Shaik Saffarudin of Taj Restaurant, Penang; Sally Ho & friends of Lorong Selamat, Penang; Mr Lai of Kwong Heng Loong, Penang, for sharing his soy sauce brewing techniques; Krishna, our guide in both Kuala Lumpur and Melaka; Jereme Leung for sharing his favourite KL hawker haunts; Ismail HJ Surin & family of Kampung Padang Bacang, Kuala Lumpur, for letting total strangers into their home; Emmanuel Prabakaran of Saloma Theatre Restaurant, Kuala Lumpur; Yusof of Tomyam Corner Seafood, Jalan Raja Muda Musa, Kuala Lumpur; Mohd Azmi Aznal of Nasi Lemak Alor Corner, Kuala Lumpur; Nancy of Nancy's Kitchen, Melaka; Yong Puay Sim, No. 1 Kopitiam, Melaka; Veronica Fong, Chef Chan Kwok & staff of Orchard Hotel, Singapore; Shiela Gomez & team, Raffles Hotel, Singapore; Chef Foo, KopiTiam, Raffles the Plaza, Singapore; Wong Wai Ling, Traders Hotel & the staff of Ah Hoi's Kitchen; Roland Lim, Roland Restaurant, Singapore; Joseph Seah of Hainanese Boneless Chicken Rice, Singapore; Salimah & Afdoli Rahmat, Singapore, for taking us to a Malay wedding; Hamidah Hashim, Samat Hashim & his lovely wife Sarimah for letting us hang out at their very busy stall on a hot Saturday morning; Annette Tan & Joycelyn Shu; the infinitely patient LP team; the folks at RGB Singapore for processing film faster than anyone else in town; and all the super-friendly hawkers who fed us, posed for us and were happy to talk with us during our weeks of rediscovering the food of Malaysia and Singapore.

Language author: Mark Tay. As a graduate of the Singapore Tourism and Education Centre Mark has considerable hands-on experience in the restaurant industry. In addition to articles commissioned for the local *Wine & Dine* magazine and restaurant reviews, Mark has been a regular contributor to the online magazines asiafoodcity.com and hotspots.com, specialising in recipes. With a Peranakan background, Mark speaks five dialects of Chinese and Malay, not to mention French and Japanese!

Mark Tay wishes to thank his wife Patricia for her support and for proofreading the Mandarin section, as well as for her constant hounding to meet deadlines.

Contributor: Rob McKeown. Rob has been writing professionally about food since he was 19 years old...but obsessing over it since birth. He is the Asia correspondent for *Gourmet* and has contributed regularly to publications like *Wallpaper**, *Travel + Leisure* and those of the Slow Food Movement. Though based between Thailand and Laos, his many *makan* addictions – to *bak kut teh, roti, teh tarik,* anything with *ikan bilis* and *nasi padang* – mean he can often be found roaming the Malay peninsula as well.

Rob McKeown would like to acknowledge Chew Hui Chin, Paige Chia, Chef Wan, Mark Lionel, Tan Su-Lyn and Aun Koh, KF Seetoh, Ruth Tobias, and the many other *makan* crazies whose lust for eating is as much an education as it is a party.

About the Photographer

Aun Koh got his first taste of working in the press at 16, training in the art and photo departments of Singapore's *Straits Times*. From there, Aun, a Columbia University graduate, embarked on a career in journalism, working at the *International Herald Tribune* in Paris, *Time Out* and *Newsweek International* in New York, and *Asia Inc* in Hong Kong. Moving back to Singapore in 1997, Aun set up and launched WHERE Singapore for Asia City Publishing. In 1999, he founded *East*, a regional lifestyle magazine. In March 2002, Aun joined Panpac Media.com Ltd, and has been working hard to launch two new lifestyle magazines on the local market, *Twenty4Seven* and *Lookbook*. Although trained in everything from graphic design to editing, his first love is still taking pictures. It is a passion that he hopes to develop further in the future.

UPDATES & READERS FEEDBACK
Things change – prices go up, schedules change, good places go bad and bad places go bankrupt. Nothing stays the same. So, if you find things better or worse, recently opened or long-since closed, please tell us and help make the next edition even more accurate and useful.

Lonely Planet thoroughly updates each guidebook as often as possible – usually every two years, although for some destinations the gap can be longer. Between editions, up-to-date information is available in our free, quarterly Planet Talk newsletter and monthly email bulletin Comet. The Upgrades section of our website (www.lonelyplanet.com) is also regularly updated by Lonely Planet authors, and the site's Scoop section covers news and current affairs relevant to travellers. Lastly, the Thorn Tree bulletin board and Postcards section carry unverified, but fascinating, reports from travellers.

Tell us about it! We genuinely value your feedback. A well-travelled team at Lonely Planet reads and acknowledges every email and letter we receive and ensures that every morsel of information finds its way to the relevant authors, editors and cartographers.

Everyone who writes to us will find their name listed in the next edition of the appropriate guidebook, and will receive the latest issue of Comet or Planet Talk. The very best contributions will be rewarded with a free guidebook.

We may edit, reproduce and incorporate your comments in Lonely Planet products such as guidebooks, websites and digital products, so let us know if you don't want your comments reproduced or your name acknowledged.

How to contact Lonely Planet:
Online: @ talk2us@lonelyplanet.com.au, www.lonelyplanet.com
Australia: Locked Bag 1, Footscray, Victoria 3011
UK: 10a Spring Place, London NW5 3BH
USA: 150 Linden St, Oakland, CA 94607

Contents

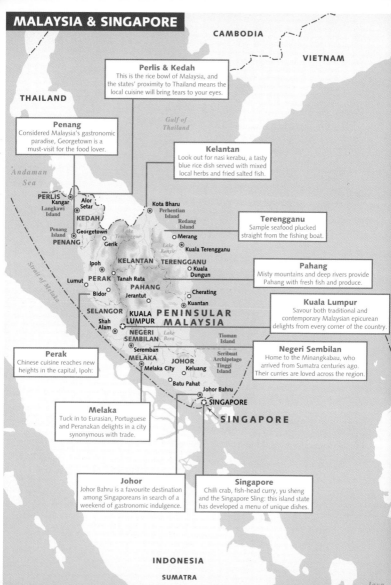

MALAYSIA & SINGAPORE

CAMBODIA

VIETNAM

THAILAND

Perlis & Kedah
This is the rice bowl of Malaysia, and the states' proximity to Thailand means the local cuisine will bring tears to your eyes.

Gulf of Thailand

Penang
Considered Malaysia's gastronomic paradise, Georgetown is a must-visit for the food lover.

Andaman Sea

Kelantan
Look out for nasi kerabu, a tasty blue rice dish served with mixed local herbs and fried salted fish.

PERLIS
Kangar
Alor Setar
Langkawi Island
KEDAH
Kota Bharu
Perhentian Island
Redang Island

Penang Island
Georgetown
PENANG
Gerik

Merang
Kuala Terengganu

Terengganu
Sample seafood plucked straight from the fishing boat.

Lake Kenyir

Ipoh
KELANTAN
TERENGGANU
Kuala Dungun

PERAK
Tanah Rata
PAHANG

Pahang
Misty mountains and deep rivers provide Pahang with fresh fish and produce.

Strait of Melaka

Lumut
Bidor
Jerantut
Cherating
Kuantan

SELANGOR
KUALA LUMPUR
PENINSULAR MALAYSIA

Kuala Lumpur
Savour both traditional and contemporary Malaysian epicurean delights from every corner of the country.

Shah Alam
NEGERI SEMBILAN
Lake Bera
Tioman Island

Perak
Chinese cuisine reaches new heights in the capital, Ipoh.

Seremban
MELAKA
JOHOR
Melaka City
Keluang
Seribuat Archipelago
Tioman Tinggi Island

Negeri Sembilan
Home to the Minangkabau, who arrived from Sumatra centuries ago. Their curries are loved across the region.

Batu Pahat

Melaka
Tuck in to Eurasian, Portuguese and Peranakan delights in a city synonymous with trade.

Johor Bahru
SINGAPORE
SINGAPORE

Johor
Johor Bahru is a favourite destination among Singaporeans in search of a weekend of gastronomic indulgence.

Singapore
Chilli crab, fish-head curry, yu sheng and the Singapore Sling: this island state has developed a menu of unique dishes.

INDONESIA

SUMATRA

Java Sea

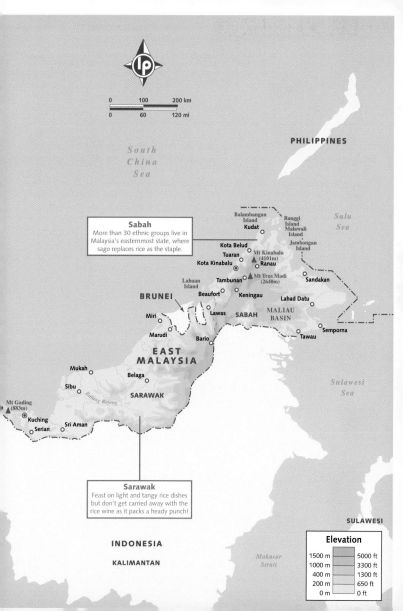

PHILIPPINES

South China Sea

Sulu Sea

Balambangan Island
Banggi Island
Malawali Island
Kudat
Jambongan Island

Sabah
More than 30 ethnic groups live in Malaysia's easternmost state, where sago replaces rice as the staple.

Kota Belud
Tuaran
Mt Kinabalu (4101m)
Kota Kinabalu
Ranau
Sandakan

Labuan Island
Tambunan
Mt Trus Madi (2640m)

BRUNEI
Beaufort
Keningau
Lahad Datu
Lawas
SABAH
MALIAU BASIN

Miri
Bario
Semporna
Tawau

Marudi

EAST MALAYSIA

Mukah
Belaga
Sulawesi Sea

Sibu
Batang Rejang
SARAWAK

Mt Gading (883m)
Kuching
Serian
Sri Aman

Sarawak
Feast on light and tangy rice dishes but don't get carried away with the rice wine as it packs a heady punch!

SULAWESI

INDONESIA

KALIMANTAN

Makasar Strait

Elevation	
1500 m	5000 ft
1000 m	3300 ft
400 m	1300 ft
200 m	650 ft
0 m	0 ft

0 100 200 km
0 60 120 mi

Variety is the spice of life. In Southeast Asia, and particularly in Malaysia and Singapore, that claim certainly rings true. Here a simple staple like rice is transformed from **bubur** (rice porridge) to **nasi lemak** (coconut rice), from **ketupat** (compressed rice) to **tuak** (rice wine). With opportunities to eat or drink around every corner, you'll never go hungry in Malaysia and Singapore, but it pays to keep yourself a little hungry as every dish offers fresh insight to the history and culture of this colourful region. A mouthful of **babi pong teh** (stewed pork) reveals how Malay cooking techniques and Chinese ingredients have found their way into a unique marriage of two cultures. In any local curry you can recognise complex spice accents – turmeric, cumin, coriander – inspired by the Arab and Indian merchants who tarried upon the shores of Malaysia. And the spicy chilli kick in any Chinese hawker noodle dish will remind you of how separate culinary traditions, when left to develop side by side, inevitably fuse to form a stimulating culinary culture.

The only way to truly experience Malaysia and Singapore is to eat your way across the region. So what are you waiting for?

the **culture** of
malaysian &
singaporean cuisine

There's no question about it. Malaysians and Singaporeans are food obsessed – even as they sit down at a laden dinner table they are drawn into discussing what they should have for supper. Often described as a chaos of races and languages, the colourful, multi-cultural traditions of the region offer the food lover a spectacular gastronomic experience like no other.

History

Have a hawker meal in Malaysia or Singapore and you'll realise that trying to describe an all-encompassing Malaysian or Singaporean cuisine is laughable – just as it's near impossible to pick out the average Malaysian or Singaporean person based on a list of physical traits. While classic dishes such as **nasi lemak** (coconut rice with fried fish) and **chilli crab** (spicy chilli and tomato-based crab stirfry dish; see the recipe) have become so closely associated with their home countries that it is possible to identify them as being quintessentially Malaysian or Singaporean, what and how locals eat in their daily lives is so diverse and changeable that it's only appropriate to speak of the cuisines, rather than the cuisine, of Malaysia and Singapore. The food of the region is as varied as its people and it thrives on a fusion afforded by a long history of trade and migration.

It is important to bear in mind that Malaysia and Singapore, as we know them today, emerged as independent countries only in the 1960s. Prior to that, the states of Peninsular Malaysia and Singapore were loosely amalgamated as a British colony. Before that, they were fragmented Malay kingdoms with disparate allegiances. Beyond influences of geographical proximity and a shared history, the culinary developments within each state were far more dependent upon the influences of neighbouring political and cultural powers (the states close to Thailand have assimilated their northern neighbours' penchant for sour and spicy flavours), the traditions of European colonialists (witness the evolution of Eurasian cuisine; see p 23) and the tenets of religion.

Today, while the states of the peninsular, together with Sabah and Sarawak, form Malaysia, the food of Malaysia is by no means homogenous across the territory. Some regions along the west coast, where Chinese and Indians have settled, exhibit different cuisine styles from the predominantly Malay and Muslim states of the east coast. **Laksa** (spicy, soupy noodle dish) served in Penang tastes nothing like its namesake in Singapore; ask for a chicken curry recipe and you're likely to be asked if you want the Indian, Malay or Chinese version of the dish.

Many historians considered the growth of Melaka (on the west coast of peninsular Malaysia) into a major port sometime around 1400 to be the starting point for the region's multicultural (and multiculinary) history. Merchants, traders and missionaries, with their idiosyncratic gastronomic preferences, were drawn to the town's shores.

Melaka's pattern of government and lifestyle became the basis of what was later termed 'traditional' Malay culture. But it would be erroneous to suppose that it was only then that the region established itself as a cultural and culinary crossroad.

Preparing a Peranakan meal, Penang

Even the Orang Asli, the aboriginal Malays, are said to have moved down the peninsular some 10,000 years ago, from the region in western China (roughly, the region called Qinghai Province today) where the great rivers of Southeast Asia originate.

Some historians say the proto-Malays, ancestors of today's Malays, were part of a later wave of immigrants who were ethnically similar to the people of Indonesia. They still share some cooking techniques and preferences for certain spices and flavours. The proto-Malays first settled in the coastal regions and then moved inland, marrying with Orang Asli and blurring the division between the two groups in the process (although you'll still find pockets of Orang Asli in Malaysia who continue to keep to their simple, nomadic lifestyles, relying on traditional crops and hunting). They brought knowledge of irrigated rice-field cultivation and the domestication of the ox and buffalo – the beginnings of agriculture. Yet, our knowledge of the early history of the region, particularly its culinary history, is still hazy. This makes it difficult to identify the specifics of its development.

By the end of the Middle Ages, when the Portuguese arrived in the region, the Malay archipelago had for hundreds of years been part of a complex trading network stretching from Africa to China. The northeast monsoon brought Chinese junks laden with silks, porcelain, pickles and other foodstuffs; Arab and Indian traders sailed in with the southwest

Palm sugar, noodles and sauces for sale on the streets, Melaka

monsoon bearing (along with precious metals, ebony and perfumes) fennel and spices such as cardamom and peppercorns. By then, Southeast Asia was already divided into two main cultural areas: one where Indian influences predominated, and the other (consisting of Tongking, Annam and Cochin China) where Chinese influences stood strong. Gastronomically and culturally, the fusion had already begun.

The traders also brought religious beliefs, as well as dietary philosophies and habits. The growth of trade with India (particularly South India) brought the coastal peoples of the Malay world into contact with two major religions, Hinduism and Buddhism. From the late 7th century until its demise hundreds of years later (when Melaka rose to take its place), the great Sumatran-based Srivijaya Empire, with its capital in the Indonesian city of Palembang, is said to have played a significant role in disseminating Hindu-Buddhist ideas in the region. More importantly, its language of government and court has been described as an early version of the Malay spoken in Melaka, the focal point from which much of Malay society developed, unchallenged, until the 19th century.

Melaka, in turn, contributed to the evolution of Malay culture by incorporating Islamic ideas into its foundations (Indian Muslim traders are said to have been an impetus for Islam's appearance in Southeast Asia) and encouraging the widespread use of Malay in the archipelago simply through its trading power and highly cosmopolitan society. The evolution of Malay cuisine, as such, is influenced by the tenets of Islam, which prohibits the consumption of pork and alcohol.

MALAY, MALAYS & MALAYSIAN

Let's get this right. Malay, or more specifically Bahasa Melayu, is the national language of Malaysia and is similar to Bahasa Indonesia, which evolved from Malay. The Malays are the indigenous people of Malaysia, although they are not its original inhabitants. The term defines them as a racial group (Malays form one of the four main races in Singapore). Their traditions and way of life are described as Malay culture. Malaysians, on the other hand, are citizens of Malaysia. This means that an individual may be Chinese and Malaysian, or Indian and Malaysian.

However, the region's culinary melting pot only truly started to bubble with the arrival of the Portuguese (1511), Dutch (1641) and British (1786), in addition to the Minangkabau from Sumatra (Indonesia) in the 17th century.

Malaysian & Singaporean Cuisine
Malay

Today's Malay food is the result of centuries of foreign interaction. Malay culture arguably crystallised around Melaka's rise as a seaport and Islamic centre. The people here developed a culinary style greatly influenced by visiting traders from Indonesia, India, the Middle East and China. Many of the ingredients central to Malay cooking were introduced by Indians and Arabs – including spices such as cardamom, pepper and cloves. Basic cooking techniques involve preparing one wet and one dry set of ingredients. Key wet ingredients include shallots, ginger, garlic, chillies and turmeric, and are usually blended using a mortar and pestle. The technique is to first combine the wet ingredients and then fry them in oil before adding dry ingredients such as ground coriander seed, cumin, aniseed, cloves, cinnamon and cardamom. Indian cooking uses the same technique.

Rice is always the foundation of a Malay meal. It may be steamed, boiled or fried, cooked on its own, or flavoured with coconut milk, spices and herbs. It can be **ketupat**, pressed rice cooked in a case made from strips of coconut fronds or **lemang**, cooked over a charcoal fire in bamboo poles lined with young banana leaves. But whichever rice is served, it's customary to have it with a fish or seafood curry, a meat or poultry dish (or both), two or more vegetable dishes and **sambal** (chilli-based condiment). Indonesian-influenced dry curries like **rendang** (beef in a thick coconut-milk curry sauce; see the recipe) have become a permanent feature at nasi lemak stalls, while more recently, Chinese dishes such stirfried **beehoon** (rice vermicelli) have even made it onto the menus of Malay weddings.

Fried beehoon is a Chinese dish popular throughout the region

Because most Malays are Muslims no pork or alcohol is served at meals; both are considered haram (forbidden). For meat to be considered halal (permitted), the animal's jugular vein has to be severed while the butcher recites the name of Allah as in the Qur'an (the Muslim holy book). Islam was introduced to the region by Indian Muslim merchants from Gujarat and Malays have, over the years, absorbed a tradition of Middle Eastern dishes interpreted with Indian overtones. Dishes include **nasi biryani** (rice casserole often layered with meat and steamed gently so that the flavours blend) and chicken **korma** (rich, thickened mild curry). In recent times, Malay homemakers are as likely to buy ready-mixed curry paste from the Indian vendor at their neighbourhood market for a fish curry as they are to use the Indian curry leaf for seasoning. Malay cooks will also whip up **roti paratha** (unleavened flaky fried flat bread), which Indians enjoy with curry; Malays, however, prefer to sprinkle it with sugar and eat it as a snack.

Roti paratha being cooked fresh at a local coffeeshop, Penang

Indian

While the region was influenced by Indian culture long before Europeans appeared on the scene, Indians only really made their presence felt in the 19th century, when the British brought them in to provide labour for their rubber plantations. Most of the Indian population is made up of Hindus from South India, where the staple food is rice (in the north it is wheat, in the form of bread). Rice is usually eaten with **daal** (cooked lentils or pulses), vegetables and pickles, although a fish and meat dish may occasionally be added. South Indian dishes tend to be searingly spicy because it is believed that in warm climates, chilli cools the body through perspiration. Coconut milk and yogurt play commanding roles, and mustard seeds are widely used as a spice. Hindus don't eat beef, and some orthodox Hindus believe that cutlery used over and over again is unhygienic, preferring to eat with their fingers. Many Hindus are strictly vegetarian.

Tandoori chicken prepared for the lunch crowds, Penang

North Indian dishes, which are also readily available, contain more meat and are less fiery. Familiar items include **tandoori** (spice-marinated meat cooked in a clay oven) dishes served with **naan** (bread made from plain flour and cooked in a clay oven). Cow's milk, cream and **ghee** (clarified butter), rather than coconut milk, tend to form the basis of curries. *Mamak* (Indian Muslim) hawker dishes (where no pork is used) are in a special class of their own: while northern Indian cuisine tends to be extremely formal, *mamak* dishes are quick, one-dish meals eaten by Muslims and non-Muslims alike. Hot favourites include **mee rebus** (thick, fresh egg noodles in a viscous, sweet and spicy sauce, served with hard-boiled eggs and freshly cut green chillies), **rojak** (the Indian version – deep-fried vegetables and seafood served with spicy-sweet sauce, and fresh cucumber, tomato and onion) and **mee goreng** (spicy fried noodle dish).

Pappadams ready to be deep fried

A SPICY SLICE OF LIFE

Singapore sure has it good – green, clean and technologically blessed. But for me its most interesting attribute is the way it grafts together influences local and global, ancient and modern, and always in places that don't receive a lot of publicity. I'm thinking mostly about Little India, a serpent-thin piece of the island nation, close to Serangoon Rd.

I spend time wandering here whenever possible, and on this trip my first act in town is to meet up with Devagi Sanmugam. She's a native Singaporean with family origins in Chennai, India. At one point she owned an Indian restaurant, which she had to close because some staff were supplementing their incomes by re-selling her crabs and shrimp. After that she ran a spice shop in the heart of Little India, which she closed to become the 'Spice Queen'. People now know her from appearances on TV, her South-Indian focused cookbooks, her lectures, and even from her line of dried curry and spice powders.

One Sunday morning I meet Devagi at Ananda Bhavan Indian Teahouse, and we are enveloped in its aromas. To get here we have to walk through the front of Tekka Market, where women have spread snake gourds, passionfruit and protein-rich greens on top of blankets on the floor. But this Ananda Bhavan, a satellite of the chain's original store, is kitted out with brushed aluminium, a retro shade of green, and hints of whitewashed minimalism throughout. The company's back-alley roots have been dropped and global design cues taken up instead. The place is packed. We're served potato **dosai** (paper-thin rice-and-lentil crêpes) on silver trays and asked if we want our **lassis** (curd drinks) salty or sweet. Our aromatic rose-water sweets are weighed by the kilo.

Devagi, who always manages to order enough food for a family of 10 (today's order: two potato dosai; one vegetable **murtabak**, panfried rice dough with vegetable pieces; a lentil cake and stew affair called **sambar idli**; lassis; and coffee), is enthusing about her new kitchen, where she hosts cooking classes and TV shoots. She's convinced a local store to outfit it to the tune of S$80,000, but she is most proud of a link-up with a French company renowned for pots. Her famed long-simmering curries will forever be made inside Le Creuset pots. 'I think my husband will be happy,' she says, thinking of home when I ask of business. Her savvy lets her ascend, but her culture centres her.

Unfortunately, Devagi has to leave as she is teaching a class today on the Ayurvedic use of Indian spices. Before she goes I ask her to accompany me down one block, exploring Little India's contradictions – its blend of cultures, and of old and new.

She takes me past Tekka Market, where one can find Indian **rojak**, where vegetables and seafood are deep-fried and served with a spicy sweet sauce and fresh cucumber, tomato and onion; and Chinese stirfries.

Then we head down Serangoon Rd, where hints of turmeric and clove, and sweet clouds of incense fill the air. Devagi motions to the Buffalo Rd sign, telling me that in years gone by, buffaloes used to be tied up here. Crossing the street she says *namaste* (hello) to some locals, stops to peruse a Bollywood video selection and show me some intriguing Indian produce: elephant ear yams and rare salted fish from the Maldives, which are used in curries and stews.

Ducking through a produce shop Devagi shows me a courtyard with a stunning Peranakan home behind. A nearby signboard advertises beauty shop services: 'steamed henna, puberty make-up, breast augmentation, hot oil massage, pedicures'. Then I look left to see the spires of a mosque, and a pre-fabricated apartment building. Devagi points to Andhra Curry Restaurant across the way, just beyond a beer garden and an Internet café, and smiles. 'They have very good food from Andhra Pradesh.'

Rob McKeown

Fish-head curry is an Indian invention that's popular throughout the region

Chinese

Like Indian culture, Chinese culture has had a strong influence on the region for a long time. But it was only in the early 19th century, drawn by the profitability of tin mining and plantation agriculture, that the Chinese population in the region grew dramatically. By 1827, the Chinese were the largest single community in Singapore, and by 1845 they formed more than half its population. Most came from China's provinces of Guangdong, Fujian and Guangxi and belonged to five major sociolinguistic groups: Teochew, Cantonese, Hokkien, Hakka and Hainanese. Each brought with them their regional cuisine.

Rice forms the basis of meals in these Chinese regions. It is usually served with an assortment of meat, seafood, poultry and vegetable dishes. It's often said that Chinese will eat almost anything; at formal occasions, the validity of that claim is constantly reaffirmed. **Yu chi tang** (shark's fin soup), **hai shen** (braised sea cucumber) and **ya jiao** (duck feet) are just some of the dishes that are considered delicacies among Chinese. But more often than not, the meals Chinese have at home are simple: a clear soup, a stirfried vegetable dish and a fish or meat dish accompanied with steamed rice. The key elements of the cuisine are the freshness of ingredients (the ingenious cook works with whatever's available) and a careful balance between tastes, textures and temperatures: sweet and sour, hot and cold, plain and spicy.

Chinese-style seafood restaurants like this one in Singapore are hugely popular across the region

Chinese sausages, Penang

To Chinese, 'meat' is near-synonymous with pork, although with growing contemporary health consciousness, chicken and fish are replacing pork as the protein of choice. Lamb was not popular until quite recently, and beef is only eaten by non-Buddhists. While they continue to eat pretty much the same food as their ancestors, Chinese in the Malaysian and Singaporean region have also modified their food in ways that reveal the long interaction they've had with other racial groups. Chinese 'cookboys' (the Hainanese have been long associated with this profession) who worked for colonial employers learnt to reproduce English food and incorporated some of the techniques and flavourings into their own food. For example, they quickly realised the potential of tomato sauce, Worcestershire sauce and HP Sauce, which they then used to flavour Chinese-style pork chops (now a favourite in its own right), fried fish and turned into a dip for **inche kabin** (spicy fried chicken pieces).

Life alongside chilli-loving Malays and Indians also inspired the Chinese to appreciate of spiciness in their food. Hawker favourites such as **wonton mee** (fine, yellow noodles served with minced pork dumplings), **char kway teow** (flat rice-flour noodles stirfried with Chinese sausage, cockles and egg in a sweet, dark soy sauce) and **Hainanese chicken rice** (see the recipe) are now served with a side dish of chilli – either pickled, chopped and topped with light soy sauce, or blended and served with minced ginger. Chilli has become just as important as the chicken and rice when a diner assesses the quality of a Hainanese chicken rice dish. Malay-style curries are also served in Chinese homes.

Peranakan

The Peranakan (or Straits) Chinese trace their roots to the 15th century when predominantly male Chinese migrant traders settled in Southeast Asia (particularly in Penang, Melaka and Singapore) and married local women. History also has it that a Chinese emperor dispatched one of his princesses to Sultan Iskandar Shah of Melaka together with a retinue of 500 handmaidens. The 'gift brides' for the local menfolk eventually produced a community of Malay-Chinese. Over time, this distinct sub-ethnic group evolved with its own language, dress and cuisine. The men became known as Baba, and the women as Nonya. The patois that developed among them was a curious amalgam of Chinese (invariably Hokkien), Malay, Portuguese, Dutch and English words.

Peranakan (or Nonya) cuisine reflects their community's cultural mix – Malay ingredients and spices such as **belacan** (fermented shrimp paste), chilli, lemongrass, galangal and turmeric are fused with Chinese cooking techniques (including a penchant for pork) and elements of Indian, Thai and Portuguese Eurasian cuisines. Classic dishes include Thai-influenced **mee siam** (rice vermicelli in a spicy, tangy sauce), **babi pong teh** (stewed pork) and **ayam buah keluak** (mildly spicy, sour chicken dish filled with **buah keluak** – black nuts from Indonesia). The wealth of the community allowed the Nonyas the luxury of devoting their time to the culinary arts and indulging in the preparation of elaborate meals. Dishes are often labour intensive to prepare, but the ensuing gossip and social interaction forms an essential part of the whole kitchen experience.

Except for one-dish meals such as mee siam, Nonya food is usually served with plain rice and eaten communally, as with Chinese food. However, the traditional way to eat is by hand.

Kuey pie tee is a Peranakan dish also known as 'Singapore top hats'

Eurasian

This term refers to anyone with a mixed European and Asian heritage. But in the context of Malaysia and Singapore, the Eurasian community stems from the arrival of the Portuguese. The descendants of 16th-century Portuguese traders, explorers and eventually colonisers call themselves Jenti Cristang (Christian people) and speak their own language, a Creole Portuguese that is now often coloured with English, Malay and Chinese phrases. The early Portuguese established a policy of racial integration that sanctioned marriage between themselves and the local people. Intent on incorporating Melaka's native cuisine into their own, they combined ingredients of the local cuisines (which were a hybrid of Malay, Chinese, Indian, Arab and Peranakan cultures) with Portuguese cooking methods.

Today, Eurasians use tamarind, lemongrass, lime and galangal to create exotic curries, sambal, soups and vegetable dishes. Occasionally they use alcohol to add body to meat and fish dishes. From the Peranakans they acquired a taste for sweet-and-sour dishes along with the art of chopping vegetables, which they stirfry the Chinese way. Signature Eurasian dishes include **curry debal** (devil's curry: spicy Eurasian meat curry; see the recipe) and **feng** (pork curry; a Christmas speciality that is best eaten a day old), as well as European conventions such as chicken pie, corned beef cutlets and shepherd's pie.

A standard formal dinner consists of seven to eight dishes: two curries, a fried or roasted dish, a pie, cooked vegetables and a salad, pickles and sambals, and a variety of cakes for dessert. Savoury dishes are placed on the table at the same time and are usually eaten with boiled rice.

Kalamansi (sour limes)

The Orang Asli & Tribes of Malaysian Borneo

There are still small, scattered groups of Orang Asli, the aboriginal Malays, in Peninsular Malaysia. In the Malaysian Borneo states of Sabah and Sarawak, around 25 different ethnic groups exist. But the simple, often basic foods of these groups have generally not entered the Malaysian and Singaporean food lexicon.

CULTURE

How Malaysians & Singaporeans Eat

With great passion and enthusiasm! It seems that they eat all the time. Breakfast is usually bought from a roadside or hawker stall on the way to work and may consist of anything: filling nasi lemak, soupy Chinese noodles, delicate **dosai** (paper-thin rice-and-lentil crêpes) or soft-boiled eggs and **roti kaya** (grilled bread with coconut egg jam).

By 10am, it's time for a snack to help tide over the hunger pangs leading up to lunch. Perhaps **epok epok** (pyramid-shaped pastries filled with spicy vegetable or meat curry) or **you char kway** (deep-fried dough stick) and a **kopi** (local coffee sweetened with sweet condensed milk). Snack options are plentiful in Malaysia and Singapore, and the multitude of food outlets make resistance all too futile.

Lunch hour starts at around noon and rarely stretches over more than 90 minutes. At the numerous hawker areas dotted across urban centres you'll discover that diners are incredibly focused on scoring themselves a clean table and seat, and will often hover over seated diners close to ending their meals, seeking to secure a table before ordering a one-dish meal. Eating is a functional (and often hot and sweaty) affair at this time of day. It is common for groups of friends and colleagues dining together to share the empty seats at their table with perfect strangers. Everyone's generally out to grab a quick but tasty bite.

Regular local fare includes: stirfried noodle dishes; Indian roti parathas served with curry; and buffet-style options where diners pick out items from an array at the stall to be served with a portion of rice (Malay, Indian and Chinese stalls have their own versions of this, and offer different kinds of dishes). In swankier, possibly air-conditioned food courts such those in shopping malls, expect, apart from local specialities, renditions of western food (fried chicken cutlets served with french fries and baked beans), Japanese rice sets, Thai noodles and soups, and other foods that reveal the intrinsic openness the locals have towards different cuisines.

For busy couples and families, dinner is also often eaten at hawker stalls. Meals are more substantial, and diners tend to mix their cuisines, sometimes opting for an Indian salad, a Malay rice dish and a Chinese dessert. Home-cooked dinners, on the other hand, tend to be based around just one cuisine, usually one traditional to the family. But it's equally common for homemakers to explore and experiment, choosing to pair a spicy fish dish with a Chinese clear soup and stirfried vegetables, for example (for more details see Home Cooking, p 101).

Then, there's always supper. At 2am, a different world of hawker stalls serves up barbecued chicken wings, peppery pork rib soups and **or luah** (oyster omelettes) to hungry night owls.

Roti kaya and coffee for breakfast, Singapore

MAKAN MADNESS

The western world has foodies and chowhounds – and that is one thing. But in Malaysia and Singapore, to eat out is to witness an obsessive passion for food that resembles a cult religion, a form of cultural expression and a Homeric journey. On my first visit to Singapore I was driven around the whole island for **char kway teow** (broad, rice-flour noodles stirfried with Chinese sausage and egg in a sweet, dark soy sauce), **cheng teng** (sweet syrupy dessert filled with nuts and dried fruit), **or luah** (oyster omelettes), **Katong laksa** (noodles in a spicy gravy, served with prawns, clams, fishcake, cockles, bean sprouts and fried beancurd) and **Peking duck** (thin slices of roasted duck served with pancakes and sauce), all in a matter of three hours. All I did was say I wanted 'some' local food. Since recovering, I've realised how important food is to locals and that deciding what to eat among friends is the mealtime equivalent of forging a political coalition.

In Singapore most food guides can't compare to *Makansutra*, the definitive guide to the local ways of consumption. Having the honesty and guts to list hawkers ahead of restaurants, this guidebook lists nearly 1000 dishes (**ayam soto**, Malay chicken soup; **lontong**, compressed rice cakes; **beef hor fun**, thick rice-based noodles cooked in a thick broth), sources the locations serving the superlative (alleys, stalls, hotels and Hokkien uncles – the name given to local older Hokkien men) and rates them on a scale from 'Good' to 'Die, Die, Must Try!' Three chopsticks is the highest rating for both low- and high-end dishes, from fish balls to modern French food. Best of all are the comments, from critical insider insight to Singlish (English spoken with a Singaporean twist) chatter. On **kaya** (coconut egg jam): 'Best to buy it in the afternoon, freshly cooked and warm'. On a great **cze cha** (pick 'n' mix) stall: 'Recommended by our friend, Heng Hwa, otherwise we would have driven right past it'. On char kway teow: 'Cooked by cool dude with ponytail'.

Almost every citizen is a walking, talking, chopsticking database that updates on a meal-by-meal basis. Like talk-show hosts, they also have their own angle – my friend Mark is known for mapping the history of local chefs from first wok to last dish.

You're always guaranteed an answer when inquiring about local food. When I asked friends for some street food recommendations, I got back an itemised list. Tapioca noodles and vegetables, it instructs, can be found in prime form in 'a shack nestled behind a Chinese primary school'. The entry for fish-head dishes, off Jalan Sungai Besi, mentions 'three shops clumped together. All dilapidated but don't worry. Don't know what type of fish they get their heads from, but I suspect freshwater. Hot sauce fish-head to die for.' There are also **niu nan mien** (beef-brisket noodles), with the comment 'before I gave up beef, I swore allegiance to these'.

Chicken rice balls, a Melaka favourite

One could go on forever. Singapore's daily newspaper, the *Straits Times,* regularly runs columns featuring taxi drivers facing off against celebrities with hawker suggestions – it took me two **yong tau hoo** (food items such as beancurd stuffed with minced meat) trips to figure out who locals trust (the taxi drivers!). In Melaka, I was given the type of clandestine left-at-this-tree-right-at-this-mah-jong-game directions used by spies. In Kota Bharu, a missed bus and confusing hike had me lost for good, or so I thought. Instead I found a **nasi kandar** (Indian version of **nasi campur,** plate of rice topped with various dishes) with some of the more haunting curries and **kerabu** (salads) I've ever encountered. Even when doing something as posh as clubbing at Zouk in Singapore, the night ends not with goodbyes or cab hailing, but with a debate over where and what to eat. That is, after all, what makes a party, night after night.

Rob McKeown

CULTURE

Etiquette

There are no complex cutlery sets to pick your way through, and no slew of wine glasses to leave you guessing which you should drink from next. Most homes and restaurants, except the most traditional, will provide you with a fork and spoon, although few provide knives (most local foods don't require much cutting action). If your host doesn't use chopsticks or eat with his or her fingers, don't ask to do so. A fork and spoon are used nearly all the time, not just in the presence of foreign guests.

As a general rule of thumb, elders should be served first. Within each culture, there is a tradition of welcoming fellow diners to partake of the food with you. Malays say *jemput makan* (please join me). Always use a serving spoon, not your own spoon, to dish out food, and serve others at the table first before you start on your own meal. And don't forget that Muslims don't eat pork or consume alcohol, and Hindus and Buddhists do not eat beef. Serving any of these to staunch believers would be a huge faux pas. At formal Malay dinners and banquets, and even some hawker centres, you'll notice teapot-like receptacles set atop large, flat-bottomed bowls covered with perforated lids. These are not for your tea. By no means should you drink the water in them. They are *pembasuk tangan* (finger bowls) to be used for washing, should you need to use your fingers to eat.

Always use your right hand to eat. In both Malay and Indian traditions, the right hand is used to give and receive, and to eat. The left hand is considered unclean. Muslims also use only the right hand to *salaam,* or wish one another well. The correct way to do it is to lightly touch as if you're shaking hands and then raise the fingers on the same hand to your heart. In the case of elders, the younger person kisses the older person's hand. But

HANDS-ON EATING

The trick to eating elegantly with your fingers is to restrict the contact with your food to just the tips of your fingers. However, remember to use serving spoons, not your fingers, to take food from the communal dish. Indians are said to prefer mixing all the different dishes into their rice, while Malays choose to mix dishes individually into each mouthful of rice. Either way is acceptable. Simply make sure that the food and rice are adequately combined (use the liquids in the curry sauces to help bind them together) before you attempt to raise a mouthful to your lips. Here, the trick is to quickly place the ball of rice directly onto your tongue. Watch your fellow diners, and you'll notice that they tend to stick the tips of their tongues out just as they spoon the food in with their fingers.

Washing before digging in, Penang

this is usually reserved for grandparents, aunts and uncles. If a member of the opposite sex fails to salaam you, don't be offended. Men generally do not salaam women, neither do women salaam men. The general rule is that if you can conceivably marry the person (and this doesn't just apply if he or she is single) you shouldn't touch or salaam him or her.

When visiting someone at home, be sure to bring a gift. Fresh fruit, cakes and other sweet delicacies are ideal. The gift doesn't have to be elaborately packaged, but your host will appreciate a gift that comes from the heart. You'll discover that in most families, feeding is an act of love. While Asian cultures do not subscribe to public shows of affection, parents and other family members will articulate their feelings by offering what's perceived as the best parts of any given dish to loved ones. When you are the object of such attention, be sure to eat all that you are given. Waste is frowned upon, and a healthy, appreciative appetite is always much welcomed.

This Malay dessert is a multi-layer jellied cake which children love to eat layer by layer

staples
& specialities

Malaysian and Singaporean pantries are mixed bags of tricks filled
with spices, herbs, grains, sauces and many other ingredients from
a host of cuisines, each continually borrowing from the other.
Rather than attempt to redraw those lines, local chefs celebrate in
the blurring of boundaries, creating distinctive local dishes that
play with the rich food choices open to them.

Nasi (Rice)

Rice is an essential element in most meals eaten among all communities in Malaysia and Singapore. Be it a simple, plain bowl of steamed rice (while the term 'steamed rice' is commonly used, it actually refers to rice cooked using the absorption method) served as an accompaniment to a spread of Malay, Chinese, Indian, Peranakan or Eurasian delights; rice steamed and then fried with other ingredients (as in the case of Malay **nasi goreng** or Chinese fried rice); grains boiled into sweet or savoury porridge; or glutinous varieties steamed and moulded into tubes or cubes, rice is invariably a major feature of local menus.

Malaysia grows its own rice, with production meeting approximately 65% of domestic demand. The northern state of Kedah, producing most of the country's rice, is often referred to as the 'rice bowl of Malaysia'. Local rice is similar to that of Thailand, although the long-grain, polished, fragrant white rice – jasmine rice – from Thailand continues to be prized for its aroma and flavour. Purists recommend against serving curry with fragrant rice because the rice works against the flavour of the curry.

Among Indians, basmati rice (translated as the 'queen of fragrance') is preferred for special occasions and particular dishes. The grains should be white, long and silky to the touch. Good basmati is supposed to be left to mature for up to 10 years! When cooked, it has a unique fragrance and distinct nutty flavour. You'll discover that basmati rice is usually served mixed with nuts and spices, and infused with the wonderful flavour of ghee. Glutinous rice is either white or black in colour, and comes in short- and long-grain varieties. When cooked, it is extremely sticky and is easily moulded into shapes. Malays use the white variety of this rice in **lemang**, a sticky-rice dish originating in Negeri Sembilan that is shaped into tubes in the hollow of long bamboo poles. Peranakans (and Malays) also use this variety in such rice-based desserts as **putri salat**, a double-layered dessert consisting of a glutinous rice base covered with a thick, sweet, green-coloured (derived from the pandanus leaf) custard-like topping. Usually made in big sheets, this dessert is then sliced into rectangular tiles of green and white.

Rice is usually consumed steamed or boiled (both terms essentially refer to the same absorption method of cooking the rice grains), resulting in fluffy white rice that has not been flavoured in any way. There are two basic methods of cooking rice in the home. The absorption method involves bringing water to the boil, and then adding the washed, drained rice. By the time the rice is cooked tender, it will have absorbed all the water, giving it the perfect consistency. The general ratio is one cup of long-grain rice to two cups of water, but the age and variety of the grain influences the amount of water you need to use. For example, you need less

Rice for nasi lemak served on banana leaves, Kuala Lumpur

water for short-grain rice. The second, most convenient method, however, is to use a rice cooker – a purpose-built appliance that cooks your rice using the same absorption method, but taking the guess-work out of it, and keeps it warm. All you do is follow the basic instructions that come with it. Almost all homes have one (see Utensils, p 113).

Rice Dishes

Nasi lemak is a common Malay breakfast dish which, in its original form, consists of lightly salted rice cooked with coconut milk and topped with **sambal ikan bilis** (dried anchovies fried and mixed with a spicy **sambal** – chilli-based condiment) and a few slices of cucumber, all wrapped up in a banana leaf. You'll find these neat little packages for sale at makeshift stalls near bus interchanges and busy thoroughfares, in coffeeshops and along the streets. You'll find long queues at the best nasi lemak stalls.

But nasi lemak has moved beyond its humble beginnings. You'll find most stalls now offer fried chicken, **rendang** (beef in a thick coconut-milk curry sauce; see the recipe), fried egg, fried Spam at some Chinese *haram* (forbidden) joints, or deep-fried fish with your coconut rice and sambal. Even-bigger stalls offer a selection of items for customers to add to the basic

dish, and instead of just coconut rice, they may also offer **nasi kuning** (yellow rice; see the recipe), which is also cooked with coconut milk. Sometimes at nasi lemak stalls, a banana leaf shaped into a cone is filled with your choice of rice before adding your choice of meat, fish or vegetable items.

This concept of picking items to go with a portion of rice is similar to that of the **nasi campur**, **nasi Padang**, **nasi kandar** and **chai peng** (economy rice) stalls. At all these stalls, the customer starts with a plate of rice and identifies what other cooked dishes, from the array on display, they wish to add to the rice. There may be a choice of plain white rice, coconut rice and yellow rice at all the different kinds of stalls, except at the economy rice stall where only plain white rice is served. Nasi campur is the Malay version, while nasi Padang originates from Indonesia. Nasi kandar, made famous in Penang, is the Indian version. History has it that enterprising Indian hawkers (see Hawker Stalls, p 177) carried their selection of dishes into rubber plantations balanced on the ends of a poles, for sale to labourers. Economy rice is the Chinese interpretation of the same concept. Essentially, the kind of dishes sold at each type of stall reflects its cuisine traditions. Nevertheless these distinctions are quickly blurring and you are likely to find Indonesian rendang at the nasi campur stall or chicken curry at the economy rice stall.

Sticky rice wrapped in leaves and steamed, Melaka

Nasi Kuning (Yellow Rice)

This delicately flavoured rice, with its beautiful yellow vibrance, is a Malay festive staple. It is also to be found at every neighbourhood **nasi campur** or **nasi Padang** stall, accompanied by a wide range of meat and vegetable dishes.

Ingredients

500g	long-grain jasmine rice
3 tbs	vegetable oil
1	onion, peeled and finely chopped
2	garlic cloves, peeled and finely chopped
250mL	coconut milk
300mL	water
1 tsp	salt
1 tsp	turmeric powder
1	pandanus leaf, tied into a knot
4	curry leaves (optional)

Garnishes

red chillies
banana leaves
fried shallots (available in small tubs from any Asian grocer both in the west and in Malaysia and Singapore)

Wash the rice in several changes of water and allow to drain in a sieve for an hour. Heat the oil in a large, heavy saucepan. Fry the chopped onion and garlic over a low heat until soft and golden. Add the rice, stirring to coat thoroughly, until each grain glistens with fat from the pan. Pour in the coconut milk and add the salt, turmeric powder and pandanus and curry leaves. Bring slowly to the boil, then turn down the heat to the very lowest and tightly clamp on the lid. Allow to steam for 20 minutes. Uncover, rake the grains well to fluff up the rice, then put the lid back on. Turn off the heat. Allow to stand undisturbed for a few minutes. Take off the lid and remove the flavouring leaves. Allow the rice to cool slightly.

To make chilli flower garnishes, slit the chillies several times lengthways, leaving the stalk end intact. Flick out the seeds with the point of a small, sharp knife. Drop the chillies into a large bowl of iced water; the strips will open up and curl. To make your own fried shallots, thinly slice shallots and panfry in vegetable oil until crisp and golden brown. Dab off excess oil with paper towels. Heap individual portions of rice onto pieces of banana leaf and garnish with a scattering of fried shallots and a chilli flower.

Serves 4

Ketupat & Lemang

While ketupat and lemang can both be classed as moulded rice, each is slightly different to the other. **Ketupat** is a pressed rice made out of regular rice (short-grain rice would be a little more sticky and help it retain its shape) whereas **lemang** is made of glutinous rice.

Ketupat cases are woven from strips of coconut fronds. They are filled up halfway with washed, uncooked rice before they are sealed. The cases are tied together in bundles of five or 10, and lowered into boiling water where they are left to simmer for four hours. To serve, the cooled rice packages are split in half lengthwise and the rice is then cut into cubes (you get anywhere from eight to 18 cubes from a ketupat case). This rice is commonly eaten with satay or curry. You are most likely to come across ketupat at satay stalls where they will be brought to the table still sitting in their split-open coconut leaf cases. To eat them, spear a cube with a satay stick, add a slice of the accompanying onion or pineapple, then dip it into the thick and spicy peanut sauce.

Lemang is eaten with curry and rendang. This speciality from Negeri Sembilan calls for bamboo poles cut into roughly 40cm lengths. Each is lined with banana leaf before being filled with pre-soaked glutinous rice and coconut milk. The poles are lined up over a charcoal fire and left to cook for about four hours. When done, the rice is extracted by splitting the bamboo. The rice is then removed from the banana leaf and sliced into short, cylindrical portions. Not easy to find at restaurants or hawker stalls, you're more likely to find roadside stalls out in the suburbs or country selling lemang to ladies who serve it to their families at home. Lemang's delicate coconut flavour and aroma and moist sticky consistency is a gastronomic experience not to be missed.

Lemang cooking over flames

Lemang revealed

In Malaysia's Kedah, another variation exists. **Ketupat pulut** seems to bring elements of the ketupat and lemang together. Glutinous rice is half-cooked in coconut milk before it is rolled into thick logs wrapped in banana leaves. The logs are then steamed before they are unwrapped and served in cylindrical slices with **serunding daging** (spicy beef floss; beef cooked to the point where it is dry and flaky so it breaks down into a coarse, thread-like consistency).

Breaking the bamboo to get to the lemang, Kuala Lumpur

Nasi Biryani (Rice Casserole)

A **biryani** is a rich, aromatic rice casserole often layered with meat (most often chicken or mutton) then steamed gently so that the flavours blend. While it is a dish quite commonly found at Indian and Malay coffeeshops and stalls, the good stuff is only to be had at special occasions where it is cooked at home. The trick is to follow the traditional Indian technique of frying the dish's dry spices in oil until aromatic, browning the onions then tossing the uncooked rice into the mixture, coating the grains with the oil. The best biryanis are flavoursome all the way through, while the meat remains tender and moist.

Bubur (Rice Porridge)

Chinese, especially Teochews, enjoy plain rice porridge (they call it **muay**), flavoured with just a hint of salt, served in place of steamed rice. Teochews like the rice grains to remain whole, so that the porridge really looks like rice in soup. They serve it with a selection of pickles, omelettes, braised and stewed meat dishes, fish and tofu. The Teochew version is a favourite supper dish in Singapore. Cantonese prefer their porridge smooth (they call it **chok/jok**), with the rice grains broken down to an almost pasty consistency. Extra ingredients are then added – classic combinations include century egg (preserved egg) and minced pork (or paper-thin slices of pork), shredded chicken, or slices of fish. You will often find these available in restaurants serving **dian xin** (dim sum), or at Chinese coffeeshops.

Hakkas have a very traditional dish that goes by the strange name **lui char fan** (thunder tea rice). *Lui* is the Hakka word for grinding, but it also means thunder. Traditionally, a pestle made from the wood of the guava tree is used to grind ingredients such as peanuts, sesame seeds, peppercorns, Chinese tea leaves, mint leaves and sweet potato leaves in a large bowl. They are then steeped in hot water, poured into a pan and brought to a boil. This soup is then poured over a serving of cooked rice, turning it into porridge. Malays also have their version, which they call **bubur**. **Bubur lambuk** (savoury rice porridge), for example, is flavoured with ginger, cinnamon, star anise and sometimes coconut, as well as coarsely chopped beef, diced chicken and diced prawns (yes, all three ingredients together).

You will find some stalls – usually open at night – serving **nasi bubur**, an East Malaysian speciality. The texture is similar to that of Teochew porridge, and as with Teochew porridge, is served with a variety of dishes you pick from a selection on display. But that's where the similarities stop. Accompanying dishes include fried stingray, fried quail, pickled garlic and cuttlefish with honey (which tastes almost candied). Salty, sweet and subtly spicy flavours dominate. **Bubur hitam**, on the other hand, is a sweet porridge made of black glutinous rice served with coconut milk.

Rice porridge, a popular breakfast and comfort food, Penang

STAPLES

Mee (Noodles)

China originally introduced noodles to the rest of Asia. The noodles used in Malaysia and Singapore are made from wheat, wheat and egg, rice, or mung beans. All come in both fresh and dried forms except mung bean, which only comes dried.

Fresh noodles, Melaka

Mian (Wheat-Flour Noodles)
La Mian (Handmade Wheat-Flour Noodles)
As most of the region's Chinese migrants were from southern China, the plain wheat-flour noodles that are a northern Chinese staple are not commonly consumed in Malaysia and Singapore. Fine, fresh, handmade wheat-flour noodles are however served at speciality Shanghai and Beijing restaurants, in soups with **wonton** (dumplings filled with meat, seafood or vegetables), or dry in **Zhejiang mian**, a one-dish meal with Beijing-style minced pork sauce.

Mian xian (dried wheat-flour noodles) are more commonly found at hawker centres, served in a clear soup with pig's kidney or liver, and sometimes with a dash of brandy for good measure. Chinese eat the dish for its restorative qualities. Peranakans use the same noodles in **mee suah tow**, a stirfry with shrimp, chicken and Chinese mushrooms. They call these 'birthday noodles'.

Jidan Mian (Egg Noodles)
Noodles made from wheat flour and eggs are more common than those made only from wheat flour. The fine, rounded egg noodle is between the thickness of angel hair pasta and spaghetti, and is the basic noodle served in **tok-tok mee** (noodles served dry and tossed in a sauce usually consisting of soy sauce, sesame oil and chilli sauce or ketchup, topped with barbecued pork, wontons, and some greens). The noodles are also served in soup. This dish is also referred to as **wonton mee** or **cha siew mee**. When the noodles are made flat, like linguini, they are called **mee pok**. You usually get to choose from the two kinds of noodles when ordering most noodle dishes. But mee pok is preferred when having **bak chor mee** – noodles doused with Chinese black vinegar and the hawker's special sauce, then topped with minced pork, fish balls, pickles, freshly chopped spring onions and toasted dried fish.

Hokkien Mee & Fujian Mian (Hokkien Noodles)
These yellow, thick egg noodles are popular not only among Chinese, but Malays and Indians as well. These noodles are central to **Hokkien mee**, a stirfried hawker favourite that's filled with squid and tiny shrimp, pork and vegetables, and rich **hay mee** (Hokkien prawn noodle soup; see the recipe). But these noodles are also used in many Malay dishes such as **mee rebus** (thick, fresh egg noodles in a viscous, sweet and spicy sauce, served with hard-boiled eggs and freshly cut green chillies) and Indian hawker dishes such as **mee goreng** (spicy fried noodles often with the reddish hue of tomato sauce and red food colouring, filled with cubes of potato, cabbage and occasionally some minced meat).

Hay Mee (Hokkien Prawn Noodle Soup)

Hokkien mee or Fujian mian, a yellow, thick egg noodle, was introduced to the region by Chinese who had migrated from China's Fujian province. This comforting noodle soup is usually sold at hawker stalls and by street food vendors.

Ingredients

500g	fresh Hokkien mee
100g	dried rice vermicelli
500g	bean sprouts
300g	**kangkong** (water convolvulus – if unavailable, substitute with spinach leaves)

Garnishes

1 tbs	vegetable oil for frying
100g	pork fat, diced
5 tbs	fried shallots (available in small tubs from any Asian grocer in the west and in Malaysia and Singapore)
2	red chillies, finely sliced into diagonal pieces
	light soy sauce

Soup stock

600g	pork ribs
2	dried red chillies, ground
600g	raw, medium-sized prawns
200g	pork fillet
2L	water
1 tbs	sugar
1 tsp	white peppercorns
1 tbs	light soy sauce
1 tbs	dark soy sauce
	salt

Bring a large saucepan of lightly salted water to the boil. Partly boil the Hokkien mee (just quickly plunge into boiling water), then tip them into a colander to drain, and run cold water over to halt the cooking process. Set aside. Soak the rice vermicelli in a bowl of hot water for 10 minutes, then drain and set aside. Scald the bean sprouts very briefly in boiling salted water, then drain and set aside. Blanch the kangkong in boiling water and drain. Snip the kangkong into 5cm lengths and set aside.

For the garnishes, heat the vegetable oil in a frying pan until very hot. Stirfry the diced pork fat until crisp. Drain on paper towels and set aside. To make your own fried shallots, simply thinly slice shallots and panfry in vegetable oil until crisp and golden brown. Dab off excess oil with paper towels. Place the crisp pork fat, fried shallots, sliced chillies, and soy sauce in four small dishes of around 1-cup capacity, leaving them on the table for people to help themselves.

Heat the remaining oil, and fry the pork ribs and ground dried chillies over a fierce heat until the meat just changes colour (ie, brown it). Transfer the bones into a large stockpot. In the frypan stirfry the prawns with their shells on until they have turned pink, which means they are cooked. This should only take a couple of minutes. Remove the prawns, cool, then peel. Add the prawn shells and heads to the stockpot. Set the peeled prawns aside. Add the pork meat, water, sugar, peppercorns and soy sauces to the stockpot, adding salt to taste. Bring slowly to the boil, and simmer until the pork meat is cooked (about 30 minutes). Fish out the pork meat and continue simmering the rest of the stock until you have a richly flavoured broth (this will take at least another 30 minutes). Cool the pork meat, slice it very thinly, and set it aside. Strain the broth through a fine sieve into a clean saucepan and bring to a rolling boil when ready to serve.

To serve, place some bean sprouts and kangkong in each bowl, and top with Hokkien mee and beehoon. Place a fan of pork slices and prawns on top of each serving, and pour the boiling broth over each portion. Serve with the prepared garnishes.

Serves 6

Mee Fen (Rice-Flour Noodles)
Kway Teow (Medium-Width Rice-Flour Noodles)
These broad ribbons of rice-flour noodle form the cornerstone of one of the region's much-loved Chinese hawker classics, **char kway teow** – stirfried kway teow noodles tossed with cockles, slivers of Chinese sausage and egg in a sweet, dark soy sauce. Every local has a favourite stall. These noodles are also served in **yu yuan mian** (fish-ball soup).

Laksa Mee (Laksa Rice Noodles)
While you'll find as many different versions of **laksa** (spicy, soupy noodle dish) as there are states in Malaysia, the noodles used remain fairly constant: white, opaque, thick rice-flour noodles similar in size to Hokkien noodles. These are also served with Chinese beef noodles. Dried versions are also available, but the texture and flavour can be quite different to fresh versions.

Beehoon/Bihun (Rice Vermicelli)
Wiry, thin and brittle, these rice-flour noodles have to be softened in water before they can be stirfried or added to soups and curries. Simply stirfried with some dried shrimp, cabbage, carrot and perhaps some chicken, they form a basic, casual lunchtime meal in most Malay and Chinese house-holds. Beehoon noodles are also served in **mee siam** (rice vermicelli in a spicy, tangy sauce), influenced by the cuisine of neighbouring Thailand, and in Chinese hawker noodle dishes (such as fish-ball soup).

Other Noodles
Tung Fen (Dried Mung Bean Thread Noodles)
These noodles look a little like beehoon tied up in a bundle, but they are actually made from mung bean flour and are difficult to cut or break in their dried state. They are also called glass noodles or cellophane noodles. They need to be soaked in water before stirfrying or boiling in soup. In most Chinese seafood restaurants, you are likely to find dishes such as **claypot tung fen** with crab or prawns. At home, the noodles are also stirfried with simple ingredients or popped into a soup to form a casual one-dish meal.

Quai Su Mian (Instant Noodles)
The variety of instant noodles available is astounding. You will find both wheat-flour and rice-flour varieties at most supermarkets, with flavours created to appeal to local palates. But the wackiest hawker dish around must be **Maggi mee goreng** – instant noodles (Maggi is the preferred brand) softened in boiling water before being fried just like Indian mee goreng and topped with an egg fried sunny-side-up. You'll find this dish at Indian stalls at suppertime. It has become so popular that there are even instant noodles packaged with mee goreng flavour sachets.

Enjoying a plate of fresh beehoon, Kuala Lumpur

Cili (Chilli)

It is impossible to conceive of a Malaysian or Singaporean meal without chilli. Even delicate **dian xin** (dim sum) is often served with a dish of chilli sauce on the side for that extra zing.

Dried chillies are a staple of all the region's cuisines

Red chilli adds colour and heat to a dish. Blended and ground with other spices, it adds depth to a curry. Sliced finely, it is tossed into anything from vegetable stirfries to fried **beehoon** (rice vermicelli), and adds a punch to most dishes. Several chillies blended on their own form the base for many a **sambal** (chilli-based condiment) and chilli sauce. Do not underestimate the importance of chilli sauce in a dish. A chicken rice dish, for example, is not simply judged by the quality of the chicken, but also by the quality and flavour of the chilli sauce – which must contain a good balance of fresh red chillies, garlic, ginger and a hint of tartness from lime juice. Some restaurants use commercial chilli pastes, others pride themselves in making their own.

Cili padi (bird's eye chilli) is by far the spiciest of them all. When a girl or woman is described as a cili padi, locals mean that the petite lady packs a powerful punch and shouldn't be messed around with. The same goes for the real thing. You'll know if you've bitten into a cili padi, as the heat will sear through your tongue and the fainthearted will experience watering of the eyes. These chillies are sometimes served sliced and in soy sauce. Just a tiny hint of chilli-soy sauce in your food will infuse a delightfully fiery heat.

Lada kering (dried chillies) lack the strong smell of fresh chillies, but often give dishes a brighter red colour. They need to be soaked in hot water until they are soft (usually just a few minutes) before they are used. In Sichuan cuisine, whole dried chillies are used in stirfries. Chilli oil is made using a base oil such as a vegetable oil, which is then infused with chilli. To make your own, simply heat one cup of oil in a small pan and stir in 10 whole dried chillies. Heat for one minute, then turn off the heat and leave to cool before straining. Use chilli oil sparingly as it has quite a spicy heat. It is usually used as a condiment rather than as part of a dish – you'll find little bottles of chilli oil at stalls serving **hay mee** (Hokkien prawn noodle soup; see the recipe). Chilli powder is used in curries and marinades. Malays believe that a few dried chillies should be put into a cook's rice bin to prevent weevils from attacking rice grains.

Green chillies are less spicy than their red counterparts, and impart a subtle flavour. At Chinese noodle hawkers, pickled cut green chillies are often served with light soy sauce as a dip to accompany light, soupy noodle dishes such as fish-ball noodles or **hor fun** (thick rice-based noodles cooked in a thick broth with seafood and pork).

If your stomach is unaccustomed to the hot stuff, be sure to indicate that you want less or no chilli in your food when you place your order. Milk provides a quick remedy for a tongue burning from too much chilli, but often this combination tends to have a nasty effect on the stomach. Other popular remedies include a good mouthful of plain rice, warm water, iced water, or **kalamansi** (sour lime) juice.

Rempah (Spice Paste)

While chilli paste is made up of large quantities of chilli blended into a paste – so as to sidestep the chore of grinding fresh chillies from scratch every time you make a dish – rempah is a mix of spices made by pounding a combination of wet and dry ingredients together to form a paste. The spice mix constantly changes depending on the dish you are making. Wet ingredients include shallots, lemongrass, garlic, chilli, ginger and galangal. Dry ingredients consist of items such as candlenuts, cinnamon, coriander seeds, cumin, cloves and peppercorns. Traditionally the ingredients are combined using a mortar and pestle; however, a food processor is often used in the modern kitchen. The wet ingredients are combined before the dry ones are added.

    The rempah is considered the heart and soul of Malay, Eurasian and Peranakan curries and sauces. It thickens curry gravies and gives dimension to their flavour, as curries flavoured with only curry powder tend to have a flat, bland taste. Beyond pounding it into a paste, the other important technique lies in frying the rempah. A significant amount of oil is needed to fry it until it is fragrant, and the oil has to be hot enough before the rempah is added to the pan. It must be constantly stirred to prevent it from sticking to the pan. Once the oil starts to seep out of the rempah, the other ingredients in your recipe (say, chicken for a chicken curry) can be added.

Sambal (Chilli-Based Condiment)

There are as many kinds of sambal (basically a chilli sauce or relish) as there are cooks. At its most simple is the **sambal ulek**, which is a combination of chilli, vinegar and salt blended either with a mortar and pestle, or in a food processor. The basic chilli paste can be served on the side with a squirt of lime or **kalamansi** (sour lime) juice as a condiment that will add a kick to your meal – you'll find it's served with anything from fried Hokkien noodles and **laksa** (spicy, soupy noodle dish), to **nasi lemak** (coconut rice with fried fish) and barbecued chicken wings. It can also be incorporated into curries and other spicy local dishes including barbecued fish and fried eggplant. By adding shallots, galangal, garlic, **belacan** (fermented shrimp paste), tamarind liquid and other ingredients at hand, different kinds of sambal are created, all with the essential spicy punch at their core. Eurasians serve **sambal cili taucheo** (onions, chilli and preserved soybeans) over fried fish or panfried **taukua** (firm beancurd). Malays love their nasi lemak with **sambal ikan bilis** (dried anchovies fried and mixed with sambal). And Peranakans cannot bear to face a meal without a helping of **sambal belacan** (chilli and belacan paste; see the recipe) – diehard fans have been known to indulge in helpings of the sambal spread on toast.

Sambal belacan Nonya style, Melaka

Sambal Belacan (Chilli & Belacan Paste)

As ubiquitous on the Peranakan table as salt and pepper shakers, this condiment is for those who want extra heat in their food. It also features as a base ingredient in other recipes, such as stuffed grilled fish or egg-plant sambal.

Ingredients

1 tbs	**belacan** (fermented shrimp paste)
4	red chillies
1/4 tsp	salt
1/4 tsp	sugar

To serve

wedges of lime

Toast the belacan in a dry pan over low heat until it is crumbly and aromatic. Strip the chillies of their seeds and set the seeds aside. If using a mortar and pestle, place the chillies on top of the belacan, add a third of the reserved seeds, and grind. Add the salt and sugar. Now, stir in the rest of the seeds. A good sambal has textural interest. The point is not to break all the chilli seeds while reducing everything else to a paste. Alternatively, use a food processor, making sure not to refine the sambal too much. Serve the sambal in little dishes with a wedge of lime for people to help themselves.

Serves 4 as a condiment

STAPLES

Terung Sambal (Eggplant with Chilli Paste)

Families stock their refrigerator with sambal made ahead of time. These pastes help add flavour and spice to quick, easy dishes such as fried fish (or any other meat, or even firm tofu) or this simple eggplant creation you're likely to see at **nasi lemak** (coconut rice with fried fish) stalls.

Ingredients

2	slender purple eggplants, left whole
	vegetable oil for deep frying
1 quantity	**sambal belacan** (chilli and belacan paste; see the recipe)

Deep fry the eggplant until tender (a few minutes on either side) and drain on paper towels. Make a central lengthwise incision in each eggplant. Spoon the sambal over, packing some into the soft flesh, and serve.

Serves 4 as a side dish to accompany plain rice and other curries or meat dishes.

Fish, Fowl & Meat
Ikan (Fish)

The region was once dotted with fishing villages, and today the fishing industry continues to thrive on the east coast of Malaysia. While the old days of buying live fish right out of the fisherman's boat are fading fast, the variety of fresh fish available continues to be mind-boggling. Depending on which regional variation of **laksa** (spicy, soupy noodle dish) you're eating, you could be tucking into **ikan parang** (wolf herring – an ingredient in **laksa Johor**, a rich, fish-based laksa served with spaghetti), **ikan kembung** (mackerel – in **laksa Pahang**, a fish-based laksa with rice vermicelli) or just **udang** (prawns – in **laksa lemak**, laksa with curry chicken or prawns).

Dried shrimp

Ikan tenggiri (Spanish mackerel) is fashioned into **ikan otak otak**, spiced rectangles wrapped in banana leaves and grilled over a charcoal fire, while **bawal puteh** (plump silver pomfret) is delicately steamed with pickled sour plums, salted vegetable and tomato wedges, Teochew style. Over at the **ikan bakar** (grilled fish) stall, grilled stingray is the hot seller. However, in select Singaporean coffeeshops it's **ka li yu tou** (fish-head curry) that rules the table. Malays generally prefer their fish fried whole and stuffed with spices or chopped into chunks or steaks and served within a spicy **asam** (tamarind) sauce. Chinese prefer to cook larger fish such as snapper, sea bass and grouper, either steamed (this is preferred when the fish is extremely fresh), fried or braised.

Kerang (Shellfish)

Clams and mussels are farmed in the coastal waters off Malaysia. In a small fishing area like Pasir Penambang (an hour's drive from Kuala Lumpur), **kerang** (cockles) are cleaned and bagged before they are transported to consumers in Kuala Lumpur, Pahang, Kelantan and Trengganu. About 5000kg of cockles pass through just one processing plant each day. They go into dishes such as **char kway teow** (broad, flat rice-flour noodles stirfried with Chinese sausage and egg in a sweet, dark soy sauce; halal versions include **kway teow kerang**) and laksa – especially in the Singapore version – or are served cooked with a simple chilli-vinegar dip on the side.

Kepah (Manila clams) occasionally feature as a mildly spicy option at **nasi campur** (plate of rice, topped with various dishes) stalls (see p 179). Peranakans stirfry these with curry paste, curry leaves and lemongrass for a dry, spicy dish.

Or luah (fried oyster omelette) is a hot favourite, and **tiram** (tiny oysters, unlike European and Australian vareties) dot this sinfully satisfying dish. While mussels make an occasional appearance in some dishes, crabs are expensive and not widely consumed. But for that special meal, **Singapore chilli crab** (spicy chilli and tomato-based crab stirfry dish; see the recipe), **black pepper crab** (sweet and spicy chilli and black pepper-based stirfry dish) or simple steamed crab (all using mud crab) are much-loved treats.

Stacked steamed crab, Kuala Lumpur

SHRIMPLY BELACAN

Geragau are the tiny shrimp found in the seas off the Straits of Melaka and in the waters of Penang. Associated with Penang and Melaka, the name geragau is sometimes used to refer to the Portuguese Eurasians of the region who used to make a living fishing for the shrimp. This is, however, considered a derogatory term.

Geragau are the shrimps used to make **cincaluk** (fermented shrimps) and **belacan** (fermented shrimp paste). Cincaluk – which is extremely salty – is either incorporated into a **sambal** (chilli-based condiment), served as an appetiser with chopped shallots, chilli and lime juice, or eaten with rice dishes. Belacan is either ground into a **rempah** (spice paste) as a flavouring in curries and other dishes, or blended with chilli and other ingredients to form a sambal.

Shrimps drying in the sun at a belacan factory, Penang

STAPLES

A fresh block of belacan, Penang

To witness belacan being made is a sight to behold and a smell to be inhaled only if you have a strong stomach (the pungent smell of belacan takes some getting used to). The shrimp is caught at night, rinsed in sea water and mixed with salt before it is left to stand overnight. In the morning, it is spread out to dry in the sun before being put through a crushing machine. It is then stored in wooden vats for a week before it is once again laid out to dry and put through the machine. It takes some weeks before the process is complete. The paste is finally put through a machine that shapes it into blocks that are then wrapped in a layer of tracing paper and another of brown paper. The best belacan doesn't smell off-putting at all (though it does take some getting used to), while lower-grade belacan smells like rotting fish. The good stuff smells of sea salt and fresh shrimp, much like a fresh ocean breeze but far more intense.

Ayam (Chicken) & Itek (Duck)

Apart from fish, chicken is possibly the most often consumed flesh in the region. While the free-range *kampung* (village) chicken is prized for its flavour and lean meat, the reality is that the chicken in your **Hainanese chicken rice** (see the recipe), **ayam buah keluak** (mildly spicy, sour chicken dish filled with **buah keluak**, Indonesian black nuts that are prized among Peranakans), **ayam soto** (Malay chicken soup) and chicken **kapitan** (a curry dish that Eurasians serve on special occasions) is likely to have never left its coop. Nonetheless, the wonderful flavours of local chicken recipes bring out the best in even the most inactive of chickens.

You can be assured that every bit of the chicken is used. The feet are marinated and served steam as a **dian xin** (dim sum) delicacy (the poetic Cantonese refer to it as phoenix claws), or boiled, de-boned and served cold at chicken rice restaurants as an appetiser. Livers, hearts and gizzards are also offered as side orders at chicken rice joints, while liver and gizzard curries are common Indian dishes.

Duck, on the other hand, is less frequently consumed. Classic dishes, though, are **itek sio** (stewed duck in coriander), **itek tim** (duck and salted vegetable soup) and **lou ark** (Teochew braised duck; served with a piquant chilli, Chinese leek and white vinegar dip).

Steamed and roasted chickens, Kuala Lumpur

Babi (Pork)

While pork is considered haram (forbidden) among Muslims, the Chinese, Peranakans and Eurasians (but not so much the Indians) revel in its flavour. Chinese especially love the fatty layers of belly pork that Hokkiens use to make **kong bak pau**, belly pork braised in a dark master stock (often consisting of dark and light soy sauce, caramelised sugar, Chinese cooking wine, star anise and Chinese cassia bark), with the pork then sliced into rectangular portions and slipped into flat buns that have pockets created just for the purpose. Pork ribs are used in the Chinese kitchen to make a peppery, herbal soup called **bak kut teh** (pork bone tea; see the recipe), that old men love to sip on while chatting with their friends at neighbourhood coffeeshops. While the soup is the focus of the meal, the tender flesh on the pork ribs must be dipped into side dishes containing sliced bird's eye chillies steeped in light soy sauce before being eaten. The spicy sensation of chilli, soy and melt-in-your-mouth pork is absolutely divine. In typical Chinese fashion, no part of the beast is wasted. **Kway chap** (a meal of braised pig's innards, pork, hard-boiled eggs, braised tofu and roughly cut sheets of rice noodles) ensures that every bit of pig is used. Awful as it may sound, when properly cleaned,

Kong bak pau, Singapore

the large and small intestines (the small one has a floury filling) are delicious. The more adventurous should also sample the glistening, smooth cubes of pig's blood on display. Can't stomach that? Then just ask for slices of pork, braised tofu and hard-boiled eggs in your bowl of rice noodles.

Peranakans and Eurasians have also got cooking pork down to a fine art. **Babi pong teh** (stewed pork) is a family favourite. Belly pork and bamboo shoots are flavoured by Peranakans with **taucheo** (fermented soybeans), cinnamon, dark soy sauce and sugar to create this hearty stew that's perfect with a bowl of steamed rice. And their **sek bak** (belly pork in a spicy black sauce), dipped in just a smidgen of **sambal belacan** (chilli and belacan paste; see the recipe), is what gastronomic dreams are made of. **Feng**, a typical Eurasian dish, is a regular Christmas feature that is best eaten a day old. Here, lean pork from the pig's hind leg is used in a curry that requires the addition of a special feng curry powder (comprised of coriander, cumin and fennel). Because cooking this dish is such a tedious process (see the recipe), a big pot of it is normally prepared early and the required amount reheated when the need arises. It is often served with a French loaf (the local baguette), **achar** (preserved mixed vegetables; a Eurasian achar usually consists of cucumber, green chillies, shallots, cabbage, garlic and ginger in a pickling liquid), fried pork chipolatas (small sausages) and meatball cutlets (minced pork balls).

Daging Lembu (Beef) & Daging Kambing (Mutton)

Both beef and mutton (you'll notice that locals use the word **kambing** – mutton – to refer to both lamb and mutton, as well as to kid and goat), are commonly served at a Malay dinner table. While Chinese do appreciate stirfried slivers of beef, the heady aroma of mutton does not quite appeal (except to the Mongolians who are not well represented in the region). Most Indians in the region are Tamils, and many are strict vegetarians. The cow, to Hindus in particular, is considered sacred, and Indians therefore never consume beef. Mutton, on the other hand, is often served in curries and biryanis.

In the Malay kitchen, dishes such as **rendang** (beef in a thick coconutmilk curry sauce; see the recipe), **daging masak kecap** (beef in soy sauce), **gulai daging** (beef curry), **daging asam** (tamarind beef), **serunding daging** (spicy beef floss) and its mutton counterparts fill the cook's prospective menu. Older meat (meaning mutton rather than lamb) is usually cooked for a long time, the results coming closer to that of a stew. But do not be surprised when your order of **daging bakar** (grilled beef) comes to you well done, rather than medium-rare, the way you may be used to having your steaks. Beef here is never served pink.

Babi pong teh, Melaka

STAPLES

Dao/Tau (Soybeans)

While soybeans are rarely used unprocessed in local kitchens, the protein-rich beans are always present, whether in the form of beancurd, fermented beans or soy sauce.

Tofu (Fresh Beancurd)

Beyond the silky smooth **silken tofu** (as locals refer to it; also known as **taofu** or **tauhu**) that we are most familiar with, Malaysians and Singaporeans have a wide variety of beancurd products from which to choose. The basic beancurd is made from soybeans that have been soaked; puréed or blended; cooked; sieved and then solidified into curds with the addition of magnesium chloride. The delicate silken tofu is often added to soups or egg (egg tofu usually comes in tubes). It can also be sliced into discs, then either panfried and served with an egg and crab-meat sauce, or individually topped with minced pork and steamed with a light sauce. A slightly firmer version of tofu (which locals simply refer to as tofu or tauhu) is panfried and used in dishes such as **tauhu goreng** (fried tofu topped with blanched bean sprouts, slivers of cucumber and a spicy-sweet peanut sauce). **Taukua**, an even firmer tofu, is used to create **taukua pau**, where it is split open to form a pocket and is then stuffed with vegetables and pieces of braised duck. **Taupok** is beancurd that has been deep fried until its insides have been transformed into a spongy hollow. These hollows are often stuffed with fish paste for **yong tauhu**, a hawker dish where diners choose items that are then dropped into a soup with noodles. Taupok can also be stuffed with minced meat and added into Eurasian and Peranakan soups. **Taukee** are beancurd sheets – the skin that forms on the surface when beancurd is made. The skin is removed, dried flat, and then folded into sheets. These need to be soaked in warm water before use. Peranakans use it in **chap chai** (a mixed vegetable dish), and Chinese use it in stirfries, braised claypot dishes and soups. **Tauhuay** (sweet beancurd; see the recipe) is commonly served at hawker stalls, particularly ones that serve **tauhuay chwee** (sweet soybean milk). This extremely delicate curd is served in bowls with a sweet syrup drizzled over it.

Tempeh (Fermented Soybean Cake)

A staple in the Indonesian kitchen, tempeh consists of boiled soybeans sprinkled with a yeast starter and then shaped into slabs and wrapped in banana leaves (it takes around 48 hours to ferment). The fermented beans form a nutritious, low-cholesterol and high-protein food that has a crunchy texture and nutty flavour. It can be panfried and served hot with **nasi lemak** (coconut rice with fried fish).

Tauhuay (Sweet Beancurd)

This sweet can be served hot or chilled, and is popular both as a dessert and as a snack.

Ingredients

1 quantity	**air soya** (soybean milk – see the recipe – halving the quantity of water and omitting the sugar)
1 tsp	powdered calcium sulphate, or gypsum, sifted
3 tbs	cornflour, sifted
125mL	hot water

Syrup

400g	sugar
250mL	water

Mix the calcium sulphate and cornflour in a large casserole dish, add the hot water, and stir until dissolved. Bring the strained soybean milk to the boil in a deep saucepan. When it boils, immediately pour the liquid over the cornflour paste. Skim off any bubbles that appear on the surface. Cover the casserole dish with a clean tea towel, and put on the lid. Set this aside for 45 minutes, by which time the liquid will have thickened into a tremulously milky jelly. Serve at room temperature or chilled.

When ready to serve, make the syrup by bringing the sugar and water to the boil in a heavy-based saucepan and stirring until the sugar dissolves. Remove from the heat, scoop the beancurd into individual bowls, and drizzle syrup over each serving.

Serves 4–6

STAPLES

Taucheo (Salted Soybeans)

Cooked soybeans are heavily salted and fermented for over a month. This results in a light coloured yellow bean sauce filled with mushy whole beans (usually packaged in jars). Salted soybeans, as their name implies, are exceedingly salty and are used sparingly in Chinese, Eurasian and Peranakan cooking. Chinese also like to use them as a dip for steamed fish. They are also crushed and mixed into food.

Jiang You (Soy Sauce)

Naturally fermented soy sauce tastes different from the mass-produced stuff we generally get in supermarkets the world over. The first extraction (much like the first oil from the olive press that is labelled 'extra virgin' and prized for its flavour) is considered the most flavoursome and has the pure saltiness that you get from tasting the best sea salt. The two basic sauces are **jiang qing** (light soy) and **hei jiang you** (dark soy). Dark soy sauce is basically light soy with caramel added before being set aside to mature for an additional period of time. Both sauce types are used as the basic flavourings in numerous stews, braises and stirfries across all cuisines.

Soy sauce made the old-fashioned way, Penang

Pulses & Nuts

Pulses are the dried seeds of legumes such beans, peas and lentils. They form the basis of many an Indian vegetarian dish and are fabulous sources of protein and vitamins. Whether it's black-eyed peas and chickpeas or yellow, red and black lentils, an Indian meal is rarely complete without a **daal** (lentil, pea or bean) curry, snack or sweet.

Dosai, a staple breakfast item, consists of paper-thin crêpes made of rice and lentils, served with coconut chutney and curry. Lentils are often used to thicken curries, and snacks such as the deep-fried and noodle-like **muruku** are made from rice and daal flours.

Masala dosai

Buah Keluak (Indonesian Black Nut)

Originally from Brazil, this black, hard-shelled nut is grown extensively in Indonesia. The black oily kernel has a slightly bitter taste, reminiscent of olive tapenade (without the salt) when cooked. The nuts need to be soaked overnight and cracked before they are cooked. Preparation is highly labour intensive. It is loved among Peranakans and forms the focus of Peranakan dishes such as **ayam buah keluak** (mildly spicy, sour chicken dish filled with **buah keluak**, Indonesian black nuts).

Sauces, Flavourings, Oils & Spices

The flavouring options across Malaysia and Singapore are astounding, as are the complexities of the region's cuisines. Here are some of the essentials most homes would use.

Sauces
Hoisin & Hao You (Oyster Sauces)

Made from salted soybeans, sugar, vinegar, sesame oil and spices such as five-spice and star anise, hoisin is used as a dipping sauce. It's also used as a meat glaze and in marinades, and spread over **Peking duck** (thin slices of roasted duck served with pancakes and sauce) pancakes before they are rolled. Oyster sauce, however, is made of oyster extract and is a Cantonese speciality. It is generally used at the end of a stirfry (to top stirfried vegetables, for example), as part of a marinade or as a dipping sauce.

Yu Lu (Fish Sauce)

Fish sauce is made from anchovies and is extremely salty and strong smelling. Thai people are fond of using it (and often use it as a dip with chopped bird's eye chillies), but in Malaysia and Singapore it is more often used to season foods such as fried rice and noodles.

Ketchup

You'd be amazed at the amount of ketchup that's used by everyone across the region. It appears in dishes as disparate as Hainanese pork chops (as part of the sweet-and-sour sauce), Singapore chilli crab, Indian **mee goreng** (spicy fried noodles often with the reddish hue of tomato sauce and red food colouring, filled with cubes of potato, cabbage and occasionally some minced meat), **wonton mee** (wonton noodle soup) and **nasi tomato** (tomato-flavoured rice served with a variety of dishes).

   Ketchup is not to be confused with **kecap manis**, which is a thick, sweet soy sauce (sweetened with palm sugar) used in **char kway teow** (broad, flat rice-flour noodles stirfried with Chinese sausage and egg in a sweet, dark soy sauce, in **pohpiah** (Peranakan spring rolls; see the recipe) and many Indonesian-influenced dishes.

Sos Cili (Chilli Sauce)

Commercial chilli sauces tend to be a little sweet and some contain garlic. These sauces are sometimes used to create meals quickly, but are more often used as dips for anything from fried chicken wings and deep-fried spring rolls to French fries from McDonald's. Thai sweet chilli sauce is also increasingly available. It is more sweet than spicy, and has visible pieces of chopped chilli floating in a semi-translucent sauce. For more information on chillies see p 48.

Soy and chilli sauce ready for dipping, Singapore

KETCHUP HOMECOMING

What's in a ketchup? Historically, that's a question Malaysians may be best equipped to answer. This now-iconic 'American' product has roots in an old Chinese fish sauce called 'ke-tsiap' that was used in ports like Melaka and Penang, where Dutch and other European settlers took a liking to it and began pronouncing it 'kejap'. Proving that taste may be the most effective ambassador of all, this condiment wound its way to Europe during the 17th century, where the pronunciation tilted towards the 'ketchup/catsup' side of things. As colonisation went trans-Atlantic, ketchup made its way to the New World. But the recipe we now know and love had yet to evolve. A recipe from 1808's *Domestic Cookery*, a classic American household tome, calls for anchovies and walnuts as main ingredients. By 1876, Heinz had begun cranking out the tomato-based condiment that has since remained the same. Yet while ketchup's popularity in the US has been eclipsed by salsa, it's now becoming a quiet player in Malaysia and Singapore. Hawkers use the modern-day tomato sauce to flavour everything from noodle dishes to Ramly Burgers.

Rob McKeown

Flavourings
Bawang (Onions)

There are a few types of onion that are commonly used in the region. **Bawang merah** is a tiny red shallot that grows in clumps similar to garlic. It is either pounded or ground to form part of a **rempah** (spice paste) in numerous Malay, Indian, Peranakan and Eurasian dishes. They are by far more pungent than white- or brown-skinned onions and add a distinctive aroma and flavour to dishes. The slightly larger red **bawang besar** (Bombay onion) is chopped and served raw with satay, and used in most dishes, although the traditional brown onion is also commonly used in its place. **Daun bawang** (spring onions/scallions) are widely used in Chinese cooking, with the green tops often finely chopped, or cut into slivers, and used as a garnish. **Koo chai** (chives) are used as a garnish over some noodle dishes and also used as a stuffing in **koo chai pau** (chive dumplings).

Bawang Putih (Garlic)

Garlic is as essential to your rempah as shallots. It is used with near wild abandon in curries, soups (in vast quantities in **bak kut teh** – pork bone tea; see the recipe), and meat and vegetable dishes. No one ever worries about having garlic breath.

Fresh garlic, Penang

Halia (Ginger)

Ginger provides a subtle heat to dishes and is believed to have medicinal qualities. It is minced and served with a fresh chilli paste with **Hainanese chicken rice** (see the recipe); steamed with fish; crushed in rempah; and even used in **teh halia** (milky ginger tea).

Kunyit (Turmeric)

This ginger-like fresh rhizome is bright orange in colour and has a slightly bitter flavour (be careful not to use too much of it). A slice of turmeric added to rice or curry will give it a bright yellow hue and it is often used in place of saffron – which imparts a warm orange tint, but is far more expensive. Primarily used for colour, turmeric is also commonly used in powdered form, known as **serbuk kunyit**.

Lengkuas (Galangal)

Also known as blue ginger, galangal looks like ginger but has a different flavour. It is used in Malay, Peranakan and Eurasian cooking, and has a faint camphor flavour. Galangal should be used sparingly as it imparts a bitter taste if too much is used.

Serai (Lemongrass)

Lemongrass imparts its delightful citrus aroma to curries, soups and tea. It is the lower, bulbous stem of lemongrass that is used (the leaves may only be used for infusions). The tougher outer layers of the stem are discarded, leaving only the pale inner portion that is sliced thinly or simply bruised. Lemongrass is used primarily for flavour and is generally not eaten. It is acceptable to leave it on your plate.

Daun Pandan (Pandanus Leaves)

These highly aromatic leaves, also known as screwpine leaves, are used by Malays, Chinese, Peranakans and Eurasians to flavour and colour cakes, drinks, rice and many other desserts. Fresh whole leaves kept in cupboards are believed to keep cockroaches away. In many taxis in the major cities, you'll notice that large bunches of pandanus leaves are left near the back window to impart a pleasant aroma (and presumably to keep the bugs away).

Cakes coloured with pandanus leaves

Daun Ketumbar (Coriander/Cilantro)

This fresh herb is not to be mistaken for **ketumbar** (coriander powder), which is made from the plant's ground seeds (a constant in most Indian and Malay spice mixtures). The roots of the herb are pounded and often incorporated into rempah or used to flavour stocks, while the fresh leaves are used as a wonderfully fragrant garnish over most curries, fried noodle dishes, steamed fish and even chicken rice.

Daun Limau Purut (Kaffir Lime Leaves)

The fresh leaves of the kaffir lime tree are used, finely shredded, in Peranakan and Eurasian – as well as some Malay – curries and **sambal** (chilli-based condiment). The leaves have a delicate lime smell and impart a subtle flavour.

Daun Kesum (Vietnamese Mint) & Daun Kari (Curry Leaf)

Despite its name, Vietnamese mint isn't of the mint family. It has narrow pointed leaves and is strikingly dark green. The leaf is most commonly chopped and tossed over **laksa** (spicy, soupy noodle dish) at the very last minute (which is why it is also called 'laksa leaf'). The curry leaf, on the other hand, is usually the first ingredient to be tossed into heated oil before the rest of the ingredients in a curry are added. Its small and pointed leaves have a unique flavour and smell, and were introduced to Malaysia through Indian migrants.

Gula Melaka (Palm Sugar)

Palm sugar is extracted from the stalks of the sugar palm, boiled and allowed to solidify in the hollow of bamboo poles (which accounts for its cylindrical shape). The rich, musky, near bittersweet flavour of palm sugar can nearly be matched by dark brown or muscovado sugar, but nothing tastes quite like the real thing. The sugar is often melted down into a syrup and used to sweeten desserts such as **cendol** (coconut-milk with green rice-flour noodles), **ais kacang** (Malaysian ice dessert) and **sago gula Melaka** (sago pudding; see the recipe). It is also used to sweeten cakes and **kueh-kueh** (little Malay and Peranakan teacakes). The best gula Melaka should be dark brown, which promises a concentrated flavour. Light-coloured versions are less intense.

STAPLES

Palm sugar on sale, Melaka

Sago Gula Melaka (Sago Pudding)

While **gula Melaka** refers to palm sugar, it plays such an intrinsic part of this popular sweet that the dessert is commonly known by that name. This is a dessert that is rarely served outside the home, except for in a few Malay restaurants, and is well worth mastering for its simplicity and delightful flavour.

Ingredients		*Gula Melaka syrup*	
1 cup	pearl sago	125g	palm sugar
5 cups	water	½ cup	water
1	pandanus leaf, tied into a knot	1	pandanus leaf, tied into a knot
1 tbs	coconut milk	*Coconut milk sauce*	
¼ tsp	salt	1 cup	coconut milk
		¼ tsp	salt

Pick over the sago in a sieve to remove any grit. Give the sieve a shake to dislodge any dust. In a deep saucepan, bring the water and pandanus leaf to a fierce rolling boil. Let the sago rain in streams through slightly parted fingers, while stirring with a flat wooden spoon using your other hand. Boil for 5 minutes. Turn off the heat, clamp the lid on, and let the sago finish cooking in the residual heat for about 10 minutes. When done, the pearls will have swelled and become translucent. Drain the sago in a large sieve (discarding the pandanus leaf) and hold under cold running water to rid excess starch. Shake the sieve of all liquid at the end. Turn the contents into a bowl and stir in the coconut milk and salt. The milk gives the sago a lovely milky white appearance. Divide the mix equally between four lightly greased dessert moulds of approximately 1-cup capacity, packing the mixture down gently with the back of a spoon. Refrigerate until set and ready to serve.

For the gula Melaka syrup, hack the palm sugar into small lumps. Heat the lumps in a small saucepan with the water and pandanus leaf until dissolved, simmering until slightly thickened. Strain the syrup through a fine sieve to remove any impurities. Chill thoroughly.

The coconut milk requires little preparation – if the milk is initially too thick (as is often case with tinned, as opposed to freshly extracted, coconut milk), thin it with a little water to a create pouring consistency. Then stir in the salt, which accentuates the flavour, and chill until ready to serve.

When each dessert is thoroughly chilled, tip it out of its mould onto individual plates. Serve each with a generous drizzle of the syrup and coconut milk.

Serves 4

STAPLES

Asam (Tamarind)

Asam jawa is the pulp obtained from the tamarind pod of the tamarindus indica tree, and packets of this are commonly available. **Asam water** (tamarind juice) is obtained by soaking the pulp in warm water. This is used in curries and soups to create a sour taste, and is central to the sourness of **mee siam** (rice vermicelli in a spicy, tangy sauce). **Asam gelugor** (dried tamarind slices), while offering a similar sourness, do not provide the full flavour of asam jawa. They are made from a different product altogether, and are sun-dried slices of the fruit of the asam gelugor tree.

Ma You (Sesame Oil)

Sesame oil, which is pressed from toasted sesame seeds, is never used for frying; it is only used to impart its special nutty aroma to dishes. When heated, it burns easily. It is most commonly tossed into dishes (such as noodles), or incorporated into dressings that are poured over Hainanese chicken (cooked lightly then cut up and drizzled with dressings for use in Hainanese chicken rice dishes) or steamed fish.

Santan (Coconut Milk)

Coconut milk is extracted from the grated flesh of mature coconuts. In wet markets you'll hear the loud mechanical whirr of coconut-grating machines that sound like whole coconuts going round in a tumble dryer. The white floss that comes out of the machine looks more like desiccated coconut than a milk. The trick is to place the grated flesh into a bowl of warm water to release its milky richness, before you sieve the liquid and squeeze the moist pulp to extract more of the milk. This is used to add richness to curries (more so for Malay, Peranakan and Eurasian curries, rather than Indian ones), desserts and drinks.

Malay desserts made with coconut, Singapore

Oils

Corn oil is most commonly used for panfrying, stirfrying and deep frying in local kitchens. But as locals grow more health conscious, they are also turning to soybean oil and canola oil. The most important thing is that the oil does not impart its own flavour to the dish (the way olive oil would). However, for extra flavour, Chinese cooks love to add a little lard (pork fat), while Indian cooks prefer ghee or butter.

Bambu (Spices)

Ketumbar (coriander powder), **jintan putih** (cumin seeds), **jintan manis** (fennel seeds), **bunga cengkih** (cloves), **kayu manis** (cinnamon), **buah pelaga** (cardamom), **lada** (peppercorns), **serbuk kunyit** (turmeric powder) and **serbuk ahlia** (ginger powder) are some of the familiar elements found in the curries, stews and braised dishes of Malaysia and Singapore. Positioned along the Spice Route in the early 1400s, the people of the region naturally experimented with the exotic aromatics that visiting merchants brought with them. Some of the spices that may need a little explaining include:

Bunga Lawang (Star Anise)

Found in China, this star-shaped pod comes from a tree belonging to the magnolia family. Bearing an aniseed-like flavour, it is used in Chinese, Peranakan and Eurasian stews and curries.

Serbuk Lima Rempah (Five-Spice Powder)

This is a Chinese mixed spice usually containing star anise, cassia bark (with a taste similar to cinnamon), cloves, Sichuan pepper and fennel seeds. It sometimes also includes cardamom, coriander seeds, dried orange peel and ginger powder (yes, that would make it more than five spices, despite its name). Not to be mistaken for allspice, five-spice (or five-fragrance) powder is used in Chinese braised dishes (including braised goose and braised belly pork), **ngoh hiang** (Teochew liver or prawn rolls) and spicy **siu yoke** (crispy belly pork).

Garam Masala

Essential to many Indian dishes, **garam masala** is a mixture of ground spices that are either incorporated into the dish or sprinkled over it just before serving. It is generally a mixture of four to six spices, but up to 15 can be included in the mix – coriander seeds and cumin seeds are always used. In North Indian cuisine, black pepper, cinnamon, cloves and cardamom are added to the mix, while in South Indian cuisine some of the spices are replaced by chilli and turmeric.

Fruit & Vegetables

Enter any wet market and you're likely to find carrots, cauliflower and potatoes from Australia, apples from America or China, mangoes from Pakistan and **petai** (stink beans) from Thailand. The point is, in a highly globalised world of trade, Malaysians and Singaporeans no longer simply consume what is indigenous to their land or even their neighbour's. Some wet markets and most supermarkets even sell Australian vine-ripened tomatoes, Japanese *kyuri* (similar to the small Lebanese cucumber) and Ecuadorian bananas.

Sayur (Vegetables)

Even the likes of **bhindi** (okra or ladies' fingers), **terung** (eggplant or aubergine) and **bok choy** (Chinese white cabbage) no longer seem exotic to an international audience. It even seems that as imports become more readily available, the variety of local vegetables available in the markets is gradually shrinking.

Timun (Cucumber)

Unlike the English cucumber, which is dark green, long and fairly skinny, local cucumbers are short, thick and have a light green variegated skin. The seeds are also larger and the flesh spongier – as if they contain more water. Cucumbers are often eaten raw in salads or shredded to make a garnish. They are also pickled in Malay, Peranakan and Eurasian **achar** (preserved mixed vegetables).

Peria (Bittergourd)

This long, ridged green gourd comes from a climbing plant. Malays slice it thinly and fry it with shrimp, while Chinese fry it in an omelette (believing it is cooling for the body) or stuff it with fish paste to make **yong tauhu**.

Kangkong (Water Convolvulus)

With a hollow stem and large, arrowhead leaves (or heart shaped, depending on how you look at it), **kangkong** is a popular vegetable often served fried with **sambal belacan** (chilli and belacan paste; see the recipe).

Bunga Telang (Butterfly or Blue Pea Flower)

This tiny, deep blue (almost violet) flower provides the natural blue colouring for Malay, Peranakan and Eurasian desserts and rice dishes. This is what gives the Kelantan speciality, **nasi kerabu** (cooked rice tossed with finely shredded herbs) its bluish tinge. A handful of these flowers are boiled in water and then squeezed. The water is strained and the resulting liquid is used.

Stink beans at a local market, Penang

Sengkuang (Yam Bean)

The white, mildly sweet, juicy flesh of the yam bean – which is really a tuber – is often eaten raw in salads. When cooked, it is one of the major ingredients in the cooked vegetable stuffing that is served with **pohpiah** (Peranakan spring rolls; see the recipe).

Kiam Chai (Salted Mustard Cabbage)

Introduced by the Chinese, salted mustard cabbage is now used in Peranakan and Eurasian soups, and sliced and added to Malay fish curries to give it that slightly sour zing. But its flavour comes to full force in **itek tim** (duck and salted vegetable soup).

Dong Gua (Wintermelon)

Wintermelon is also known as wax gourd. It comes in round or elongated shapes (similar to the different shapes watermelons come in), and has translucent flesh similar to that of cucumber. When hollowed out (it has many seeds and membrane in the middle like honey dew), the Chinese use it as a soup pot and soup bowl (it goes straight from the steamer to the table), and the flesh on the walls of the melon are scraped out and eaten. When cooked this way, it offers more texture than flavour. Candied wintermelon is basically peeled and chopped wintermelon (with the seeds removed) that is candied and dried. This has a distinct flavour akin to caramelised sugar.

Other Vegetables

Other common vegetables include **choy sum** (Chinese flowering cabbage), **gai lan** (Chinese broccoli or kale) and **por choy** (Chinese spinach). All of these vegetables can be added to stirfries or simply tossed into soups and fried noodles.

Kelongtong (Fruit)

Fruits are usually served raw, ripe and sliced, in a big, mixed fruit platter. They are sometimes used in salads such as **rojak** or **kerabu** (often the unripe fruit is used). They are rarely cooked.

Durian

One simply has to start this list with 'the king of fruit'. Love it or hate it, it's near impossible to stay neutral about the durian. The creamy, bitter-sweet flesh is eaten fresh, as **durian pengat** (porridge-like sweet made by cooking durian pulp, coconut cream and palm sugar), piped into choux puffs, slathered onto cakes, or turned into polite – ie, not so stinky – tubes of **durian kueh** (chewy, fudge-like durian-flavoured snack). Aficionados go to the extent of believing that while it is a terrible thing if a person lives his life without knowing love, it is an equally terrible thing to live a life without having tasted durian. Malays also believe that durian is a powerful aphrodisiac, hence the old adage, 'when the durians go down, the sarongs go up'.

STAPLES

VARIATIONS ON A STINKY THEME

When it comes to durian, Malaysians are not happy to leave a great thing be. If this is indeed the king of fruit, then surely it has a long line of successors. Delicacies savoury and sweet include: **durian pengat**, a porridge-like sweet made by cooking durian pulp, coconut cream and palm sugar until gooey-thick; the black saccharine chewiness of **dodol durian**; and Nonya-style **yulian gao**, a cake sold in cylindrical 20cm sticks. Vendors add durian to their **ais kacang** (ice dessert), **roti** (bread) and Chinese mooncakes; batter and deep fry it, tempura style; and make it into chips. Restaurants serve durian gâteau and tiramisu. Extremists may want to try **tempoyak**, fermented and near-alcoholic durian pulp mixed with fish curry, **sambal** (chilli-based condiment) and rice. My vote, though, goes to durian pancakes served at the Mandarin Oriental in Kuala Lumpur. They're really a veil of batter, like a crêpe, draped over layers of durian flesh, and cream that has been folded through puréed durian. The whole thing is too big to eat in one mouthful – instead, biting through and pulling away the outer pancake layer mimics the act of eating the fruit itself. Physical output is rewarded with the stinky, lush and primordial durian ooze within, which plays counterpoint to the floury dough without.

Rob McKeown

STAPLES

Manggis (Mangosteens)
Almost always sold alongside durians, this dark-purple fruit (roughly the size of a tennis ball) has deliciously sweet white flesh inside. It is supposed to balance out the 'heatiness' of durian. (See p 234 for an explanation of the Chinese philosophy of 'heaty' and 'cooling' foods.)

Rambutan
Red and hairy, rambutan may not look like the most appealing fruit to eat. But peel away the thick, leathery skin and you find sweet, succulent, semi-translucent white flesh. The rambutan is a relative of the lychee.

Mangosteens

Nangka (Jackfruit)
It's hard not to miss jackfruit as it looks like an alien pod. Its bumpy shell emits an unappealing odour, and oozes a sticky sap when cut. But the jackfruit's yellow flesh is sweet and wonderfully fragrant. Jackfruit flesh is sometimes boiled, sliced and tossed in a spicy salad (flavoured with sambal belacan) called **kerabu nangka**, or added into curries such as **ikan tenggiri masak nangka** (braised mackerel fillet with coconut milk and jackfruit). The **biji nangka** (jackfruit seeds) are sometimes cooked in curry dishes, and they taste a little like potatoes.

Jackfruit flesh revealed

Belimbing Manis (Star Fruit)
The star fruit is so named because the cross section of the juicy fruit resembles a star. It is eaten ripe (locals also like it blended into a juice) or half-ripe, flavoured with a little salt.

Rambutan for sale by the bunch, Penang

Ciku

The flesh of the **ciku** takes a little getting used to. While it is soft and sweet, the texture is a little sandy and the flesh is brown in colour. The fruit is brown on the outside and is either round or oval.

Jambu (Rose Apple)

The inverted **jambu** looks like a bell and, when ripe, is bright pink with a waxy skin. Its flesh is watery and sweet. Locals enjoy it sliced and dipped in a combination of dark soy sauce and sliced chillies.

drinks of malaysia & singapore

To provide respite from the heat and humidity, enterprising stall holders offer a plethora of soothing hot and cold drinks. Don't be thrown by mysteriously black or pink-hued concoctions. The real challenge lies in learning to sip your drink, precariously packaged in a little plastic bag pinched together at the top by draw-string handles, from a straw without spilling it all on yourself!

Non-Alcoholic Drinks
Fruit Juices

Freshly made fruit juices are readily available at most hawker centres and even in some shopping malls. Look out for colourful displays of cut fruit and the loud whirr of a juicer going at full speed. You'll find that sipping juice is the best way beat the heat and still ensure that you keep up your daily vitamin intake.

Familiar options include watermelon, orange, apple (specify whether you want red or green apples) and pineapple. Don't expect celery, but a local favourite in both Singapore and Malaysia is carrot and orange juice. More local options include: sugar cane juice, which is extracted from the cane with a purpose-built press and is an amazing thirst quencher when served with a wedge of lemon; star fruit; and soursop, a dark green, prickly fruit with a slightly acidic, tropical-flavoured pulp (the black seeds found in the pulp are not meant to be consumed). While more-recent, and somewhat exotic, additions to the selection cover anything from honeydew with milk, (which first made it big in Taiwan) to the rich, Indonesian-influenced avocado with a hint of instant coffee – and a shot of cognac if you pay a little extra. Be warned that most stalls add a generous tablespoon of sugar syrup to your juice and some tend to fill your glass up with too much ice (which leaves you with more ice than juice). Feel free to request that they don't add sugar to your juice. A request for 'no ice' will usually incur a surcharge.

Sugar cane is crushed to extract a deliciously refreshing drink

DRINKS

A glass of fresh watermelon juice, Kuala Lumpur

DRINKS

Lime Juice

Lime juice is a less common option at fruit juice stalls, but you are likely to find it on the menus of coffee-shops where **ka li yu tou** (fish-head curry) or chicken rice (chicken and rice with chilli-ginger sauce), and other spicy dishes, are sold. Don't cringe at the thought of drinking it. In taste, it's closer to lemonade than pure juice. Tiny dark green local limes (also referred to as kalamansi), two-thirds the size of a golf ball and with pale orange flesh, are used. The sweetness of the drink, which is nearly always enhanced with sugar syrup, is believed to soothe the palate after a spicy meal, and its ever-so-slightly sour bite cleanses the palate after a rich, greasy meal the way a lemon or lime sorbet would. At larger establishments, the 'fresh' juice is often either a cordial or a commercially extracted product. Hand-squeezing those little limes is far too time-consuming to be commercially viable. You may also come across a variation of the drink. It's referred to as **guai bee** (which literally means 'weird flavour' in Hokkien). According to our friendly waiter at Fatty Loh Chicken Rice in Penang (37-G Cantonment Road), it is a glass of lime juice served with a few dried sour plums that have been soaked in a sugar solution. Sweet, sour and just a little salty, it is an odd, yet oddly appealing, concoction that hits the spot after a long day spent pounding the streets and taking in the sights.

Enjoying fresh lime juice, Melaka

Air Kelapa (Coconut Juice)

While coconut juice isn't exactly a juice – the liquid you drink is not extracted in any way, the nut is simply cracked open and the liquid in it offered to you – it is a drink that would most logically fall under the category of juices. The milky liquid, also known as coconut water, is mildly sweet and provides a soothingly pleasant counterpoint to spicy food. It is usually available at roadside stalls (where you'll see green, whole coconuts on display) and most hawker centres (especially the ones that cater to tourists). The tops are trimmed to a three-cornered point and with the swish of a cleaver, the tip is removed to reveal a pool of liquid and a layer of tender white flesh. You drink the liquid, and then, with the aid of a metal spoon, scrape off the flesh, which can be eaten – as long as it's a fairly young coconut that you've been given. It'll have the delicate flavour of coconut, but without the richness that you've come to associate with coconut milk or cream. Other places serve the juice with the coconut flesh scraped out and mixed through the juice (which is handy if you intend to walk with drink in hand).

DRINKS

Young coconuts at a drink stall, Penang

Local Street-Stall Drinks

The only advertising that streetside drink stalls seem to need is a display of distinctively coloured local drinks laid out in tall, transparent containers. At most, each stall serves three varieties. You're likely to be able to tell which drinks they do sell from a long way down the road, simply by looking at the colourful liquids on show.

Bandung

Possibly the most eye-catching drink available, this milky pink thirst quencher is made from a combination of rose syrup (a commercial product consisting of rose essence, sugar syrup and pink colouring) and evaporated or condensed milk. It makes a great accompaniment to Malay food. You should only drink this cold.

A drinks vendor prepares his ingredients, Kuala Lumpur

Air Cincau (Chin Chow & Grass Jelly Drink)

This black-coloured drink filled with black strings of jelly may look a little dodgy, but it's considered a great herbal tonic. The jelly is made out of **agar-agar** (a gelatine-like substance obtained from seaweed) and **chin chow** (a type of Chinese cabbage leaf), which can be bought at Chinese medicinal shops. The liquid consists of sugar syrup flavoured with pandanus leaf. Ready-made chin chow jelly, as well as canned versions of the drink, can be bought at supermarkets. Some prefer to have it with a hint of fresh lemon juice.

Air Soya (Soybean Milk)

Soybean milk consists of beans that have been liquidised with water and then strained, before being boiled and sweetened with sugar. This makes it quite unlike the soy milk you're likely to find in health food stores both locally and in the west. It has a beany flavour that is usually masked with the addition of pandanus leaves at the boiling stage. A popular drink served both hot and cold, you are likely to find many stalls selling this milky white liquid. Because it is rich in protein, many locals choose to drink a glass of it each day. Soy milk in cans and cartons can also be found in most supermarkets.

Air Soya (Soybean Milk)
Be warned: this drink is not designed to be a milk substitute.

Ingredients

200g	soybeans
	tepid water for soaking
	(enough to just cover the soybeans)
8L	water
2	pandanus leaves, tied into a knot
400g	to 600g white sugar

Soak the soybeans overnight in enough tepid water to just cover them. Drain the beans, rinsing them thoroughly and discarding the soaking water. At this stage, there are two schools of thought. Some insist on rubbing off the skins, claiming that leaving them on contributes an earthy flavour to the drink. Others find it a hassle, and leave the skins on. Whichever route you choose, grind the beans in an electric blender – you may find adding a little water facilitates the process. Scrape the paste into a deep saucepan and add the 8L of water and the pandanus leaves. Bring slowly to the boil, stirring frequently. Turn the heat down and simmer the mix for 15 to 20 minutes. Remove from the heat and set aside to cool. Strain the liquid through a fine sieve that has been lined with muslin. Return the strained liquid to the heat and add the sugar. Bring to the boil, adding more sugar to taste, if necessary. Reduce the heat and simmer until all the sugar is dissolved. Serve hot, or well chilled.

Serves 4–6

DRINKS

Air Barli (Barley Water)

You're most likely to find air barli served homemade at coffeeshop stalls serving chicken rice. It is made from barley boiled with water to create a murky, white liquid, and its primary flavouring comes from the rock sugar dissolved in it as it boils. When consumed at home, **dong gua tang** (candied wintermelon) is sometimes added, creating a caramelised bittersweetness (akin to the flavour of molasses). It can be served either hot or cold. As a canned drink, lemon-barley is a popular combination.

Air Mata Kuching (Longan Water or Tea)

The Chinese serve air mata kuching during the Chinese New Year. Despite its name, this ultra-sweet beverage doesn't actually contain any tea leaves. It is a combination of **kurma** (red dates) and dried **mata kuching** (longan) boiled in water. It is the sweet, dried longan (which are similar to lychees) that gives the drink its amber-brown hue. Likewise, the chilled version of the drink sold at roadside stalls is sometimes referred to as tea, but also isn't tea. It is just a drink consisting of dried longan boiled in water and then chilled. Some hawkers claim that they add secret herbs that make their version of air mata kuching even more of a tonic.

Cendol (Coconut Milk with Green Noodles)

While cendol is a drink, it is more often consumed as a dessert. The liquid element of the drink is made up of coconut milk (where the flesh of the coconut is grated and squeezed to produce a milk) sweetened with palm sugar syrup – the freshness of the coconut milk and the quality of the palm sugar can make or break a cendol. But approximately a quarter of your glass is first filled with fine, short strings of cooked green-bean flour dough (the finer the strings, the better quality the cendol). The palm sugar syrup is then added, followed by the coconut milk. That's all topped with some shaved ice. So be sure to give your cendol a good stir before you sip it! Either suck the little noodles up your straw (if you're drinking it out of a cup), or spoon them, along with the sweet liquid, and chew.

Canned Drinks

Popular soft drinks such as Coke, Pepsi, 7-Up and Sprite are readily available, although you are only likely to find one cola brand, or lemonade brand, at any establishment. Diet versions are also appearing in some restaurants. Don't be shocked if a local friend adds a pinch of salt into his or her cola. The belief is that the salt reduces the bubbliness of the drink – presumably thus making you less likely to burp after a tall glass. Other favourites among locals include Fanta Orange, Kickapoo (grapefruit) and Sarsi (sarsaparilla).

You'll also discover a host of fizzy apple juices from China, fruity soft drinks from Japan and other local drink products. Among the nonfizzy drinks, there are also canned versions of most of the popular drinks you find at roadside stalls. Other interesting variations include jasmine tea (served sweet and cold – terribly untraditional), wintermelon tea (essentially candied wintermelon boiled in water) and chrysanthemum tea (made by steeping dried chrysanthemum in boiling water, sweetening it and serving it cold in a can).

Buying drinks at the National Mosque, Kuala Lumpur

DRINK TO VIRILITY

Most cultures have their own health tonics and purported aphrodisiacs. **Tongkat ali**, a root found deep in Malaysian tropical rainforests and other forests of Southeast Asia, is considered the herb of 100 healing qualities. Traditionally regarded, through local folklore, as having restorative and rejuvenative properties, the root is also believed to be a potent aphrodisiac that can be used to enhance sexual energy in men. It is common to find hawker or coffeeshop stalls serving it as a drink. And they don't usually suffer from any lack of customers! Of late, the drink is even being sold in canned form. But rather than harp on about Tongkat ali's Viagra-esque qualities, producers are focusing on its nongender-specific ability to help both men and women recharge from fatigue.

Yogurt-Based Drinks
Yogurt-based drinks are not commonly found at restaurants, coffeeshops or hawker stalls. But at home, many drink Yakult (a fermented milk drink) or Vitagen (a cultured milk drink) for its health benefits – both drinks are supposed to be good for your intestines, aiding digestion. In high-rise residential areas you may even catch sight of the Yakult lady, with her little trolley in tow, making weekly deliveries.

Lassi
Lassi, an Indian drink based on curds, is available only at Indian coffeeshops and restaurants. It can be served plain, savoury (seasoned with a little salt, pepper and cumin) or sweet (flavoured with sugar, puréed mango or with rose-water).

Teh (Tea)

The per capita consumption of tea in Malaysia alone is about half a kilogram a year. The dominant variety grown and used is an Indian Assam tea, *Camellia assamica*. The total annual demand is for nine million kilograms. Local production is less than five million kilograms, the rest is imported (some imports are considered inferior, others superior). Locals take great pride in knowing exactly where they can find the best tea (and coffee) made the local way. Be prepared for a unique taste sensation when you sip on your first local tea. You'll only find them at coffeeshops and hawker drink stalls. This style of tea is rarely prepared at home.

Unlike the delicate teas of China and Japan, which are served plain, or even the British teas served with milk, Malaysian and Singaporean tea is brewed for longer to give it stronger flavour. It is often served with thick condensed milk, which is both sweet and rich. This style of tea preparation is probably closer to the tea-making methods practised in parts of India, where tea is infused with a mixture of water and milk (according to Indian custom, the more important the guest, the milkier the brew should be, but this is no longer widely observed in India or in Malaysia and Singapore).

Cups of tea with condensed milk, Penang

While various options are available to you (tea without milk but with sugar; tea with evaporated milk and sugar – see the boxed text 'Coffeeshop Lingo' on p 218), the one tea you must try is **teh tarik** (pulled tea) otherwise known as **teh terbang** (flying tea). The act of making the tea has become part of the region's tourism landscape, but it is nonetheless a visual experience not to be missed. The teh tarik master is invariably an Indian man, and you should really only order this at an Indian drink stall. His unique art involves pouring your tea – sweetened with condensed milk – from a metal container held high above his head down into another metal container he holds somewhere close to his waist-level (the two should be about a metre apart). The process is repeated a couple of times until a layer of froth appears and the tea has cooled a little. He then pours your drink into a cup. This is a teh tarik. The benefit of this process is that the drink is cooled just enough not to burn your tongue when you sip it.

Making teh tarik, Penang

DRINKS

Be aware that iced tea served at coffeeshops will invariably be a local tea (yes, with the condensed milk) served with ice. Modern east-meets-west concoctions include **teh-cino** (inspired by cappuccinos), which is a bizarre tea served with a bottom-half layer of milky tea, and a top half that is frothy and milky white. For full effect, it's served in a glass mug, of course. If you're feeling a little under the weather, ask for a cup of **teh halia** (milky ginger tea). It's a restorative pick-me-up that most locals swear by.

Other Teas

Besides the predominant local teas of the coffeeshop and hawker stall, there is a host of teas that are served at restaurants and teahouses. At Chinese restaurants, expect a basic selection of Chinese teas that will be served with your meal. The more stylish the restaurant, the more likely you are to find exquisite, rare teas. Generally, Chinese tea, served in little teacups containing little more than a thimble-full of tea, is designed to be appetite enhancing (if served at the beginning of a meal) or cleansing (if served at the end of a meal). Pale-yellow chrysanthemum tea is often served sweet. Japanese restaurants will have basic *ocha* (green tea), but little more

Iced tea, Penang

than that. At Indian restaurants, you can indulge in a rich **masala** (spice blend) tea that is milky, sweet and spiced with cardamom, cloves and cinnamon. Tea served the British way is readily available at local cafes and European restaurants. Specialised teahouses focusing on herbal teas (such as camomile, lavender and mint) are growing in popularity and can be found in Kuala Lumpur and Singapore.

Kopi (Coffee)

While the likes of international chains such as Starbucks and The Coffee Bean & Tea Leaf are rapidly growing in popularity in the region, the good old local coffeeshop holds sway in most locals' lives. The preference is for coffees characterised by a heavy body, earthiness and yet a mellow smoothness. As with tea, coffee in Malaysia and Singapore generally comes with a generous helping of condensed milk. You will not find espressos, lattes or flat whites on the menu. But the strong, heady, local black coffee forms the basis of many a coffee drink. You'll find locals start and end their days with a coffee. The old-timers prefer to pour some of their piping hot coffee into saucers to hasten the cooling process before casually sipping the dark, smoky brew from the lips of the little dishes. On a hot day, a **kopi peng** (iced coffee served with condensed milk) offers the perfect relief from the heat and the sun. If you're on the move, look for **kopi kong** (coffee served in a recycled condensed milk tin; see the boxed text 'Coffee-shop Lingo' on p 218 for more information on the different coffees you can try.

Coffee to go is served in a recycled condensed milk tin

DRINKS

Alcoholic Drinks

Obvious alcohol consumption in Malaysia is frowned upon as the nation has a predominantly Muslim population. Alcohol is, however, available and consumed by non-Muslims and tourists.

Bir (Beer)

Tiger and Anchor are the two beer brands you get to choose from when you ask for beer in Malaysia or Singapore. Tiger is an easy-to-drink, smooth lager that goes well with local food, and the brand was started in 1932 as a joint venture with the Dutch Heineken brewery. Anchor is a pilsener beer that is crisp, refreshing and made with aromatic European hops for a rich, full-flavoured taste. Both are most readily available in restaurants and some coffeeshops. You are even likely to find ABC Extra Stout in stock. Locals strongly believe in the medicinal value of stout!

Coffeeshop, Penang

DRINKS

Other beers such as Heineken, Carlsberg, Stella Artois and Corona are available in bars, nightclubs and western-style restaurants. While boutique beers are a little harder to come by, there are outlets that carry them. Notably, microbreweries have sprouted in Singapore, a phenomenon not quite expected in an Asian country.

Makeshift and mainstream advertising, Melaka

Cocktails

Gone are the days of 'pink ladies' and 'sex on the beach'. Today's cocktail lounge lizards know a proper cosmopolitan when they taste one. Flavoured vodka martinis are all the rage, but stay right away from chocolate martinis – lychee ones are natural winners. And if you want a vodka gimlet, you'll be asked exactly what kind of vodka you like – the point being that local tastes are fairly sophisticated.

While the Singapore sling is more for the tourists than the locals (locals consider it rather touristy), it warrants a mention here. The Raffles Hotel (where it was first created early in the 20th century) serves around 2000 slings each day, which is no mean feat. History has it that Hainanese bartender Ngiam Tong Boon created it as a ladies' drink (which explains why it's pink). No first-time visit to Singapore and the stately Raffles Hotel is complete without trying one (see the recipe).

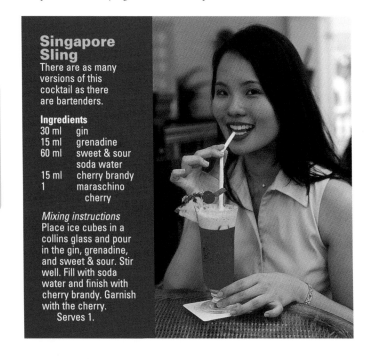

Singapore Sling

There are as many versions of this cocktail as there are bartenders.

Ingredients
30 ml   gin
15 ml   grenadine
60 ml   sweet & sour
          soda water
15 ml   cherry brandy
1   maraschino
          cherry

Mixing instructions
Place ice cubes in a collins glass and pour in the gin, grenadine, and sweet & sour. Stir well. Fill with soda water and finish with cherry brandy. Garnish with the cherry.
Serves 1.

DRINKS

BOTTOMS UP

Lychee martinis may be a new invention, but the ability to mix a good drink goes way back in Malaysian history – all the way to when the Portuguese first came to Melaka. At the time, **toddy**, which is made from fermented sap of the coconut flower, was the only known alcoholic drink of the region. Enter Cristang culture (see p 23), with its fiesta funk and Asian grace, and a roster of special-occasion tipples was born. The flavours of Malaysian drinks are equally reflective of local ingredients, Moorish foodstuffs and European tastes. And they make many of today's out-of-balance and too-sweet cocktails seem like child's play. The following examples can be found in a fabulous cookbook called *Cuzinhia Cristang* by Celina J Marbeck.

Codial floris sapatu	(hibiscus cordial): hibiscus tea dosed with lime juice, two types of sugar, ginger and water.
Nona rostu bremeilu	(maiden's blush): sweet red wine mixed with lemonade and fresh rose petals. Served in goblets with rose petals on top.
Lembransa brancu	(white memories): anise liqueur blended with water chestnuts, evaporated milk, carnation petals, water and sugar. Served in cocktail glasses with flower garnish.
Soldadu chocolat	(chocolate soldier): milk, chocolate, **kopi o** (black coffee), brown sugar, rum, almond slivers and a trace of nutmeg or cinnamon. Served hot in mugs.

Rob McKeown

DRINKS

Wain (Wine)

Over the past decade, wine has overtaken hard liquors such as cognac and whisky as the alcohol of choice. While the latter still has a strong following, the market for wine (especially red wine) has grown dramatically. While the trend applies more to Singapore, wine consumption across the entire region has matured. Most restaurants (except for Malay/Muslim establishments) have a modest wine list. Fine dining western restaurants and even some high-end Chinese restaurants carry extensive wine lists that cover both Old and New World wines.

While the earlier wave of wine connoisseurs went for French wines, the more recent wave of wine lovers are more open to Australian and American wines and those of other New World wine regions. As evidence of this growing market, many supermarkets now have wine sections, and wine stores are mushrooming in the larger cities – most notably in Kuala Lumpur and Singapore.

While you would expect that white wines would be far more appropriate in the tropical heat, locals generally prefer red wines. Champagne, however, is growing in popularity.

Toddy (Palm-Sap Wine)

The fresh toddy is extracted from the central part of the young stem of a coconut palm. It ferments within a few hours. From this fermented sap you get palm wine, a sour, potent brew. This is illegal to make and considered a 'poor man's' drink.

Tuak (Rice Wine)

This is a potent rice wine made by the Iban tribes of Borneo. If visiting a longhouse, be prepared to down copious amounts of tuak, which is a milky and tastes like a sweet, fruity white wine. Sustained consumption of tuak, by both hosts and visitors, is a major part of the local welcome.

home cooking & traditions

Eating and cooking are so closely woven into the fabric of Malaysian and Singaporean lives that even the most clueless local food lover knows exactly what should go into a proper **pohpiah**. The rules of gastronomic tradition are learned in the home kitchen and at the dining table, as are the very tenets of life.

Flip through a few Malaysian or Singaporean cookery books and you're likely to find different ingredient lists for seemingly standard recipes like **kari ayam** (chicken curry). It's only been in the last few decades that authors and culinary historians have attempted to document the variety of Malaysian and Singaporean cuisine. Expectedly, the task is a daunting one. For example, in Singapore, Penang and Sarawak, **laksa** (a spicy, soupy noodle dish) has very distinct variants on the same theme. Each is, however, authentic. And how to document dishes from the domestic kitchen? What about a recipe for the ultimate **curry debal** (devil's curry: spicy Eurasian meat curry; see the recipe)? One granny's definitive version will be at utter conflict with another's secret recipe.

Food is central to home life in Malaysia and Singapore. Rather than stick religiously to recipes, your typical passionate home cook will be more than ready to try out her neighbour's special version, all in the name of improvement (if she can get her hands on it, that is). Whether this readiness to adapt can be traced to the migrant mindset, or wanting to add variety to the traditionally

Meat is added to porridge for flavour and texture

cloistered lives of female home cooks (mothers, wives, grandmothers, aunts, sisters, daughters and/or daughters-in-law), we'll leave the social historians and authorities on gender studies to speculate. What's for certain is the institution of *agak* (estimation).

Cooking is a craft that has always been passed on from generation to generation, from mother to daughter. A familial legacy, recipes were not so

Preparing lunch for her family, Kuala Lumpur

HOME COOKING

Curry Debal (Devil's Curry)

Eurasian cuisine is very much a pleasure relished behind closed doors. As such, there are as many legitimate variants of this devilishly hot curry as there are Eurasian households – everyone will claim their granny's or mum's debal is *the* definitive version. What they all have in common, however, is a wonderful gravy of tongue-tingling fieriness balanced by mouthwatering acidity, which coats a tender assortment of meats.

Ingredients

1	large chicken, chopped into large pieces
1	cucumber
1 tbs	salt
5 tbs	vegetable oil
4	potatoes, peeled and quartered
2.5cm (1 in)	piece of ginger, julienned
1 tsp	black mustard seeds
$^2/_3$ cup	water
	salt
	sugar
250g	Chinese roasted belly pork, cut into 2.5cm (1 in) thick slices
6	cooked pork or chicken sausages, cut into 2.5cm (1 in) thick slices
	big handful of bacon bones
8	white cabbage leaves, cut into bite-sized squares
2 tbs	vinegar, or to taste
	English mustard powder (mixed with a little water to form a thin paste), to taste

Marinade

1 tsp	pepper
1 tsp	sugar
2 tsp	dark soy sauce
2 tsp	vinegar

Paste

6	onions, peeled and chopped
4	candlenuts (or macadamia nuts)
$^1/_2$ tbs	turmeric powder
10	dried red chillies, soaked and drained, then chopped
10	fresh red chillies, chopped
1 tbs	ginger, chopped
$^1/_2$ tsp	English mustard powder

Combine the pepper, sugar, soy sauce and vinegar and marinate the chicken in this for 30 minutes. In a blender, grind all the ingredients for the paste, adding a little water to facilitate the process. Set the paste aside. Cut the cucumber into 3 sections, then quarter each section and de-seed. Rub the salt into the cucumber segments to draw out the water. After 10 minutes, drain off the excess liquid and set aside the cucumber.

Heat the vegetable oil in a frying pan on medium heat. Fry the pieces of chicken in the oil until they are nicely browned, then transfer them into a large casserole dish. In the same frying pan (and with the residual oil), fry the potato pieces over a brisk heat until a golden crust forms. Remove and add to the chicken. Fry the julienne of ginger until golden, then remove and add to the chicken and potatoes. Now place the mustard seeds in the frying pan, and when they start to pop, add the blended paste. Fry these over a low heat, diligently stirring all the while, until the oil separates and becomes a brick-red hue (about 20 minutes).

Scrape the paste into the casserole dish and add the water, along with salt and sugar to taste, stirring to mix well. Bring this slowly to the boil, and let simmer for 5 minutes. Next, add the roast belly pork, sausages and bacon bones, stirring thoroughly and simmering over a very gentle heat for 10 to 15 minutes. Add the cabbage and prepared cucumber, and cook until the cabbage is tender. Finally, stir in the vinegar, and add mustard to taste. Serve with plain white rice, or thickly sliced baguette to mop up the addictive gravy. Left overnight for the flavours to intermingle, curry debal tastes even better.

Serves 8

much instructions set in stone as the passing down of techniques gleaned from observation. Grocery shopping was a daily affair carried out at the crack of dawn in the neighbourhood wet market. Measurements such as grams, tablespoons and cups were meaningless – learning what a small handful of this or a generous pinch of that could do helped you bring out the best of what came from the butcher and vegetable seller, or harvest the nicest leaves from the **daun kesum** (Vietnamese mint) plant in the back yard. You could only gauge how much you needed for your **rempah** (spice paste) when you knew the size and freshness of your lemongrass and chillies. Young girls would hone their skills through painstaking trial and error, acquiring the experience that would prepare them for prospective marriage. Whether Malay, Indian, Chinese, Eurasian or Nonya, a women's ability in the kitchen was very seriously regarded as a measure of her desirability as a wife and future mother.

The modern-day kitchen, however, is a completely different place. As modernisation occurs, the *kampung* (village) way of life erodes, and women play an increasingly vital role in the world beyond the home, the domestic insularity of yore is no longer. Both husband and wife are likely to put in equally hard hours at work. Dinner can be quickly rustled up or a takeaway bought from a nearby hawker centre. High-density living, particularly in land-scarce Singapore, means economically planned spaces – kitchens are usually large enough to just accommodate a four-plate burner or electric

Enjoying a meal with family and friends, Kuala Lumpur

stove, a sink and a few electrical appliances (a rice cooker and a microwave for reheating food being the most common). There is often precious little workspace. Unless it's already built-in with the apartment, only baking enthusiasts and keen cooks will have a convection oven (although many find the grill/broiler functions a close substitute for the charcoal burners of the past). As refrigerators and freezers are commonplace, food shopping is usually carried out once a week (very often at the supermarket) rather than every day.

Given the harried pace of modern urban life, complex dishes involving labour-intensive preparation and patient simmering are saved for special occasions, celebrations, festivities or convivial gatherings of friends and family. An everyday home-cooked meal will revolve around the staple steamed white rice, served in individual bowls or on plates. Eating with hands or chopsticks has been largely replaced by the fork and spoon. Meat and vegetable dishes (there will be at least two) are served on communal platters in the centre of the table. For ease of use, the lazy Susan is a popular contraption in many homes. Accompaniments that may be laid out on the table include little saucers of **sambal belacan** (chilli and belacan paste; see the recipe), **cincaluk** (fermented shrimps) mixed with a squeeze of lime and thinly sliced shallots, or sliced chillies (red or green) in soy sauce. To say that Malaysians and Singaporeans love their food spicy and savoury is an understatement.

Get that into ya, Kuala Lumpur

Pohpiah (Peranakan Spring Rolls)

The dish that best articulates the intimacy between family and food is **pohpiah**, a fresh (as opposed to deep fried) spring roll. Preparation of the many ingredients can be a raucous family affair as mothers and aunts, cousins and daughters gather in the kitchen to chop, peel, slice and pound. The other part of the fun lies in the DIY assembly. The ingredients and sauces are laid out on a large dining table that everyone gathers around. Consisting of three parts – the wrapper, the filling, and the many tasty garnishes – each person gets to add a portion of each ingredient to taste. Much talk and laughter is exchanged among family and friends amid the filling, wrapping, and eating. The list of ingredients may look long, but don't be put off – these are well worth the effort.

Ingredients

Filling

4 tbs	vegetable oil
2	squares of **taukua** (firm beancurd), diced
500g	belly pork, boiled and diced
10	garlic cloves, peeled and finely chopped
4 tbs	**tau cheo** (fermented soybeans), mashed to a paste
500g	small raw prawns, peeled
500g	Chinese sweet turnip, peeled and finely shredded
800g	canned bamboo shoots, rinsed, drained and shredded
1 tbs	dark soy sauce
1 tbs	sugar
	salt

Garnishes

10	red chillies, ground to a fine paste
10	garlic cloves, peeled and ground to a pulp
	kecap manis (sweetened dark soy sauce)
	leaves of one large lettuce, rinsed and patted dry
1	cucumber, finely shredded
250g	bean sprouts, parboiled
6	**lap cheong** (Chinese preserved sausage), steamed for 10 minutes and sliced
500g	prawns, boiled and peeled
200g	fresh crab meat, flaked
4	eggs, beaten and fried into thin omelettes, then sliced into ribbons
4 tbs	vegetable oil, for frying the minced garlic
20	garlic cloves, peeled and finely chopped
	bunch of fresh coriander, separated into small sprigs
2	packets (30 pieces) egg roll wrappers

For the filling, heat a little of the oil in a wok and fry the diced beancurd until golden brown. Remove the beancurd and set aside. Add the rest of the oil, and stirfry the belly pork over a low heat until the fat begins to run. Add the minced garlic and tau cheo and stir over a low heat until a garlicky aroma arises. Toss in the small raw prawns and give a good stir. Now add the sweet turnip, bamboo shoots, soy sauce and sugar. When well mixed, add the reserved fried beancurd and salt to taste. Bring slowly to the boil (the turnip will have released much water by this stage), then simmer uncovered until almost dry (around 45 minutes).

For the garnishes, set out small separate bowls and pile one with the chillies, one with the pulped garlic gloves, and so on (not including the vegetable oil or 20 minced garlic cloves). Heat the vegetable oil and fry the minced garlic slowly until golden. Remove the pan from the heat and let the garlic finish cooking in the residual heat of the oil. When cool, drain off the oil and place the garlic in a small bowl.

Stack the wrappers on the table, along with the filling and garnishes. Everyone helps themselves and assembles their own pohpiah according to taste. Here's how it's done – place an egg roll wrapper on a plate, then dab it with a smear each of pounded chilli, raw garlic paste and kecap manis. Place a lettuce leaf on top, then add the cucumber, bean sprouts and some of the pohpiah filling. Add the lap cheong, prawns, crab, eggs, the crisp fried garlic and a sprig of coriander. Roll up the wrapper, tucking in the sides as you roll so that the ingredients are completely encased. Eat immediately before the wrapper goes soggy.

Serves 6–8 people (2–4 rolls per person)

Catching up while preparing pohpiah, Singapore

Pantry Essentials

Most households keep an array of dried goods, seasonings, flavourings and condiments on standby in the cupboard. Peer into any kitchen cabinet and you'll see candlenuts, cartons or tins of coconut milk, dried red chillies, dried prawns, belacan, palm sugar, tamarind pulp, dried tamarind slices, white rice, glutinous rice, dried egg noodles and rice vermicelli. Amongst the canisters of whole and ground spices, you'll spot cloves, coriander seeds, turmeric, cinnamon, cumin, star anise, fennel seed, nutmeg, and white and black pepper. Sealed in airtight containers or little resealable bags, these ingredients stay fresh for several months. There will also be the odd commercial packet of ready-mixed curry powder and bottle of spice paste, for days when the cook has no energy to start from scratch. Once again, certain ingredients are more culture-specific. A Chinese kitchen, say, would also stock tinned bamboo shoots, water chestnuts, straw mushrooms, dried shiitake and 'cloud's ear' mushrooms, lap cheong, salted duck's eggs, dried tangerine peel, Sichuan pepper, five-spice powder, hoisin sauce, and an array of fermented black bean and soybean pastes.

Bottles and packets kept within grabbing distance from the stove might include chilli sauce, vegetable oil, light and dark soy sauces, **kecap manis** (sweetened dark sweet soy sauce), **shao shing** (Chinese cooking wine), sesame oil, oyster sauce, and black and red Chinese vinegars. In addition, containers of cornflour, salt and sugar aren't too far out of reach. In a tiered wire or plastic basket nearby, there will be heads of garlic and a purple papery mass of shallots.

In the fridge, small quantities of galangal, ginger, lemongrass, fresh red and green chillies, spring onions, pandanus leaf, laksa leaf, curry leaf, fresh coriander, kaffir limes and lime leaf are likely to be spied, each neatly wrapped up in newspaper (which helps absorb moisture and prolongs the shelf life of such perishables).

Chilli sauce, an essential in restaurants and in the kitchen, Singapore

Utensils

A **kuali** (wok) is an essential piece of equipment. While many latter-day variants fashioned from aluminium or stainless steel are readily available, serious cooks still insist on good old-fashioned cast iron. A brand new cast-iron wok needs to be seasoned before use. The Straits Chinese way is to first fry freshly grated coconut in the ungreased wok until the pulp is toasted and dry. The coconut is then discarded and the wok is rinsed. Next, the inner surface of the wok is rubbed all over with the cut side of an onion. The onion is then taken out, bruised, and fried in a few tablespoons of vegetable oil. The onion is discarded and the wok rinsed. It is now ready for use – the more frequently you use the wok, the more seasoned the surface becomes, and the more 'nonstick' it gets. To clean after use, the wok is simply rinsed with water then wiped thoroughly dry. It is never scoured with steel wool or abrasive agents of any sort as this causes rust.

BATU LESONG – A NONYA'S METTLE

A Nonya lady was trained from an early age in all the domestic arts (cooking, sewing and demure subservient behaviour), these being the quintessential qualities sought-after in a good Peranakan daughter-in-law. Such importance was placed on a girl's prowess in the kitchen that matchmakers often called in before meal times, while the kitchen was bustling with food preparations and when the **rempah** (spice paste) was being pounded. This was to investigate if the prospective bride fulfilled key criteria – it was said that matchmakers could detect by the sound of the **batu lesong** (mortar and pestle) which ingredient was being pounded and whether the person pounding was an experienced cook. A rhythmic pattern to the pounding gave away a good cook's presence. Mastering the art of the batu lesong was a Nonya's rite of passage – the pounding of an assortment of different spices to just the right degree of pastiness: smooth yet not liquid, textured yet not coarse.

Despite the advent and convenience of electronic household gadgetry, the dedicated believe nothing can quite replicate the texture of a rempah skillfully pounded by hand. A new mortar and pestle, hewn from granite or stone, needs to be seasoned before use. The point is to smoothen the inner surface as much as possible. Frequent correct usage is rewarded by an improved ease of use. Firstly, pound sand. Discard the sand and pound vegetable trimmings and peelings. Discard those then pound raw rice to a fine powder. Discard the rice; it will be grey from picking up the grit in the bowl. Repeat the pounding process with raw rice in several batches until both mortar and pestle are smooth, and the resulting rice powder is white.

Rempah is the foundation of any curry, be it Malay, Nonya or Eurasian. This spice paste is conventionally prepared with the **batu lesong** (mortar and pestle) or **batu giling** (rectangular grinding stone). These days, however, convenience often dictates that the electric blender or food processor takes its place in the kitchen.

When stirfrying in a wok, a wide spatula with a long handle is used to toss the ingredients. An assortment of perforated ladles also comes in handy, especially when deep frying, parboiling or blanching food such as noodles. These ladles are basically strainers with a long handle, with the best being made of wire mesh with bamboo handles (bamboo is a poor conductor of heat). For steaming, many cooks still use bamboo baskets, specifically designed to fit inside the wok. Whether used singularly or stacked in multiples, they sit above the simmering water in the wok.

Chopping boards are usually substantial wooden affairs, and used for all manner of food preparation. The home kitchen relies on few knives, with the most indispensable being the Chinese cleaver. Usually forged from carbon steel, the blade is approximately 10cm (4 in) wide and 25cm (10 in) long. Despite its hefty appearance, it is a truly multipurpose utensil. The blade cuts, chops, slices, shreds, trims, peels, smashes and minces with equal ease.

With rice being a staple food, the electric rice cooker takes the guesswork, trepidation and hassle out of preparing the grain in many a Malaysian and Singaporean household. Hardly anyone cooks rice via the absorption method anymore. With a rice cooker, all you need do is throw in the grains, top up with the requisite level of water, and there you have it – perfectly fluffy rice every time.

Aluminium or enamel saucepans and stockpots are used for preparing soups, stocks, braised dishes, stews and curries. It should also be noted that recipes requiring large volumes of coconut milk are not cooked in cast-iron pans because they discolour the coconut gravy.

Certain utensils, of course, are culture-specific. An Indian household, for instance, would be in possession of not one but several **blangah** (earthenware vessels for slow cooked curries) and **tawa** (flat cast-iron griddles). Available in various diameters, tawa are used to cook a glorious assortment of **roti** (bread) and **chapati** (griddle-fried breads). On the other hand, a Chinese household wouldn't be without a well-seasoned pot-bellied clay (or sand) pot for sealing in the delicious flavours of a 'red-cooked' dish.

celebrating
with food

Malaysians and Singaporeans love to eat. At times, it feels like eating takes priority over everything else in life. Little surprise then, that in this region, special occasions are marked by great and unique foods. Whether it's a birthday, New Year celebration or wedding banquet, each festival demands its own very special menu.

Celebration Calendar

Malaysians and Singaporeans often boast that they live to eat. How fitting then that so many of their major milestones, both public and personal, are marked by great feasts. With three major races and twice as many cuisine types, the diversity here is astounding. Every event, from the Chinese New Year to the Muslim Hari Raya Puasa to the Indian Diwali, is a banquet of delights, each unique but equally scrumptious.

Few countries of the world have calendars filled with so many festivals and rituals as Malaysia and Singapore. There is rarely a month in the region that's devoid of a celebration. And beyond the sheer number of holidays celebrated here, perhaps the most exhilarating thing is that everyone – regardless of their cultural or religious background – takes every festival to be a celebration for all and an excuse to feast.

Chinese New Year food for sale, Singapore

Christmas

Despite the heat, during Christmas Kuala Lumpur and Singapore are covered in twinkling fairy lights and fake snow. You'll find plastic firs draped with tinsel and shiny baubles in every home. Everyone celebrates the Eurasian Christmas with presents, parties and plenty of food. But the best indication of how nondenominational the celebration has become in the region is the growing tradition of serving roasted turkey stuffed with a mix of glutinous rice, braised pork and chestnuts. This stuffing is usually used to make **bak chang** (pyramid-shaped dumplings, normally associated with the Chinese Dragon Boat Festival; p 123). Whole honey-baked hams and fruit cakes are also commonplace, although they are likely to be placed beside a dish of **kari ayam** (chicken curry) or **pohpiah** (Peranakan spring rolls; see the recipe).

While house parties with friends are common in the weeks leading up to Christmas Day, Christmas dinner itself is a family affair. A Christmas meal culturally specific to this region is the Eurasian dinner. Eurasians have a complex heritage, the result of years of intermarriages between Malaysians and Singaporeans with European traders and colonisers. Their dishes blend exotic ingredients drawn from a variety of cultural backgrounds – a dash of Portuguese, Dutch and British together with Indian, Chinese and Malay, mixed liberally with other European and Asian traditions. For Eurasians, who are mostly Catholic, Christmas is a major festival marked by hours slaving over a hot stove to create specials such as: **curry debal** (devil's curry: spicy Eurasian meat curry; see the recipe); **feng** (pork curry, a Christmas speciality that is best eaten a day old); roasts made with a soy-based marinade and served with chilli dips; Eurasian chicken pies; **coubes gulung** (stewed cabbage rolls); and **sugee** (moist, ultra-sweet sponge cake). Families traditionally head for midnight mass before going home, at 2am, to a table laden with these delicacies and a turkey fresh out of the oven.

Raffles Hotel illuminated with Christmas decorations, Singapore

Chinese New Year

Just as Christmas decorations are being removed, preparations are usually under way for the Chinese New Year celebrations. Born out of an agricultural tradition, the celebrations mark the coming of spring and were once the only time Chinese farmers took a break from working the fields. These days, few Chinese are farmers. The holiday represents more of a spiritual renewal than a physical one, offering new beginnings, new opportunities and a reaffirmation of family ties.

For most of the traditional 15-day celebrations, Chinese New Year practices remain similar to those in Hong Kong and China – Malaysian and Singaporean Chinese also clean their homes to get rid of last year's dust and misfortunes; settle all debts; buy new clothes and shoes; and visit one another to exchange *hong bao* (lucky red envelopes filled with money).

There are, however, other traditions unique to the region. On New Year's Day, visitors are offered tidbits: orange segments for good luck, and sweets and cookies for a sweet future. Peranakans of Penang, Melaka and Singapore – descendants of mixed marriages between Chinese men and Malaysian women – have added love letters, otherwise known as **kueh Belanda** (Dutch cake), to the selection. The round, thin and crispy sweet rice-powdered wafers are rolled up in little scrolls or folded in quarters to look like Chinese fans. The round shape of an unfolded love letter is significant.

Duck on sale during Chinese New Year, Singapore

The Chinese character for round, *yuan*, also means satisfaction or a cycle of life, so the round love letter therefore connotes success in one's cycle of life. **Ayam siyow** (chicken in tamarind sauce), another Peranakan Chinese New Year favourite, grew out of more pragmatic needs. As shops and markets often stayed shut during the festivities, and refrigerators were once a rarity, Peranakans would buy several chickens and cook them with spices and tamarind to preserve the meat. They thus had a handy dish that could be served during any meal.

What differentiates Singapore from Malaysia is the custom of eating **yu sheng**, a salad of paper-thin raw fish, finely grated vegetables, candied melon and lime, red and white pickled ginger, pomelo sacs, sesame seeds, jellyfish and peanuts tossed in a dressing. This salad is to be eaten on the seventh day of the New Year. Singaporean families and business associates first toss the salad with their chopsticks shouting *'lo hei'* ('toss the fish') – a wish for prosperity and abundance – before the salad is eaten. Four enterprising Singaporean master chefs created the salad to appeal to Chinese beliefs, attributing special qualities to each ingredient and giving it a name that sounds similar to the Chinese phrase 'rising abundance'. The Chinese find yu sheng appealing as it has come to hold symbolic meaning. With yu sheng they can eat their way into a prosperous New Year. This practice has now spread to Malaysia and Hong Kong. But it is in Singapore that it is religiously consumed.

Decorations for Chinese New Year, Singapore

A PERANAKAN REUNION

'Welcome to my world. Won't you come on in?'

The old gramophone belts out a familiar tune in Nek Nek's (Grandmother and Matriarch) hall as she patiently slaves over the stove in the back kitchen. Si Yi (Fourth Auntie) is lamenting as usual about my cousin's inability to find a mate, while the rest of the young ones try time and again to sneak something off the dining table.

It is the eve of Chinese New Year and all three generations of my family have gathered in my grandmother's house for the traditional reunion dinner. Preparations for the meal began as early as 5am two days previously. Grumpy and suffering from lack of sleep, I am unceremoniously dragged out of bed to accompany my grandmother and her *ah sam* (maid) to the market. Everything seems to whizz by and before I know it we are home, laden with tons of food.

Being the eldest grandchild, I enjoy the special privilege of helping Nek Nek with the preparations. The duck is washed, rubbed down with salt and immersed in the pot to braise for six hours; the **buah keluak** (Indonesian black nuts) are cleaned and soaked in hot water to soften; the beef is sliced and marinated with a mix of oyster sauce, sesame seed oil and pepper; the vegetables are washed and stored away in the cold box – there are a thousand and one things to be done!

Zi Gao Mei (the 29th day of the lunar calendar – Lunar New Year's Eve) is finally here. The kitchen bursts to life with Nek Nek issuing commands like a field marshall: dice this; wash that; *'Aiyah Ah! Boy not like that. Nanti you potong long chong eh finger then you mati!'* – Nek Nek was never one to mince her words (she basically said that I'd cut off my fingers if I continued to chop things as I did). Tua Pek (Eldest Uncle) finally arrives from Melaka with the **belacan** (fermented shrimp paste) that Nek Nek insists on; he gets quite an earful for arriving so late. After all, the belacan has to be fried over slow heat and pounded with the chilli.

In time, everyone trickles in and the hall sounds like a busy market on a Sunday morning. From the kitchen, over the clanging of pots and commands shouted by Nek Nek, smatterings of gossip can be heard – *'You know Pek Neo's son last week hor ... Yah lor! That Nancy-ah always ... Johnny! Johnny oi, come and let Tua Ee sayang ...'.* To this day, I thank the heavens for keeping me in the kitchen by Nek Nek's side through all of this.

The long-awaited hour finally arrives (Nek Nek always magically has everything ready at the same time year after year). Peranakan custom dictates that all the elders of the family pride of place at the main table while second-generation uncles and aunties sit at the adjoining tables. Third-generation *anak anak* (children) are delegated to look after the surrounding floor area. In Nek Nek's home, this philosophy is left at the

The streets of Chinatown decorated with lanterns for Chinese New Year, Melaka

door – everyone enjoys a place at the table and we all get to choose where we want to sit, although the seats to Nek Nek's immediate right and left are always reserved for her youngest son and eldest grandson – my dad and I.

Dinner always begins with a prayer, thanking God for the safe return of all present and for the coming year to be fruitful. In no time, the bowls are emptied and the bones stripped bare. This is the hour we children look forward to the most – it is time for us to receive our *ang pows* (red packets). In Chinese custom, red signifies good luck, while the money in the packets purportedly stems one from ageing. I never quite understood the theory behind it, but generous donations are always welcomed in my bank account.

As midnight, uncles and aunties start herding the children off to bed. Another year has passed and another begins ... Welcome to my world.

Mark Tay

Hari Raya Puasa

The third major festival in the region marks the end of the Muslim fasting month of Ramadan, a time when faithful Muslims abstain from eating, drinking, smoking and other sensory pleasures from dawn to dusk. In Malay, Hari Raya means 'a great day', and Puasa is derived from Sanskrit meaning 'fasting or abstention'. So Hari Raya Puasa actually means 'the festival marking the end of a period of fasting'.

The blue-tiled Malabar Muslim Jama-Ath Mosque, Singapore

Ramadan falls on the first day of Syawai (10th month in the Muslim calendar) and is a time for Muslims to visit elders and seek forgiveness for their wrongdoings. The day begins with prayers in the mosques for the men, and visits to cemeteries followed by a substantial brunch. The women, who pray at home, spend their time preparing the brunch. The meal usually consists of **ketupat** (rice cakes wrapped in coconut leaves), **rendang** (beef in a thick coconut-milk curry sauce; see the recipe), **sambal goreng** (prawns, meat and soybean cake cooked in chilli and coconut milk) and **serunding** (desiccated coconut fried with chilli). For the rest of the day, friends and family visit one another and guests are pampered with every type of dish, cake and delicacy imaginable. These days, dishes are exchanged between neighbours to the point where tables groan under the weight of dishes and plates. The food is usually accompanied by tea, coffee, syrupy drinks (rose-flavoured ones are favoured) and soft drinks.

Diwali

Hindus celebrate Diwali, the Festival of Lights marking the triumph of good over evil, on the new moon of the seventh month of the Hindu calendar (usually in October or November). Rows of earthenware oil lamps are lit to welcome Lakshmi, goddess of wealth, and a vast variety of Indian dishes are created for the occasion. **Muruku** (a deep-fried noodle-like snack made of rice and lentil flours), **dosai** (paper-thin rice-and-lentil crêpes) and **putu mayam** (string hoppers, or rice noodles) are just some of the delicacies painstakingly prepared for friends and relatives who join in the festivities.

Indian laddus, eaten at weddings and other special occasions

Statues adorn Sri Srinivasa Perumal Temple, a large complex devoted to Vishnu, Singapore

Duan Wu Jie (Dragon Boat Festival)

Celebrated on the fifth day in the fifth month of the lunar calendar, this festival marks the death of Chinese patriot-scholar Qu Yuan, who drowned in Hunan's Milo River in 296 BC. Fishermen threw rice in bamboo leaves into the river so that fish would eat the rice instead of his body. Today **bak chang** (dumplings stuffed with meat, chestnuts and mushrooms), among many other dishes, are eaten in his memory during the month leading up to the festival.

Rendang (Beef in a Thick Coconut-Milk Curry Sauce)

A time-consuming dish to prepare, the rendang's appearance on any menu marks a special occasion at the Malay family table.

Ingredients

1 tbs	coriander seeds
1 tsp	cumin seeds
1 tsp	black peppercorns
1 tsp	fennel seeds
1	onion, chopped
10	dried red chillies, soaked in warm water (10–15 minutes) and drained, then de-seeded (if preferred, for less heat) and chopped finely
4	garlic cloves, chopped
1 tbs	fresh ginger, chopped
1 tbs	galangal, chopped
1 kg	beef (stewing cut), cubed into approximately 2.5cm (1 inch) cubes
4 tbs	vegetable oil
1	onion, sliced
1	cinnamon stick
5	cloves
1	lemongrass stalk, bruised
4 tbs	desiccated coconut, toasted
5 cups	coconut milk
1 tbs	tamarind, soaked in ¼ cup water, with liquid strained and reserved
	salt
	sugar

Toast the coriander seeds, cumin seeds, black peppercorns and fennel seeds in a small, dry frypan until they are aromatic. Set aside to cool. In a blender, grind together the chopped onion, chillies, garlic, ginger, galangal, coriander, cumin, black pepper and fennel seeds to a fine paste, adding a little of the coconut milk to help the process along. Scrape the paste into a large mixing bowl. Turn the cubed beef into the bowl and give everything a good stir. Set aside.

Heat the oil in a deep saucepan over medium heat. Add the sliced onion, cinnamon stick, cloves and lemongrass. Fry over a medium heat, stirring constantly until the onions are translucent and are just beginning to colour. Add the beef and fry until it browns slightly. Add the desiccated coconut, coconut milk, tamarind liquid, and salt and sugar to taste. Bring slowly to the boil, stirring all the time. Boil at a moderate pace for 10 minutes, being careful to scrape the bottom and edges of your saucepan as you stir. Then turn the heat right down. Simmer uncovered – giving everything a good stir now and then – until the meat is tender and the gravy reduced. Depending on the size of your pan and the quality of your beef, the process should take at least an hour. Should this evaporation and caramelisation occur before the meat is cooked to meltingly tender, top up with a little water.

Serves 8

Zhong Qiu Jie (Mid-Autumn Festival)

Also known as the Mooncake Festival, Zhong Qiu Jie is observed by Chinese on the 15th day of the eighth lunar month as a celebration of autumn harvests. The **yue bing** (mooncakes) savoured at this time are made of pastry filled with sweet red bean or lotus seed paste and **xian ya dan huang** (salted duck egg yolks). These cakes were once used to hide messages during the Chinese rebellion against the Mongols in the Yuan Dynasty.

Wooden mooncake mould   *Pressing into the mould*   *Ready for baking*

Gawai Dayak Festival

The Dayaks (Borneo's non-Muslim people) of Sarawak celebrate the Gawai Dayak, which marks the end of the paddy-harvesting season. This week-long festival (officially, it falls on 1 and 2 June, but the ceremony starts days earlier and stretches beyond these dates) observed by the Iban and Bidayuh communities involves much merry-making, dancing and the drinking of **tuak** (potent rice wine) in addition to cockfights, war dances and blowpipe competitions. Exotic delicacies created for this occasion include **tempoyak** (fermented and near-alcoholic durian pulp) and **ikan kasam** (fermented preserved fish with black beans).

Mooncakes, Singapore

Personal Celebrations
Weddings

While Christmas, Chinese New Year and Hari Raya are huge occasions, nothing brings people together better than a wedding. Locals love weddings both for what they represent but also for the massive banquets that follow. Modern couples now prefer to host wedding banquets at hotels, but traditional weddings can still span days of feasting. Many of the dishes served hold symbolic significance. A Peranakan mother-in-law, for example, presents a special **nasi lemak** (coconut rice with fried fish) to the mother of her son's bride, to acknowledge that the bride is a virgin. At Malay weddings, guests are presented with ornate, beautifully packaged gifts of hard-boiled eggs when they leave – a wish for fertility and offspring.

Malay weddings can be huge affairs involving hundreds of guests, who all must be fed. Throughout the celebration guests stop by to convey their good wishes, and stay for a meal of **nasi minyak** (a rice dish cooked with clarified butter and spices) or **biryani dam** (Indian and Arabic speciality where rice and meat is laid out layer upon layer), as well as **kari ayam** (chicken curry) and rendang. Cooking for such huge numbers is a time-consuming affair so chefs set up a makeshift open-air kitchen (most weddings are held in open, communal spaces) at least a day ahead. The cooking sometimes goes through

Malay wedding preparations, Singapore

Wedding couple at Kek Lok Si Temple, Georgetown

the night, and someone has to spend the night simply watching over the food. Similarly, at an Indian wedding, the food section presents a veritable feast: **biryani** (dish of steamed rice oven-baked with meat, vegetables and spices) is served at a Muslim wedding; **macher tarkari** (fish curry) at a Bengali one; and **murg makhanwala** (butter chicken) at a Punjabi do. And the festivities can span days.

TAPAI – MUST TRY!

Looking longingly at the water in the drinks cooler at a *mamak* (Indian hawker) stall in Putrajaya, I notice small plastic containers containing a milky white substance. Excited to think that my yogurt addiction may soon be sated, I open the frosted door and retrieve a container. I unknowingly peer at it – confused and hungry.

'Tapai,' issues a nearby voice from a stately Tamil man at the register. 'Very traditional, must try,' comes the follow-up. I open the lid and reveal grains of rice bathed in a pungent liquid. I'm handed a wee plastic spoon to give it a try. Tapai, an old Malay dessert served at weddings, made from sticky rice and **gula Melaka** (palm sugar), touched with powdered yeast and left to its own ageing devices. Not my beloved yogurt, but a cousin in ferment and just as good a sweet-and-sour coolant. It numbs the mouth, slakes the thirst and somehow feels healthily indulgent. I buy three for the road.

Rob McKeown

Waiting for other wedding guests, Singapore

Chinese weddings are less drawn out, celebrated with one big dinner. Most couples legally marry through a civil ceremony, attended only by family and close friends. Sometimes, couples elect for a church wedding. But it's the tea ceremony and the banquet that are important.

On an auspicious day picked out from the Chinese almanac by the couple's parents or relatives, the groom visits the bride's house, paying his respects and 'bargaining' for her hand. This can involve anything from

CHINESE WEDDING BANQUETS

A Chinese wedding banquet is both a joy and a stress-inducing, logistical nightmare. As times have changed, banquets have become as much about celebrating a young couple's love for each other, as they are opportunities for proud parents to show off to friends. Furthermore, in Malaysia and Singapore, people often speak of 'wedding face', which has been behind the trend towards larger and larger banquets. Quite simply, 'wedding face' means that if you have been invited to someone's child's wedding, you are bound to invite them to your child's; to not do so is a loss of face, something Chinese take very seriously. High-society wedding banquets are often attended by up to 1000 people – some are even held over several nights.

The banquet itself is a Chinese culinary extravaganza, usually held at a hotel or a restaurant. In the past, shark's fin soup was a staple dish; parents ordered it not only because it was delicious but also because it demonstrated wealth. These days, more and more modern couples are taking shark's fin off their menus for both ethical and budget concerns. That said, most dinners usually offer 10 courses – serving any less than that is considered 'cheap'. The first courses are often served with a sound-and-light show, a chance for the venue to show off its innovative packaging and hopefully attract more custom (with 20,000 weddings a year in Singapore alone, hosting banquets is big business). In fact, it's common for waiters to serve the first course, lit up with sparklers, accompanied by the *Star Wars* theme.

Toasts are common at these events. Chinese love to toast and do so by bringing their glasses of whisky, cognac or more recently, red wine, together and yelling *'yam seng'*. More specifically, they yell *'yam'* for as long as they can, followed by an emphatic *'seng'*, after which the glass is downed.

At the close of the banquet, the happy couple and their parents line up, forming a farewell party at the doorway, signalling the end of the evening with their desire to personally thank all their guests. At big weddings, smart guests get up quickly; you can only imagine how long it takes to shake 1000 hands.

answering silly questions about her to exchanging money. Once accepted, the groom takes the bride to his family home, where they go down on bended knees to serve his parents and older relatives a specially brewed tea. The whole ceremony acts as symbol for the young bride's acceptance to serve and care for her new relatives. The groom's family usually brings gifts of food to the bride's parents – a whole roasted suckling pig coloured red is a traditional offering.

Birthdays

To celebrate births across most cultures in Malaysia and Singapore, the baby's first month is marked with a banquet. On the 100th day, some Chinese families cook a chicken and its tongue is rubbed on the baby's lips to ensure the child will be an eloquent speaker.

Peach buns are a birthday tradition, Singapore

To mark each subsequent birthday, most modern locals throw a party and take it as an excuse to tuck into a good meal. Some classic traditions, however, do remain. **Shou tao** (longevity peach buns) shaped like peaches and filled with red bean or lotus seed paste are an enduring favourite. Peaches and peach trees have always been symbolic; it is believed that bad spirits fear peach wood. Chinese also believe that peaches symbolise spring-time and beauty.

In Peranakan and Chinese families, the birthday person is served **diam mee**, fine egg noodles and hard-boiled eggs (some use quail eggs) in a sweet, sugary soup. The noodles represent long life. One should take care never to break the noodles while lifting them up, as this represents a life cut short (but feel free to chew on them once they're in your mouth).

regional
variations

Different, yet similar. The people of Malaysia and Singapore are staunchly proud of their regional food. While the casual visitor may see little difference between Hainanese chicken curry and **kari ayam** (chicken curry), locals are conscious of every different ingredient and variant cooking technique between the two.

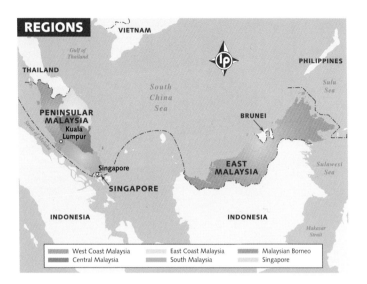

REGIONS

West Coast Malaysia | East Coast Malaysia | Malaysian Borneo
Central Malaysia | South Malaysia | Singapore

The food of this region is as varied as its people. It thrives on a fusion created by a long history of trade. While it's impossible to speak of an overarching Malaysian or Singaporean cuisine, the regional differences across the two countries are very subtle. Variation is found in the slightest difference in the choice of fish used in a **laksa** (spicy, soupy noodle dish) or whether the rice is served shaped into balls rather than heaped on a plate. The food variations across Malaysia and Singapore are perhaps more interesting in the way they have been influenced by history rather than geographical differences. With today's communication and transport, the availability of ingredients and cooking methods can no longer be restricted to specific territories or locations within the two nations.

Selling nasi lemak at Jalan Alor in Kuala Lumpur

West Coast Malaysia

The west coast of Malaysia, the stretch of the peninsular starting from Perlis (at the Thai border) and reaching all the way down to the capital Kuala Lumpur, is the most industrialised and populated part of the country. The various states lining the west coast are located along historic trade routes. Bear in mind that by the end of the Middle Ages the Malay archipelago had for hundreds of years been part of a trading network stretching from Africa to China. Coupled with their wealth of natural resources (such as tin around Kuala Lumpur), the states lining the west coast have long attracted traders, merchants, entrepreneurs and individuals seeking to eke out better lives for themselves and their families. Settlement in Kedah, for example, goes back to the Stone Age. It was also one of the first places in the peninsular to come into contact with Indian traders. With each successive wave of European investors, Malay farmers, Chinese merchants and Indian traders (and into the 20th century, workers from Tamil Nadu), the cuisine of this region attained yet another multicultural facet. Here, you are more likely to find evidence of colourful culinary contrasts and fusion borne of a thriving, cosmopolitan environment.

Fishing boats docked at Pulau Langkawi, Kedah

REGIONAL VARIATIONS

Perlis & Kedah

These two states, which border Thailand to the north, are known as the rice bowl of Malaysia. They produce over half of the country's domestic rice supply and are covered with lustrous paddy fields. Historically, they have close associations with Thailand (the Siamese conquered the region in 1842). You will find that many Thais have settled here and their preference for hot, spicy flavours paired with sour accents has found its way into the regional cuisine. Lemongrass, kaffir lime leaves, lime juice and fish sauce are more common in kitchens here. Stalls selling **tom yam** (spicy and sour Thai seafood soup) line the streets of Padang Besar, the border town to Thailand. The version served here is clear (misleading you into thinking it isn't at all spicy), unlike the fiery red versions popular in Kuala Lumpur.

Locals insist that **laksa Kedah** (laksa served sour, without coconut in its broth) differs from its similarly sour and spicy counterpart, laksa Penang. The restaurant manager at Restoran Rasa Utara, an eatery specialising in Kedah cuisine in Kuala Lumpur explained that laksa Kedah uses blended eel rather than the sardine flakes found in laksa Penang. What is consistent, however, is the fact that both use rice noodles. In Kedah and Perlis,

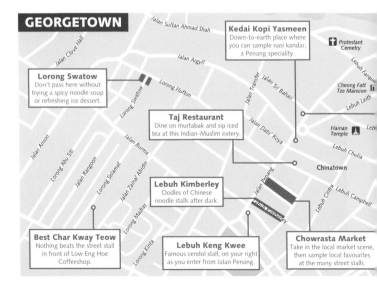

GEORGETOWN

Jalan Sultan Ahmad Shah

Jalan Clove Hall

Jalan Argyll

Kedai Kopi Yasmeen
Down-to-earth place where you can sample nasi kandar, a Penang speciality.

Protestant Cemetery

Lebuh Farquhar

Lorong Swatow
Don't pass here without trying a spicy noodle soup or refreshing ice dessert.

Lorong Hutton

Lorong Swatow

Jalan Transfer

Jalan Sri Bahari

Cheong Fatt Tze Mansion

Lebuh Leith

Taj Restaurant
Dine on murtabak and sip iced tea at this Indian-Muslim eatery.

Jalan Dato' Koya

Jalan Burma

Hainan Temple

Lebu

Jalan Anson

Lorong Abu Siti

Jalan Rangoon

Lorong Selamat

Jalan Zainal Abidin

Jalan Madras

Lebuh Chulia

Chinatown

Lebuh Kimberley
Oodles of Chinese noodle stalls after dark.

Jalan Penang

Lebuh Cintra

Lebuh Campbell

Best Char Kway Teow
Nothing beats the street stall in front of Low Eng Hoe Coffeeshop.

Lorong Kinta

Lebuh Keng Kwee
Famous cendol stall; on your right as you enter from Jalan Penang.

Chowrasta Market
Take in the local market scene, then sample local favourites at the many street stalls.

a helping of **otak udang** (prawn sauce) tempers the sourness of the dish and shares centre stage with a garnish of shredded cucumber, onions, torch ginger bud, chilli and mixed herbs.

In contrast to the cuisine of the other western states, the cuisine of Perlis and Kedah remains more staunchly Malay, possibly because both states remain strongly Islamic. The region, populated by rice farmers and fishermen, focuses on simple food such as **ikan bakar** (grilled fish), **kanji Kedah** (Kedah porridge filled with chicken or beef and prawns, flavoured with ginger, lemongrass and fenugreek) and **ketupat pulut** (glutinous rice half-cooked in coconut milk, rolled into tubes, steamed in banana leaves and served with spicy dried shredded beef).

Penang

Penang includes the mainland port town of Butterworth as well as Pulau Penang (literally, betel nut island), a short ferry ride away. Founded as an outpost of the East India Company in 1786, Penang grew to become a trade hub connecting Bengal, Burma, the Dutch East Indies and treaty ports of China. By the next century, it was considered one of the finest

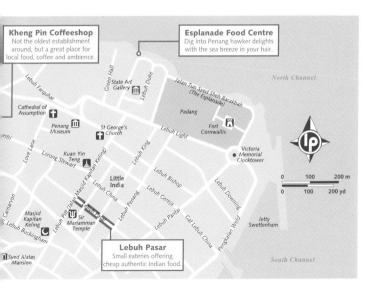

Kheng Pin Coffeeshop
Not the oldest establishment around, but a great place for local food, coffee and ambience.

Esplanade Food Centre
Dig into Penang hawker delights with the sea breeze in your hair.

North Channel

Green Hall

State Art Gallery

Lebuh Farquhar

Jalan Tun Syed Sheh Barakbah (The Esplanade)

Lebuh Duke

Cathedral of Assumption

Penang Museum

St George's Church

Lebuh Light

Padang

Fort Cornwallis

Love Lane

Kuan Yin Teng

Lorong Stewart

Lebuh King

Lebuh Bishop

Victoria Memorial Clocktower

Little India

Lebuh China

Lebuh Penang

Lebuh Gereja

0   100   200 m
0   100   200 yd

Masjid Kapitan Keling

Lebuh Buckingham

Jalan Masjid Kapitan Keling

Lebuh Pitt

Sir Mariamman Temple

Lebuh Pantai

Lebuh Downing

Gat Lebuh China

Pengkalan Weld

Jetty Swettenham

Syed Alatas Mansion

Jalan Carnarvon

Lebuh Pasar
Small eateries offering cheap authentic Indian food.

South Channel

islands in the world for nutmeg and cloves. The growth of the city's spice trade was accompanied by the arrival of immigrants: Malays from Kedah, Chinese from Canton, Acehnese from Sumatra, Tamils from India, Thais from across the border and Burmese. The food of Penang reflects the inter-mingling of these dynamic cultures and is a gastronomic highlight on your culinary tour.

Dishes such as **murtabak** (pan-fried rice dough with minced or pieces of chicken, beef or mutton, or vegetables), **jiu hoo char** (stirfried shredded cuttlefish with yam bean) and **pasembur** (Peranakan salad of cucumber, yam bean, bean sprouts, beancurd, cuttlefish and prawn fritters topped with sweet, sour and spicy gravy) represent the region's spice trade-centric history. Peranakan cooking in this region (also referred to as northern

DON'T MISS

- **Char kway teow** – broad, flat rice-flour noodles stirfried with Chinese sausage and egg, topped with shrimp. Penang has some of the best in the region.

- **Perut ikan** (fish stomach) – fish innards cooked in a coconut curry lightly scented with mint, presented on top of sliced beans and pineapple.

- **Nonya tok panjang** (Nonya long table meal) – Peranakan festivities are celebrated with an elaborate buffet-style spread. Jump in and experience one if you're lucky enough to chance upon an occasion.

- **Pong piah** – Hokkien speciality of flaky puff pastry filled with white molasses. Variations include **tau sar piah** (filled with red-bean paste) and **tambun piah** (filled with yellow-lentil paste).

- **Teh tarik** (pulled tea) – a deliciously rich, frothy and sweet tea that the coffeeshops of Penang do so well.

Nonya cooking) is heavily influenced by Thai cuisine. Chillies, lime juice and tamarind pulp are used to create distinctly sour, lip-numbingly hot sensations. The classic example of this is **Penang asam laksa** (rice noodles topped with a spicy and sour fish gravy, flakes of mackerel and garnished with fresh pineapple, cucumber, chilli, mint, finely shredded torch ginger flower and a dollop of shrimp paste).

Perak

Perak is the second largest state on the peninsular and is renowned for its tin deposits. It also played a key role in the rubber industry, another mainstay of the Malaysian economy. The tin mines attracted Chinese immigrants, which accounts for the fame of state capital, Ipoh, for its Chinese food. One of the best known Chinese dishes is **Ipoh kway teow** (rice noodles topped with sauce, shredded chicken and mushroom). The noodles used in this dish are unrivalled for their smoothness, which is attributed to the specificities of the water in Perak.

The local Malay dish, **rendang tok** (beef left to marinate with grated coconut, sliced coconut flesh and coconut milk then simmered) is is often served at festive celebrations with **nasi himpit** (compressed rice cakes).

REGIONAL VARIATIONS

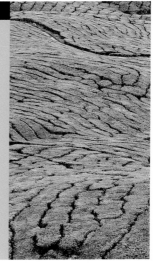

DON'T MISS

- **Tea Plantations** – Perak's highlands are a great place to hike. They are also where much of Malaysia's tea is produced
- **Tempoyak** (fermented durian) – locals scrape the durian flesh of the seeds, mix it with salt and leave it in an airtight jar in the refrigerator for at least three days. Tempoyak is most commonly mixed with pounded chilli to make a **sambal** and eaten with rice. It can also be incorporated in curry dishes.
- **Ipoh kway teow** – the delicious Chinese noodle dish named after the state capital. Look for it at street stalls and hawker centres
- **Rendang tok** – this local curry is an extremely rich, spicy stew of meltingly tender beef.

Selangor & Kuala Lumpur

It's inevitable that when one speaks of Selangor, Kuala Lumpur eventually drifts into the conversation, as it was previously the state's capital (the new state capital is Shah Alam). The histories of both the Federal Territory of Kuala Lumpur and Selangor (which surrounds it), much like that of Perak's, are tied to the success of the tin trade and the wave of immigrants the lucrative industry attracted.

In its 120 years, Kuala Lumpur has grown from a tin-mining town into an affluent modern Asian capital. The city remains unrivalled in terms of the variety of food it offers – a melange that has been made possible by the confluence of its diverse population. You'll find region-specific Chinese, Malay and Indian eateries offering Cantonese, East Malaysian or South Indian specialities. Its food doesn't bear the sour, Thai influence of the cuisines found further north, although the penchant for spiciness remains.

Kuala Lumpur's culinary strengths lie in the cuisines of the Malays, Chinese and Indians who dominate the population (don't expect exceptional Peranakan food, for example), and in the unique culinary heritage that the British left behind. Savour laksa Kedah along one street, then tuck in to Penang asam laksa along another. Diversity also stretches to the style of dining available: you may choose to dress up and sample modern French creations with a Japanese twist one evening, and go absolutely casual the next, when you eat standing on the kerb by a satay stall on wheels.

DRY DISCOVERY

The appearance of a new dish is heralded with the fervour of revolution on the Malaysian peninsular, so when I heard whispers of a so-called 'dry' version of **bak kut teh** (pork rib soup; see the recipe) being served in the port town of Klang, I called my friend Paige, who rang her friend Chew, and two days later we were en route to the town in Selangor. Sprawling Klang is said to be where bak kut teh originated and became king – and the city supposedly has a doubly high incidence of heart disease to prove that. The bak strain we discovered was recognisable in its greasy and herbal overtones. But here it went further – the stock was put into a clay pot with salted fish, squid, pork and roasted chillies, and reduced until everything communed into a silken whole. The choice of cooking vessel caramelised the contents and the addition of okra bound the whole with vegetal slipperiness. It tasted like the Klang I'd always heard about – salty breezes off the water, porky goodness on the palate, and a breadth of flavour that is wholly Malaysian.

Rob McKeown

REGIONAL VARIATIONS

DON'T MISS

- **Diverse dining** – Kuala Lumpur has it all, from street-side fare packed in paper pyramids to sophisticated silver service.
- **Inche kabin** (fried chicken) – An unusual, Hainanese-style fried chicken served with Worchestershire sauce. Found only in old colonial haunts like Coliseum Café on Jalan Tun Abdul Razak.
- **Appam** (hoppers) – Taste these Indian fermented rice cakes freshly made. You'll recognise an appam stall by its row of tiny woks, each just big enough for one appam.
- **Maggi mee goreng** (fried instant noodles) – Just the speciality to hit the spot after a night of partying in the nation's capital. Instant noodles are softened in boiling water before being fried and topped with an egg fried sunny-side-up.

CHEF WAN – Faces of Gastronomy

Everybody in Malaysia knows Chef Wan. He is rock star, talk-show host, comedian and ambassador all in one. During the last 15 years, he's hosted cooking shows in Malaysia, Singapore, the Philippines, Australia, England, South Africa and the US. He has published dozens of cookbooks and has even starred on the stage in the lead role of the musical, *A Funny Thing Happened on the Way to the Forum*. Forget about food. Chef Wan is a culture of his own.

So what is Chef Wan like? His face is boyish and has a smooth and welcoming quality. Floppy yet stylish hair grazes his forehead and, while short, his vivacious personality makes him seem taller. Sometimes his tone is machine-gun excitable, and often he is surprisingly soft-spoken, but he is always sincere. It all combines to give an audiovisual portrait that much of Asia has memorised. During two days with him in Kuala Lumpur, there isn't a place we go that he isn't recognised.

'Hi Chef, we love your show,' teenagers shout while passing.

'Good evening, Chef,' smiles the valet at the Mandarin Oriental.

'How are you, Chef?' bows a durian seller.

We meet up around dusk in downtown Kuala Lumpur. The air is heavy, darkness is beginning to fall and the fairy-light exteriors of the Petronas Towers are coming into their own. I mention being a bit hungry. 'Ooh. Do you like **nasi lemak** (coconut rice with fried fish)?' Wan questions in a cooing voice. He then veers off Jalan Sultan Ismail onto a smaller street. The unpretentious rows of tented stalls and two-wok kitchens we find here represent the spirit of old and new that defines this city – and my guide. Baby-blue plastic tables are lined up under neon-strip lighting. Four young diners dressed in baggy clothes and wearing baseball caps look up and then notice Chef Wan. He nods and they back-and-forth about what they're eating and the bands and DJs they'll be seeing that night.

Shifting into expert mode, Wan guides me to tables full of options to garnish the plates of coconut rice being prepared nearby. 'Very fragrant, their rice. It's steamed with fenugreek and ginger.' Without losing a beat in our Q&A exchange, he orders and soon we are seated. Each plate is a Gauguin-ish portrait of green banana leaf geometry, a white canvas of rice grains, and three swaths of protein colour made up of beef rendang, cockle sambal and prawn sambal.

'Sambal is very much the heart of a lot of our cooking. Chillies, onions, **belacan** (fermented shrimp paste), garlic and tamarind.' Bright lights, people aplenty, nonstop recipes. The free-flow of information and fun is addictive.

Wan's upbringing helped him to embrace the diversity of Malaysian cuisine.

'I was an Air Force brat,' he says with deadpan humour, 'so we moved everywhere: Kedah, Sarawak, Penang, Selangor. When really young I used to love my Mom's morning breakfast of **nasi goreng** (fried rice). I tried making it, but all we had around was belacan, garlic and onions. I made it five days in a row until my father got completely sick of it . After that I just cooked all the time.'

Between his familial roamings, a Malaysian father, and a Singaporean mother, Wan (born Redzuwan bin Ismail) managed the feat of learning multiple Malaysian cooking styles almost naturally. Most Malaysians' knowledge of cooking is bound to their immediate family background – which, granted, can be pretty exotic – but Wan can glide from teaching the cooking of Indian stews to contemporary Mediterranean fare without blinking an eye.

'I find it both a pleasure and a challenge,' he says of the multiple gears of cooking in Malaysia and Singapore. 'Malay is my culinary background, from street food to regional foods. Indian I feel comfortable with, but now I am trying our kind of Chinese food: chilli crab that you only have in Singapore.'

Even in the two days I spend with Chef Wan he manages more than most do in a career. Post-nasi lemak we stop at the Mandarin Oriental for a cocktail. Then onward to Jalan Alor for Chinese-style laksa and **ikan bakar** (grilled fish). He tells me about a wedding feast he just cooked for a Malaysian prince, which included a heavenly dessert. 'It has five layers: cassava, sweet potato, green bean, rice flour with egg and custard, and mung bean. Lots of sweet spices in the old Moorish way and flavoured with pandanus leaves and rose petals. Each layer is cooked for six hours in a copper cauldron. I had to have three cooks continuously stirring. It was a major, major thing.' The 2000-person guest list included the Sultan of Brunei and President Clinton. Wan pauses and adds: 'Traditional desserts are my hobby. I'm researching them all around the country.'

One hour, two durians, and plates of oyster omelette and char kway teow later our night is over. Tomorrow Chef Wan must get up early. He has a trip to Egypt to plan, a movie script to read, and recipes to test.

Rob McKeown

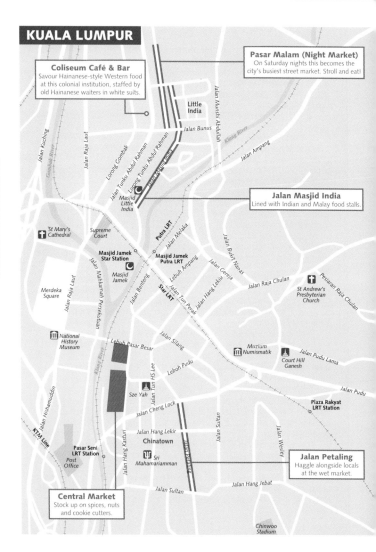

KUALA LUMPUR

Coliseum Café & Bar
Savour Hainanese-style Western food at this colonial institution, staffed by old Hainanese waiters in white suits.

Pasar Malam (Night Market)
On Saturday nights this becomes the city's busiest street market. Stroll and eat!

Jalan Masjid India
Lined with Indian and Malay food stalls.

Jalan Petaling
Haggle alongside locals at the wet market.

Central Market
Stock up on spices, nuts and cookie cutters.

Little India

Jalan Munshi Abdullah

Jalan Bunus

Klang River

Jalan Ampang

Lorong Gombak

Jalan Tunku Abdul Rahman

Lorong Tunku Abdul Rahman

Jalan Masjid India

Masjid Little India

Jalan Kuching

Jalan Raja Laut

Trimbak River

St Mary's Cathedral

Supreme Court

Putra LRT

Jalan Melaka

Jalan Bukit Nanas

Masjid Jamek Star Station

Masjid Jamek Putra LRT

Masjid Jamek

Jalan Ceria

St Andrew's Presbyterian Church

Pesiaran Raja Chulan

Merdeka Square

Jalan Raja Laut

Jalan Malhamah Persekutuan

Jalan Bentong

Star LRT

Lebuh Ampang

Jalan Tun Perak

Jalan Hang Lekiu

Jalan Raja Chulan

National History Museum

Lebuh Pasar Besar

Jalan Silang

Muzium Numismatik

Jalan Pudu Lama

Court Hill Ganesh

Jalan Pudu

Klang River

Jalan Hitbamuddin

KTM Line

Leboh Pudu

Sze Yah

Jalan Tun HS Lee

Jalan Cheng Lock

Jalan Sultan

Jalan Wesley

Plaza Rakyat LRT Station

Pasar Seni LRT Station

Post Office

Jalan Hang Kasturi

Jalan Hang Lekir

Chinatown

Sri Mahamariamman

Jalan Petaling

Jalan Sultan

Jalan Hang Jebat

Chinwoo Stadium

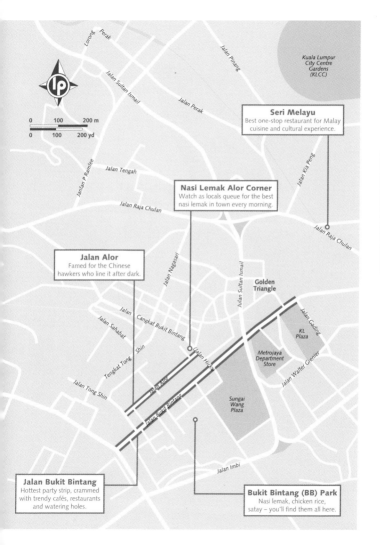

Seri Melayu
Best one-stop restaurant for Malay cuisine and cultural experience.

Nasi Lemak Alor Corner
Watch as locals queue for the best nasi lemak in town every morning.

Jalan Alor
Famed for the Chinese hawkers who line it after dark.

Golden Triangle

KL Plaza

Metrojaya Department Store

Sungai Wang Plaza

Jalan Bukit Bintang
Hottest party strip, crammed with trendy cafés, restaurants and watering holes.

Bukit Bintang (BB) Park
Nasi lemak, chicken rice, satay – you'll find them all here.

Kuala Lumpur City Centre Gardens (KLCC)

REGIONAL VARIATIONS

0 100 200 m
0 100 200 yd

Central Malaysia
Pahang

Pahang is the largest state in peninsular Malaysia. It was one of the last states to attract the interest of British colonialists and is still relatively less developed. Once the preserve of Orang Asli, prospectors eventually started to arrive in Pahang when rich tin and gold deposits were discovered. However, even then, the thick forest, network of rivers mountain ridges made most parts of the state impenetrable – which may account for the reason why the cuisines of the east and west coasts of Malaysia have remained fairly separate. Since the 1980s, the growth of timber, rubber and palm-oil industries have attracted people from other regions.

While you're likely to find a selection of Malay, Indian and Chinese eateries in the main towns of Pahang similar to the ones you'd find any-where else in Malaysia, the distinct cuisine of the region must be the food of the Orang Asli – although you're unlikely to taste it in a restaurant. The food of the Orang Asli is simple: fish is grilled or barbecued, tapioca leaves are boiled, and for much-needed carbohydrates rice is boiled or tapioca is left to cook on an open fire.

Pahang is also home to Malaysia's longest river, Sungai Pahang, and its tributaries are teeming with such fish as **ikan jelawat** (sultan fish), **ikan kelah** (greater brook carp) and **ikan patin** (fork-tailed catfish). Ikan patin, an oily fish with a fine texture is highly prized. It has no scales and is often served Chinese style, steamed with soy sauce or in either a coconut-based or tamarind-flavoured curry. Temerloh, a small town in the middle of the state, is a great place to try these fish dishes.

REGIONAL VARIATIONS

Above: Boys on their boat in Kuantan, Pahang
Left: Summer protection on the streets of Kuantan, Pahang

East Coast Malaysia
Kelantan & Terengganu

Compared to the more populated and industrialised west coast, the states of Kelantan and Terengganu have a far stronger sense of Malay culture. This is very evident in their cuisine. Kelantan and Terengganu were considerably isolated from the rest of the country, and received few Chinese and Indian immigrants. Consequently regional specialities have remained staunchly Malay.

Both Kelantan and Terengganu thrive on fishing and their famous white beaches are dotted with fishing villages. In Terengganu, the locals enjoy the luxury of being able to savour seafood that's fresh from the fisherman's net, and have created countless ways to prepare these wonderful fruits of the sea. Here **epok epok** (deep-fried pyramid-shaped pastries) are filled with fish fried with grated coconut.

Satar is a local delicacy consisting of fish, tamarind water, grated coconut, chilli, belacan, onion and sugar. The ingredients are blended, then wrapped in cones fashioned out of banana leaves and grilled. The sugar makes satar a little sweet, and some regard this regional penchant for sweetness as an influence from the states' northern neighbour, Thailand (both states were once vassals of the Thai kingdom of Ayuthaya).

Another fishy local delicacy is **keropok lekor** (crackers made from fish and sago flour). Many locals will boil their keropok lekor and then dip it into chilli sauce. The chilli sauce served with keropok lekor is a little more sweet than spicy and contains a swig of tamarind juice, yet another indication of Thai influence.

Another noteworthy regional flavour lies in the way laksa is created in Terengganu. **Laksang**, as locals prefer to call laksa, is made with noodles that are rolled up and sliced sheets of steamed rice flour. The laksang gravy is white and consists of fish, thin coconut, garlic and shallots. What's more, laksang is usually eaten cold and garnished with shredded raw long beans, bean sprouts and cucumber, as well as chillies and belacan.

Yet another dish that draws from the state's Thai ties is **sanggang**, a fish soup made with lemongrass, galangal, chilli and tamarind juice (which gives the dish a sour tinge).

The state of Kelantan boasts some unique specialities such as **nasi ayam percik** (barbecued chicken marinated with spicy coconut gravy) and **nasi dagang** (red or brown glutinous rice served with coconut milk, flaked fish, desiccated coconut and a variety of herbs and sauces). But the speciality of Kelantan has to be **nasi kerabu**, a rice dish tinted blue using the petals of the **bunga telang** (a local flower also referred to as clitoria). It's served with fish crackers and fried salted fish.

Nasi kerabu, Kuala Lumpur

South Malaysia

The three states that make up the south of Malaysia play significant roles in the life, and the cuisine, of the nation. Each has a cultural and culinary history built upon the arrival of immigrants – especially in Negeri Sembilan and Melaka.

Negeri Sembilan

The small state of Negeri Sembilan (literally, nine states) was once a loose federation ruled by Malay chiefs before they were united under the British. During the 15th century, many Minangkabau people from Sumatra settled in the area. Their cuisine has influenced the Malay food of Negeri Sembilan. Most of their dishes are flavoured with a generous helping of chilli, creating a searingly spicy kick. And their **rendang** (thick coconut-milk curry), while time consuming to prepare, is considered to be unsurpassed in flavour. To thoroughly enjoy Minangkabau rendang, it should be eaten with delicately salty yet sweet **lemang**, glutinous rice flavoured with coconut milk and cooked over an open fire in bamboo poles lined with young banana leaves.

Making the Negeri Sembilan speciality, lemang

Melaka

The growth of Melaka can be attributed to the trade of spices, silks, ivory and gold. Melaka first fell to the Portuguese, who remained for more than a century (making the port one of the mightiest in the east), then to the Dutch for another century and a half.

Melaka's colourful history has left it with an equally colourful culinary heritage. The stand-outs in Melaka's already renowned food scene are its Peranakan and Eurasian specialities. Unlike the Peranakans in Penang, who tend to favour sourer flavours in their dishes (due in no small part to their proximity to Thailand), Peranakans in Melaka tend towards the Malay penchant for coconut milk, chillies and fragrant roots. Curries are generally richer and creamier due to the amount of coconut milk added.

DON'T MISS

- **Cendol** – dessert consisting of coconut milk sweetened with palm sugar syrup, and with fine, short strings of green-bean flour dough, all topped with shaved ice. The best one is at No. 1 Kopitiam, No. 1 Jonker Street.

- **Gula Melaka** (palm sugar) – a speciality of Melaka, sap is extracted from the stalks of the sugar palm, then boiled and allowed to solidify in the hollow rounds of bamboo poles.

- **Satay celup** (skewered food items) – an assortment of meat, seafood, vegetables, fishballs and hardboiled quails eggs are skewered and cooked in a boiling stock before they're eaten with a peanut sauce.

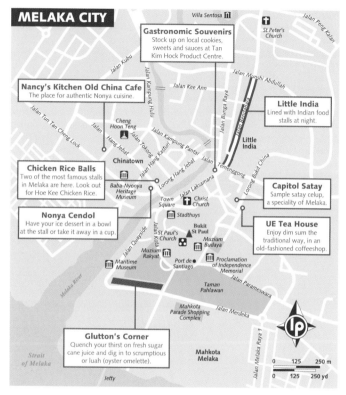

MELAKA CITY

Gastronomic Souvenirs
Stock up on local cookies, sweets and sauces at Tan Kim Hock Product Centre.

Nancy's Kitchen Old China Cafe
The place for authentic Nonya cuisine.

Little India
Lined with Indian food stalls at night.

Chicken Rice Balls
Two of the most famous stalls in Melaka are here. Look out for Hoe Kee Chicken Rice.

Capitol Satay
Sample satay celup, a speciality of Melaka.

Nonya Cendol
Have your ice dessert in a bowl at the stall or take it away in a cup.

UE Tea House
Enjoy dim sum the traditional way, in an old-fashioned coffeeshop.

Glutton's Corner
Quench your thirst on fresh sugar cane juice and dig in to scrumptious or luah (oyster omelette).

Villa Sentosa
St Peter's Church
Jalan Peng Kalan
Jalan Kubu
Jalan Kee Ann
Jalan Munshi Abdullah
Jalan Kampung Hulu
Jalan Tun Tan Cheng Lock
Cheng Hoon Teng
Jalan Hang Jebat
Jalan Tokong
Jalan Kampung Pantai
Jalan Bunga Raya
Jalan Bendahara
Little India
Chinatown
Jalan Hang Kasturi
Jalan Hang Jebat
Jalan Temenggong
Lorong Bukit China
Baba-Nyonya Heritage Museum
Lorong Hang Jebat
Jalan Laksamana
Town Square
Christ Church
Lorong Hang Jebat
Stadthuys
Bukit St Paul
St Paul's Church
Muzium Budaya
Jalan Kota
Jalan Quayside
Muzium Rakyat
Maritime Museum
Port de Santiago
Proclamation of Independence Memorial
Melaka River
Jalan Parameswara
Taman Pahlawan
Mahkota Parade Shopping Complex
Jalan Merdeka
Strait of Melaka
Mahkota Melaka
Jalan Melaka Raya 1
Jetty

0 125 250 m
0 125 250 yd

Johor

The southernmost state of Malaysia, Johor, is covered in pineapple, palm and rubber plantations. In the 16th century, when Melaka fell to the Portuguese, Johor's rulers became the protectors of the western states. Even though the demand for pepper in the 19th and 20th centuries attracted an influx of Chinese immigrants, today Johor continues to boast of a strong Malay culture and cuisine. **Satay Johor** may look much like satay you find in the rest of the region, but is different in that before being grilled, each skewer of meat is basted with a mixture of coconut milk and oil, brushed on with a stalk of lemongrass. This process is repeated as the meat cooks, giving it a delicate lemongrass flavour. The local version of laksa is **laksa Johor**, which contains coconut milk, flaked fish (most commonly wolf herring) and tamarind liquid that gives it a sour zing. It's also garnished with mint leaves, cucumber and bean sprouts.

But to suggest that the cuisine of Johor consists only of Malay classics would be inaccurate. Its capital city, Johor Bahru, is linked to Singapore by two causeways. This means that the two cities are drawn closely together physically, but also gastronomically. You are likely to find prime samples of char kway teow, **nasi biryani** (rice casserole) and murtabak here. But Johor Bahru is most popular among food-loving Singaporeans for its cheap seafood, particularly at Tepian Terbau Food Centre and Selera Sungai Chat Food Centre, both on Jalan Abu Bakar.

REGIONAL VARIATIONS

The colourful fruit of a palm tree, Johor

LAKSA 101

It's hard to walk the length of a block in Malaysia without being offered laksa. Even harder is trying to ascertain just which one to have, as every hawker seems to profess to serving the 'real' laksa. The truth is, there is no one such thing. But there are plenty of varieties to which you might pledge allegiance. To find the one you like best takes preparation and a little bit of knowledge. Hot gravy (the stock or broth), aroma, well-chosen and cooked noodles, and a crunchy and herbaceous garnish are the foundation to any decent laksa.

Sarawak Laksa
Kuching's breakfast of choice has a burnt-sienna-coloured base, given its hue from toasted rice and coconut. This is offset by the acid-sweet perkiness of kalamansi lime, with an intriguing chicken-shrimp combo adding protein oomph.

Asam Laksa
Very much a benchmark, this sour laksa strain is loved and hated for its hefty use of tamarind that comes in moist blocks. Flaked fish is the base of the aromatic gravy, along with wild ginger buds and belacan. Shredded pineapple makes for a sweet garnish. Penang is the ancestral home of this laksa version.

Laksa Lemak
Also known as curry laksa, this is mostly found in Kuala Lumpur and is frowned upon by some purists as 'not a laksa'. It lives up to its name with a generous dosing of coconut milk and curried chicken. Mung-bean sprouts and deep-fried beancurd further fortify the dish. Prawns are sometimes included.

Ipoh Curry Laksa
The old town of Ipoh on the west coast of Malaysia serves a curry laksa with bicultural tweaks that are unforgettable. Firstly the addition of Chinese barbecued roast pork, and secondly a stock made with oh-so-Indian curry leaves.

Laksa Johor
Believe it or not, this is an even richer version of laksa lemak. The gravy of laksa Johor is fish-based, made from oily swimmers such as mackerel or wolf herring. It is hugely complex, with flavours of cumin, coriander seeds and turmeric, and is coconut-milk lush, with a roasted note of dry-fried shredded coconut meat. The boldest inclusion may be the use of spaghetti. Laksa Johor is finished with slices of cucumbers, bean sprouts and Vietnamese mint.

REGIONAL VARIATIONS

Asam laksa gravy prepared for a wedding banquet, Penang

Singapore Laksa

Enter the laksa of the famous Nonya women. It was once the centrepiece of a 'laksa war' in modern-day Singapore. The gravy is rich, sour and deep in flavour, and includes deep-fried anchovies, coconut milk and belacan. It has an iconic garnish of fish cakes – in a more authentic version, these are homemade.

Laksa Kedah

From the Malaysian state of the same name, this thick laksa uses tamarind in dried slices and has a purple appearance. The garnish for laksa Kedah is roughly julienned cucumbers, shards of raw onion and ribbons of lettuce.

Rob McKeown

Malaysian Borneo

Sabah, Malaysia's northernmost state, together with Sarawak, make up Malaysian Borneo. While Sabah offers the challenge of Mount Kinabalu (one of the highest mountains in Southeast Asia), gorgeous beaches and coral reefs, Sarawak is filled with rainforests, wildlife and caves. Both are a world apart from the peninsular.

Sarawak

Sarawak is home to numerous indigenous tribes, including Dayaks, Ibans and Melanau. The latter group live in and around Mukah, a small town on the coast north of Sibu. A traditional Melanau fisherman's lunch is **umai** (thin slivers of raw fish – **ikan pirang**, a yellow fish with small bones is a regional preference, but Spanish mackerel, black pomfret and shad are also used – marinated with shallots, chilli, salt and tamarind liquid or lime juice). This is usually eaten with a bowl of toasted sago pellets. Another Melanau speciality is **siat** (sago grubs stirfried with shallots and ginger). Because of their swampy environment, where the soil is unsuitable for paddy cultivation, the Melanaus use the sago palm as the main starch component in their meals. Sago-based dishes include **linut**, a thick translucent sago paste which is eaten hot with sambal. Other specialities such as wild boar and deer are Sarawak favourites, and tasty vegetable dishes made with jungle ferns and **paku** (fernshoots) are not to be missed.

DON'T MISS

- **Forests & Farms** – visit verdant Sarawak, beyond the growing cities.
- **Siat** (sago grubs) – stirfried, these fat grubs are a protein-rich delicacy.
- **Tuak** (rice wine) – whether home brewed or served at a pub in town, Sarawak's traditional welcome drink packs a heady punch.

Sabah

The people of Sabah (who hail from over 30 different ethnic groups) enjoy an abundant supply of seafood, fish, deer, wild boar, game, wild plants, herbs and fruits from their forests. While rice is cultivated both in the hills and in irrigated fields, it is not necessarily the staple food of Sabahans. In the north, corn and tapioca are preferred.

Sabah has its own raw fish dish called **hinava** (fish marinated with lime juice and herbs). The Kadazans (Sabah's main tribal community) are famous for **hinava tongii**, a combination of fresh Spanish mackerel, chilli, ginger and shallots drenched in lime juice. We're told that the secret ingredient of this dish, however, is the grated seed of the **bambangan**, a variety of mango found only in Sabah.

Just as in Sarawak, in many swampy areas of Sabah the wild sago palm flourishes and sago starch forms part of many Sabahan meals. The Muslim Bisaya people, who live on the Klias peninsular, make a gluey porridge with sago starch which they call **ambuyat** (it's much like Sarawak's linut). The thick, sticky mixture is twirled around a chopstick and dipped into an accompanying sauce. The Murut, who live in the hilly southwestern region of Sabah, are famous for their **jaruk**, chunks of raw wild boar or river fish packed into a bamboo tube together with salt and cooked rice. The bamboo is sealed with leaves and the contents left to ferment for several weeks or even months. It is finally eaten in small portions with rice or tapioca starch.

The Kadazan, who live in the west of the state, love sour flavours and use bambangan, unripe mangoes, limes and **belimbing asam** (carambola) to add the tangy zing to their food. Other favoured ingredients include dried shrimp and anchovies, ginger, chilli, fresh turmeric and galangal.

Nearly all of Sabah's non-Muslim tribes make their own rice wines from steamed glutinous rice and dried yeast. **Tapai** (otherwise known as **pengasai**) is much loved by the Kadazan and Murut. It is consumed from communal jars through bamboo straws. But be careful of **montaku**, a distilled form of tapai and much more potent. **Lihing**, a gold-coloured rice wine, is believed to be particularly good for post-natal mothers. It also used to cook the Kadazan favourite, chicken soup with rice wine and fresh ginger.

REGIONAL VARIATIONS

Sunset over Kota Kinabalu, capital of Sabah

Singapore

Where do we start? Food is a national obsession in Singapore. The first thing a Singaporean friend says when you meet is 'Have you eaten?' Much like the trade-centric cities of Malaysia, namely Penang, Kuala Lumpur and Melaka, Singapore is blessed with a fascinating melting pot of food traditions. Having served as the crossroads of Asia for thousands of years, yet not having any local produce to call its own (today, the tiny 646 sq km island has no agriculture to speak of), Singapore has a food tradition that can only be called evolutionary – one that has gradually developed from the original that its migrant people brought to its shores.

In the Peranakan and Eurasian enclave of Katong, stalls serving Singapore laksa compete with tea-cake counters, chicken rice sellers and char kway teow hawkers. In Little India, the busy Tekka Market draws Indian Muslim, Hindu and Chinese housewives, as well as European *taitais* (local term for ladies of leisure) and feisty Nonyas (Peranakan ladies) – all out to get the freshest ingredients for their dinner tables at the best price. **Teh tarik** (pulled tea), arguably a drink of Indian origin, is accepted as the best thing to wash down anything from **roti paratha** (flaky fried flat bread) to **roti kaya** (grilled bread slathered with coconut egg jam).

While there are only subtle differences between, say, Penang and Singapore char kway teow, the truly idiosyncratic dishes of Singapore are the ones that were creations cooked up by innovative local chefs. Three dishes: **chilli crab** (stirfried crab with spicy chilli and tomato sauce; see the recipe), fish-head curry and **yu sheng** (raw fish salad), have become so much part of Singaporean cuisine

Chilli crab, a Singaporean invention

DON'T MISS

- **Fish-head curry** – Go on, it tastes fabulous, especially the soft muscle around the eyeballs.
- **Durian** – Sure, the fruit isn't cultivated on the island, but the experience of digging into the spiky shells alongside locals at tables lining Geyland Road is a gastronomic experience not to be missed.
- **Singapore Laksa** – A couple of years back, a veritable war broke out between a handful of competing laksa stalls in Katong. Find out what the fuss is about!
- **Chilli Crab** – Dig into the scrumptious local speciality with your fingers, then mop up the eggy, thick sauce with French bread or deep-fried **man tou** (plain Chinese buns, a northern Chinese staple).

that few people realise that they've evolved from dishes that enterprising chefs concocted and added to their restaurant menus.

While crab curries do exist within the Indian culinary oeuvre, Singapore chilli crab has a thick, sweet and spicy sauce that is close to what's considered sweet and sour sauce in the West. The creation of the dish is attributed to Lim Choon Ngee, who owned a seafood restaurant along the Kalang River. Today, his son Roland keeps the family tradition alive at Roland Seafood on Marine Parade Central.

REGIONAL VARIATIONS

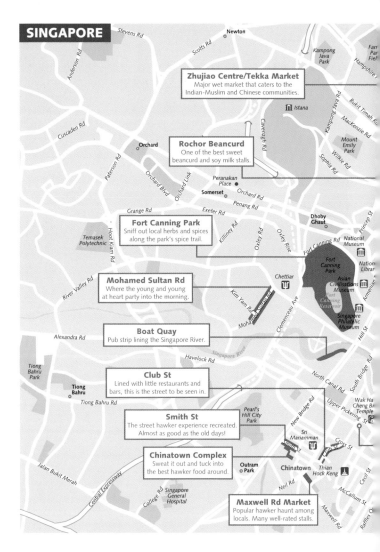

SINGAPORE

Zhujiao Centre/Tekka Market
Major wet market that caters to the
Indian-Muslim and Chinese communities.

Rochor Beancurd
One of the best sweet
beancurd and soy milk stalls.

Fort Canning Park
Sniff out local herbs and spices
along the park's spice trail.

Mohamed Sultan Rd
Where the young and young
at heart party into the morning.

Boat Quay
Pub strip lining the Singapore River.

Club St
Lined with little restaurants and
bars, this is the street to be seen in.

Smith St
The street hawker experience recreated.
Almost as good as the old days!

Chinatown Complex
Sweat it out and tuck into
the best hawker food around.

Maxwell Rd Market
Popular hawker haunt among
locals. Many well-rated stalls.

Stevens Rd
Newton
Scotts Rd
Kampong Java Park
Farr Par Fiel
Hampshire
Anderson Rd
Cuscaden Rd
Istana
Cavenagh Rd
Kampong Java Rd
Bukit Timah Rd
MacKenzie Rd
Mount Emily Park
Wilkie Rd
Sophia Rd
Orchard
Paterson Rd
Orchard Blvd
Orchard Link
Peranakan Place
Somerset
Orchard Rd
Penang Rd
Grange Rd
Exeter Rd
Dhoby Ghaut
Temasek Polytechnic
Hook Kiam Rd
Killiney Rd
Oxley Rd
Oxley Rise
Fort Canning Rd
National Museum
National Library
River Valley Rd
Chettiar
Kim Yam Rd
Clemenceau Ave
Fort Canning Park
Asian Civilisations Museum
Armenian St
Fort Canning Reservoir
Mohamed Sultan Rd
Singapore Philatelic Museum
Hill St
Alexandra Rd
Havelock Rd
Singapore River
North Canal Rd
South Bridge Rd
Tiong Bahru Park
Tiong Bahru
Tiong Bahru Rd
Pearl's Hill City Park
New Bridge Rd
Upper Pickering St
Wak Ha Cheng Bi Temple
Sri Mariamman
Cross St
Jalan Bukit Merah
Central Expressway
College Rd
Singapore General Hospital
Outram Park
Neil Rd
Chinatown
Thian Hock Keng
McCallum St
Cecil St
Maxwell Rd
Raffles Q

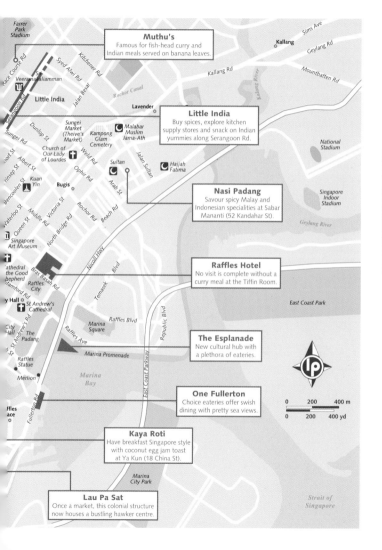

Muthu's
Famous for fish-head curry and Indian meals served on banana leaves.

Little India
Buy spices, explore kitchen supply stores and snack on Indian yummies along Serangoon Rd.

Nasi Padang
Savour spicy Malay and Indonesian specialities at Sabar Mananti (52 Kandahar St).

Raffles Hotel
No visit is complete without a curry meal at the Tiffin Room.

The Esplanade
New cultural hub with a plethora of eateries.

One Fullerton
Choice eateries offer swish dining with pretty sea views.

Kaya Roti
Have breakfast Singapore style with coconut egg jam toast at Ya Kun (18 China St).

Lau Pa Sat
Once a market, this colonial structure now houses a bustling hawker centre.

Farrer Park Stadium
Race Course Rd
Syed Alwi Rd
Kitchener Rd
Veeramakaliamman
Little India
Jalan Besar
Rochor Canal
Kallang
Sims Ave
Geylang Rd
Kallang Rd
Mountbatten Rd
Kallang River
Lavender
Serangoon Rd
Sungei Rd
Dunlop St
Sungei Market (Theive's Market)
Kampong Glam Cemetery
Malabar Muslim Jama-Ath
Church of Our Lady of Lourdes
Weld Rd
Wold Rd
Ophir Rd
Sultan
Jalan Sultan
Hajjah Fatima
Albert St
Kuan Yin
Bugis
Arab St
Rochor Rd
Beach Rd
National Stadium
Bencoolen St
Waterloo St
Queen St
Middle Rd
Victoria St
North Bridge Rd
Singapore Art Museum
Cathedral the Good Shepherd
Bras Basah Rd
Stamford Rd
Raffles City
City Hall
St Andrew's Cathedral
City Hall
The Padang
St Andrew's Rd
Raffles Ave
Raffles Statue
Merlion
Raffles Place
Fullerton Rd
Nicoll Hwy
Temasek Blvd
Marina Square
Raffles Blvd
Marina Promenade
Republic Blvd
East Coast Parkway
Marina Bay
Singapore Indoor Stadium
Geylang River
East Coast Park
National Stadium
Marina City Park
Strait of Singapore

0   200   400 m
0   200   400 yd

LP

Fish-head curry was famously created by an Indian cook named Gomez at his restaurant on Tank Road. The dish appealed to his Chinese diners who considered fish head a delicacy. These days, you find the dish on menus across both Malaysia and Singapore.

The same goes for yusheng, a salad of paper-thin raw fish, finely grated vegetables, candied melon and lime, red and white pickled ginger, pomelo sacs, sesame seeds, jellyfish and peanuts tossed in a dressing. It's eaten on the seventh day of the Chinese New Year in the belief that it brings diners prosperity and good luck (see p 118).

shopping
& markets

For Malaysians and Singaporeans, shopping for food is a passion.
The markets of Malaysia and Singapore are a celebration of great
produce, culinary fusion and multiculturalism. Offering a glimpse
of local life, market shopping is an experience worth getting your
feet wet (and your backs sweaty) for.

At the Market

Markets play a big part in the everyday life of Malaysians and Singaporeans. The cook of the family sets off around 6am to the market armed with baskets, bags and shopping trolleys to get the best bargains and freshest produce. The market is also a meeting place, where haggling over the freshest food becomes a social occasion. The atmosphere is convivial and bargaining is the norm as shoppers raise the noise quotient by several decibels even if it's just to knock 10 cents off the price of a bag of bean sprouts. The stallholders often give as good as they get, but outnumbered by the determined shoppers that descend upon them, they usually concede to shaving a few cents off the price.

A typical market is a one-stop shop sectioned by the kinds of meat, produce and sundries sold. Lining the perimeter of most markets are shops that sell clothes, shoes and other daily necessities like brooms, mops, pails, clothes pegs, pots, pans, cutlery and crockery. Following the general rule of thumb in Malaysia and Singapore, where there's human traffic, there are hawkers and other food sellers, so never far away from any market will be a hawker centre or coffeeshop where shoppers can enjoy a cup of coffee sweetened with condensed milk and a breakfast fry-up before returning to their homes to start the day's cooking.

While neighbourhood markets empty out by noon, there are central ones that stay open throughout the day, to cater to those who prefer to do their shopping after school or work.

Pasar Malam (Night Markets)

These open-air market stalls literally spill out onto the pavements at night and tempt you with the sheer variety of goods on sale. As their name suggests, night markets open for trade in the early evening and close just before midnight – sometimes later, depending on the area. Here you'll find clothes, costume jewellery, CDs, cassettes, toys, grooming products, mattresses, bed linen, food, drink, fruit and much, much more. It can take hours just to walk through an entire night market and it's a lot of fun. If you're in for a long haul, come dressed in cool clothing as it can get really hot and sweaty under the bright lights and tarpaulin tents.

Bargaining is the norm at night markets and stallholders often quote a high price to start off. Don't be shy to haggle them down to what you think is a reasonable price. Stick to your guns and walk away if you have to. More often than not, the stallholder will back down and accede to the price you've asked for. You'll know you've gone too far when they let you walk away without buying anything. But don't worry as there will surely be another stall selling the same goods not too far down the row.

Fresh vegetables for sale, Penang

The highlight of a night market is always the food. Go on an empty stomach because you'll find an abundance of foods like grilled chicken wings, skewered fishballs, **ikan otak otak** (spiced fish rectangles wrapped in banana leaves and grilled over a charcoal fire), **roti kaya** (grilled bread with coconut egg jam), roasted chestnuts and **char dan** (braised eggs in tea), as well as desserts and sweets like **cendol** (cold coconut-milk dessert), **mua chee** (cooked rice dough shaped into strips and cut into bite-sized pieces then tossed in a chopped peanut and sugar mixture) and **kueh-kueh** (tea cakes). Some night markets also host entertainment with singers crooning hits in Malay, Mandarin, Cantonese and English.

Roast pork, Penang

Pasar (Wet Markets)

Wet markets are so named for their concrete floors that are washed down to clear away dirt and waste, leaving a slopping layer of water lingering on the thin aisles that separate the small stalls. Many stallholders are decked out in gumboots or galoshes (almost always black or bright yellow), while some opt for wooden clogs. Such footwear is best suited for the slippery floors; if wearing normal shoes, ensure you don't lose your footing while haggling over a piece of fish. Don't be intimidated by the noise and funky smell of fresh produce mingling in the air. Take a deep breath, dive in and explore. You'll be amply rewarded.

Wet markets are usually divided into distinct sections. Fruit stalls will be located at one end, loaded with stacks of bananas, furry red rambutans, sweet-smelling pineapples, mangoes, apples, oranges and all manner of other tropical fruit. Some stallholders will let you have a taste before you buy.

In the vegetable section, you'll find everything from local spinach and **daun kari** (curry leaves) to watercress and cabbage. Many vegetables are freshly picked from the market gardens in Malaysia and Singapore, while others come from as far as China and Australia. Look out for things like fresh water chestnuts as well as exotic tubers, young bamboo shoots, turnips and small eggplants. Another common sight in the vegetable section is a lady sifting through a pile of bean sprouts removing their dirt and 'tails'.

Not far from the area selling vegetables will be stalls selling fresh noodles. These stalls also stock wonton wraps as well as soybean products like silken tofu, **taukee** (beancurd sheets), all sorts of soy sauces and preserved soybeans. Nearby, eggs – fresh or preserved – can be bought from stalls that sell them individually or by the carton. Eggs covered in black soot are **kiam neng** (salted eggs, usually duck), and those in flecks of dark brown sawdust are **pei daan** (century eggs).

The wettest part of the market is where the meat and fish are sold. If you're squeamish about raw meat and blood, you should avoid this section where great slabs of meat are hung from hooks and the occasional pig's head or a pail full of entrails share space with the butchers and their hefty meat cleavers.

Beef, lamb and pork get separate departments in the wet market. And since there is a large Muslim community in Malaysia and Singapore, halal (forbidden) meats are sold in different sections. For the most part, livestock is slaughtered daily and when choosing your meats look for a good, bright colour and ensure that they are not dry. Note also that the Chinese eat almost every part of an animal, so don't be surprised to see tongues, trotters and intestines on sale too. Inform the butcher of the cut you want and how much of it, and they will cut it for you.

Longans, Penang

Chopping chicken to order, Penang

SHOPPING & MARKETS

Plucked for your convenience, Penang

Fresh fish fillets, Penang

Some stalls still sell live poultry and, if you like, you can pick out the plumpest chicken and have it weighed before you go home to chop its head off and pluck its feathers. Alternatively, you can have the stallholder do it for you. For the less adventurous, most other poultry stalls sell already-slaughtered whole chickens or ready-to-cook cuts like wings, breasts, feet, liver and parson's noses. Haram stalls should sell ducks as well. Some stalls sell **kampung chicken**, free-range poultry that tend to be leaner and hence a healthier choice.

At the fish section, you'll find an extensive selection of the night's fresh catch. If you're unsure about what kinds of fish are on display, just quiz the fishmongers, who are a mine of information on these exotic creatures. Among the most highly prized (and highly priced) fish are the **bawal puteh** (silver and white pomfrets) that are best served steamed with chilli, ginger and soy sauce. Large fish like **ikan tenggiri** (mackerel) can be sold whole or in fillets. When choosing, note that fresh fish should be firm to the touch and have shiny scales, red gills and bright eyes. A sure sign that a fish is not fit for consumption are eyes that are cloudy. Some fish stalls also sell homemade fish balls that you can throw into a soup at home.

Piles of **sotong** (squid), **kupang** (mussels) and **udang** (prawns) of all sizes are also readily available. Look for prawns with shiny shells that are not soft and limp. Large baskets of

MARKET TALK

The language used in the markets of multicultural Malaysia and Singapore represents an entire vocabulary of its own. For example, the Portuguese brought to the Melakan marketplace many new products such as **terung** (eggplant), known commonly as brinjal. Thanks to the region's colonial history, vegetables are known by their British names rather than their American one. For example, the crunchy-on-the-outside-slimy-on-the-inside vegetable is called ladies' fingers instead of okra (it's called **kacang bendi** in Malay). And because of the mishmash of languages and dialects that locals use, some vegetables have been given entirely new, made-up names like 'ko-le-chai-hua' for cauliflower ('ko-le' is a play on 'cauli', 'chai' means vegetable, and 'hua' means flower).

Here is a guide to some herbs, spices and vegetables that aren't commonly known by their English names.

candlenuts	**buah keras, kemiri**
cardamom	**buah pelaga, kapulaga, krawan**
coriander/cilantro	**ketumbar, wang swee**
lemongrass	**serai**
small limes	**limau kesturi**
nutmeg	**buah pala, anis**
fermented soybean cakes	**tempeh**
salted soybeans	**tau cheo**
tamarind	**asam**
turmeric	**kunyit**
water convolvulus	**kangkong**

SHOPPING & MARKETS

live **ketam** (crabs) are another typical feature at the seafood section. There are basically two types of crab that are sold – the **ketam renjong** (blue swimmer crab or flower crab) that comes from the sea, or the **ketam batu** (mud crab) that live in the mangrove swamps. Don't miss out on the plethora of shellfish and other fruits of the sea like **kerang** (cockles), **kepah** (Manila clams), **siput** (razor clams) and a popular sea slug used in Chinese cooking, called **trepang** (sea cucumber).

Florists also have a home at the wet markets and they are a cheap source of tropical buds like carnations, chrysanthemums and orchids sold by the stalk. Also, dried-goods stalls that line the market's edges display sacks of rice, onions and garlic, and are the stalls to visit if you're looking for packets of **hay bee** (dried shrimp) and mushrooms, bottles of soy sauce and oyster sauce, beans or wraps.

Dried goods, Penang

By and large, the wet market is the best place to catch an authentic glimpse of local everyday life. All sorts of people trudge through here – bored expats whiling their mornings away, servants fulfilling their shopping duties and happy to have time away from their employers' homes, mothers rushing to buy ingredients for family meals, old men sitting around a makeshift checker board and kids wandering around touching everything in sight. At the end of a long and sweaty shopping trip, the hawker centre, usually located nearby, beckons with samples of a fine number of local dishes. Dining here may also inspire a second visit to the wet market in an attempt to recreate one of the invariably delicious dishes you will taste.

Specialist Stalls in the Wet Market
Herb Stalls

To find the unusual selection of herbs and vegetables used in Malay and Peranakan salads, head to the **ulam** (herb) stall. Here you'll find ginger, galangal, coriander shoots, lemongrass, fern fronds, **bunga siantan** (torch ginger buds), **daun kaduk** (wild pepper leaf, used in several North Malaysian herb rice dishes), **daun cajus** (young cashew leaves) and the like. The same stall also supplies herbs for soups and drinks, ingredients for betel-leaf chewing, and seasonal fruits like jackfruit, soursop and guava. Also look out for tubers and rhizomes for curries; citrus fruits like lime and lemon; and even pickled fish liver and roe preserved in brine.

> ## Measurements
> Malaysia and Singapore use the metric system of measurements, but in many older markets, vendors still sell based on the weight measure of kati (catty) and tahil.
>
> | | |
> |---|---|
> | 1 kati | 653g |
> | 1 tahil | 41g |
>
> See also the Measurement & Conversion tables on the inside back cover.

Indian Spice Stalls

Indians are masters of spices and no wet market experience would be complete without a visit to the Indian spice stall. Usually located close to the meat section, the Indian spice stall will assault your senses with every imaginable spice from star anise, cumin and cardamom to turmeric, cloves and, of course, curry powder. In large plastic tubs or dishes are the secrets to a good curry and all it takes is a simple request for 'fish curry for two' or 'mutton korma for four'. In a flash of twirling hands, the stallholder will then scoop a little bit of this and that from several tubs into a plastic bag, give it a little shake and hand over an unbeatable spice mix.

Coconut Stalls

Coconuts are essential in local cooking, and the coconut seller usually takes up a small spot near the vegetable section or outside a provision shop. Freshly grated coconut with or without the brown exterior can be bought here, as well as freshly squeezed coconut cream and milk. This should not be confused with coconut water, which is the liquid found inside the coconut. **Santan pekat** (coconut cream) is made by squeezing the grated coconut with little or no water added. **Santan kental** (coconut milk) is made in the same manner but with more water. Sometimes, a pinch of salt is thrown in to enhance the flavour and help preserve the coconut cream or milk.

Things to Take Home

The markets in Malaysia and Singapore offer a treasure-trove of utensils and cooking equipment to take home. You may not put them to use in your kitchen, but these items will certainly add character to its décor, evoking an old-world Asian charm.

Cooking Utensils

Most Chinese and Malay foods are cooked in a wok and the market is the best place to find a good quality one at a reasonable price. Other utensils and cooking equipment to look out for are Indian copper pots, in which curries are best cooked, bamboo steamers that retain heat most effectively, porcelain pots (otherwise known as double-boilers) for double-boiling soups and Chinese clay pots for optimum stewing.

Some shops in Malaysia still sell typical Peranakan cooking utensils like a **parut**, a special implement for grating coconut, **batu giling** (a grinding stone for making spice pastes) and **batu lesong** (the normal bowl-shaped mortar and pestle made of stone, ideal for pounding small amounts of spices). Also take the opportunity while you're at a market to buy a good Chinese cleaver that will be much cheaper than cleavers at home. A knife-sharpening block made of stone is also a good buy and will help keep your knives sharp for a lifetime.

All your kitchen needs, Penang

SHOPPING & MARKETS

Moulds & Cookie Cutters

Look out for old-fashioned cake and jelly moulds made of aluminium or sometimes copper that locals use for festive occasions. A favourite for Chinese New Year is a jelly mould in the shape of two carp, which signifies good luck and prosperity. Also pick up cookie cutters, wooden-and-net flour sieves, wooden mooncake moulds and hefty **kueh pie ti** (a Peranakan snack) moulds that are fast disappearing.

SHOPPING & MARKETS

Creative cake moulds, Penang   *Showing off a set of shell moulds, Penang*

Food

Dried **keropok** (crackers) are great snacks to take home. When you get back, dry them out in the sun for a couple of hours before deep frying in vegetable oil and then keep them in airtight tins to enjoy whenever hunger strikes. **Belacan** (fermented shrimp paste) is a key ingredient when recreating Peranakan dishes at home, so stock up (it can keep for months in the fridge). Another favourite is **pada** (salt-fish pickle), which is sold in most shops in Melaka. It is a great accompaniment to plain rice. **Cincalok** (fermented shrimps) is another Melakan speciality, which goes well as a condiment with grilled fish and rice. **Gula Melaka** (palm sugar) also keeps for months in the fridge and is essential when recreating local desserts like sago pudding.

Air drying shrimp crackers in Pasir Penambang

where to
eat & drink

It's nearly impossible to go hungry (or thirsty, for that matter) in a region where you can find an opportunity to snack, sup or sip round every street corner. To eat or drink in Malaysia and Singapore is far more than an act of sustenance, it is a social experience – a chance to let your tastebuds savour the cultural melange of these two countries.

Street Food

Recently, great effort has been made to raise the hygiene standards of hawker food preparation by moving hawker carts off the streets and into permanent stalls at hawker centres and food courts. But locals will argue that the best food can still be found at the compact little kitchens-on-wheels that line alleyways and street corners, fill whole hawker enclaves, and cluster around popular coffeeshops.

That said, it's difficult to define street food purely as food served at these roadside stalls. There is very little difference between the types of dishes served from a hawker cart along the street and a hawker stall in a hawker centre or food court (and in Singapore these carts have almost disappeared, although they are still to be found throughout Malaysia). In fact, many pushcart stallholders will position themselves close to popular eating establishments so as to tap into their pool of diners. Of course, popular pushcarts similarly help entice diners into choosing to stop at the nearby coffeeshops. The business relationship between the roadside hawker and the coffeeshop owner can develop to an extent where should you choose to have your meal in the comforts of the coffeeshop (as opposed to eating standing on the street) you'll be charged a small premium for the convenience – especially if the pushcart stall offers no tables and seats at all.

The top of Swatow Lane, famous for its ice kacang stalls, Penang

The hawker meal is central to the experience of eating in Malaysia and Singapore. This is how a majority of locals eat on a regular basis. While stay-at-home mums or grandmothers take the time to prepare home-cooked meals for their families, many young couples and families in which both parents work will have most of their meals at the neighbourhood hawker corner or centre. Obsessive foodies may have splendid dinners at home, but still choose to head out to their favourite supper joints for an extra hawker fix.

Most significant of all, is the fact that the hawker meal best reflects the multicultural nature of these two countries. No meals need be cuisine specific. You can choose to start with an Indian **rojak** (deep-fried vegetables and seafood served with spicy-sweet sauce, and fresh cucumber, tomato and onion), go on to tuck into a Chinese **char kway teow** (broad, flat rice-flour noodles stirfried with Chinese sausage and egg in a sweet, dark soy sauce) with a side dish of Malaysian **sop ekor lembu** (oxtail soup), then complete your meal with an **ais kacang** (Malaysian ice dessert).

Char kway teow stall on Jalan Selamat, Penang

Diners can dine communally the way most Asians do, or simply order a single portion of what they feel like eating. Most hawker dishes are designed as single portions – a bowl of noodle soup, a plateful of fried rice or noodles, a single serve of dessert. In fact, the quickest way to upset a hawker is to order just one plate of his food and ask for multiple sets of cutlery. But there are exceptions to the rule. Most stallholders expect veg-etable dishes such as **kerabu taugeh** (bean sprout salad), and meat dishes such as **satay** (spicy grilled meat skewers; see the recipe) to be shared. Some rice dishes such as chicken rice can be ordered in portions suited to the number of diners sharing the meal – meaning that you'd get a serving of chicken on one plate placed in the middle of the table, with individual plates of rice for each diner.

The important thing to note is that most stalls specialise in only one dish. The following list isn't so much a categorisation of different kinds of stalls, but of stalls selling different kinds of food.

WHERE TO EAT & DRINK

Rice Stalls

There are two kinds of rice stalls: those that offer a wide selection of dishes to accompany your rice (you tell them what you want) and those that serve one kind of dish with rice. **Nasi lemak** (coconut rice with fried fish), **nasi campur** (rice with a choice of dishes), **nasi Padang** (the Indonesian version, almost identical to nasi campur), **nasi kandar** (the Indian version) and **chap chai peng** (economy rice) stalls fall under the former category. Pick the kind of rice you prefer (at economy rice stalls you'll only get plain steamed rice; at the others, you're likely to get a choice of plain rice, coconut rice or possibly **nasi kuning** – yellow rice; see the recipe), then let your fingers do the pointing.

The other kind of rice stall is either a chicken-rice stall, or a roasted or barbecued meat stall. It is usually identified by the rows of whole cooked chicken, roasted duck, slabs of crisp, roasted belly pork and lengths of **cha siew** (barbecued pork) displayed in its window. Depending on whether you're ordering a dish for one person or more, the meat you've chosen will be sliced and placed on top of a serving of rice (if for just one diner) or placed on a separate dish to be shared between diners (if for more than one). The meat will usually come heaped over cucumber slices, but at some stalls also over side orders of stirfried vegetables. A bowl of soup customarily comes with the meal.

Shopkeepers prepare for business, Penang

STREET HAWKERS, HAWKER CENTRES & FOOD COURTS

The food choices you'll get at any of these dining locations – the street-side hawker stall, the hawker centre and the food court – will not vary dramatically. Sure, you're more likely to find a Thai or Japanese food stall in a food court rather than on the street, but the primary concept remains the same: quick, simple and affordable meals.

Street hawkers, whether permanent or mobile, are the precursors of hawker centres and food courts. Hawkers once carried their wares over their shoulders (often two bundles consisting of foodstuff and equipment, balanced on either end of a pole swung over their shoulders), and set up shop at busy street corners and at plantations where hungry labourers sought quick, hearty meals; or simply took to the streets, announcing their presence by the 'tok-tok' of short bamboo sticks tapped against one another (which explains why they were also called tok-tok vendors), only stopping when an order was placed. Dishes were assembled on the spot. Some hawkers had more elaborate equipment – satay vendors would set up stoves and grill their sticks of chicken, mutton and beef over a charcoal fire. Women would come to the makeshift stall bearing their own plates and bowls. But this is a tradition that no longer exists in the big cities.

Lunch at Swatow Lane hawker centre, Penang

Chee cheong fun at an outdoor hawker stall, Penang

More common now are pushcart stalls with fires powered by large gas canisters. Some remain in one spot all the time, others move from location to location. Many gather at an agreed location and set up tables and chairs for their shared diners (often in the open air). Chances are, you'll find one or two close to, or situated right in, major markets in each town. Some street hawkers associate themselves with coffeeshops which have indoor seating, others offer minimal seating built into their carts, and some don't offer seats of any sort.

Hawker centres are created in purpose-built structures with basic services such as electricity, running water and washrooms provided. There are many tables, and you are likely to find a greater selection of food. Food courts are even fancier, and are often air-conditioned. You are likely to find them in shopping malls and large office buildings. The stalls usually have a small kitchen attached and refrigeration facilities, unlike the cramped quarters of most hawker centre stalls.

Hainanese Chicken Rice

A dish brought to Malaysia and Singapore by settlers from Hainan, China, chicken rice in Malaysia and Singapore has become closely associated with the cuisine of this region. There are people who claim to be able to eat chicken rice every day and still not grow weary of its flavour! In Melaka, more so than in other parts of the region, you'll also find the same chicken served with rice balls rather than rice. The rice is shaped into golf ball-sized orbs and served alongside the chopped chicken. This dish is eaten the same way you would eat the regular version, making sure to get a portion of chicken, some rice and the soy and chilli condiments into each mouthful.

Older chefs argue that the rice was originally shaped into balls because it needed to be kept warm from the time it was cooked (often earlier in the day) until mealtime. The rice balls, when stored in wooden containers, apparently stayed warm for a longer time. The other theory is that the rice balls were more portable and were easier for labourers working on plantations to transport from home. Today, rice balls are appreciated more as a novelty than anything else.

You'll find chicken rice sold at hawker centres, food courts and even stylish hotel coffeehouses. But the chicken rice shops, often housed in old coffeeshops, remain the place to go. Traditionally family-owned businesses, some of the region's chicken rice shops have been in operation since the early 1900s. Though low on fancy restaurant ambience, they are full of local colour. The peerless combination of silkily tender chicken, pungent chilli sauce (which is not part of the Hainan original), and richly flavoured rice is enjoyed at all times of the day, in venues ranging from humble hawker centres to the Mandarin Hotel's justly famous Chatterbox Coffeehouse.

Hainanese Chicken Rice Recipe

Ingredients

Hainanese chicken

1	fresh whole chicken, about 1kg
1 tsp	salt
1 tbs	light soy sauce
1 tsp	Chinese rice wine, or substitute dry sherry
2	pieces of ginger, 2.5cm (1 in) thick, lightly bruised
1	garlic clove, peeled and lightly bruised
1	spring onion
2L	water
2L	iced water
1 tsp	sesame oil

WHERE TO EAT & DRINK

Chicken-flavoured rice

2 cups	long-grain jasmine rice
2¹/₂ cups	chicken stock (from cooking the chicken; see below)
chicken fat	(from preparing the whole chicken; see below)
1 tbs	ginger, finely chopped
5	garlic cloves, peeled and finely chopped
1 tsp	sesame oil
1	pandanus leaf, tied into a knot
1 tsp	salt

Chilli and ginger sambal

10	fresh red chillies, seeds removed from half, chopped
10	garlic cloves, peeled and chopped
2 tbs	ginger, peeled and chopped
1 tbs	vegetable oil
1 tbs	chicken stock (from cooking the chicken; see below)
	salt, to taste
	sugar, to taste
	kalamansi (sour lime) juice, to taste

To serve

1	cucumber, halved lengthways and thinly sliced
1 handful	coriander sprigs
4 tbs	dark soy sauce
	salt, to taste
	ground white pepper, to taste
2	spring onions, finely sliced

Remove the fat from the cavity of the chicken and set aside for use in flavouring the rice later. Vigorously rub the inside and outside of the chicken with the salt, ¹/₂ tablespoon of the light soy sauce and all of the rice wine. Place ginger, garlic and spring onion in the cavity. Set aside for 1 hour at room temperature. Add the water to a deep pot and bring to the boil. Lower the chicken into the pot – it should be completely immersed. Immediately turn off the heat and put the lid on. Leave to stand for 1 hour, at 15-minute intervals lifting the chicken and draining the water from the cavity to ensure that the chicken cooks inside as well. After 30 minutes, reheat the water almost to boiling point, then turn the heat off again. Never having been allowed to boil, the chicken is cooked to succulent and juicy perfection. At the end of the hour, remove the chicken from the pot, and plunge it into a large bowl containing the iced water, to prevent further cooking. Once cool (about 20 minutes), drain the chicken thoroughly either by sticking a wooden spoon into the cavity and lifting it out of the stock while using another spoon to prevent it from slipping around or, if it is cool to touch, simply lift it out gently with your fingers. Rub it down with the remaining 1/2 tablespoon of light soy sauce and sesame oil. Snip off the chicken wing tips, neck and legs. Toss these into the liquid left in the pot. Set the rest of the chicken aside, covered, until ready to serve.

To prepare the rice, rinse in a sieve under cold running water until the water runs clear. Drain thoroughly. Bring the pot with the chicken stock to the boil, simmering until the liquid is reduced to about 5 cups (40 fl oz), skimming off any scum that rises to the surface. Strain the stock. Measure out 2 1/2 cups (20 fl oz) for cooking the rice. Reserve the rest. Place the chicken fat set aside earlier in a medium saucepan. Cook on a low heat to render the fat (there should be about 3 tablespoons). Add the ginger and garlic, and fry gently until aromatic without browning. Add the drained rice and sesame oil, stirring well to coat each grain with fat. Add the chicken stock to the rice, and bring to the boil. Add the pandanus leaf and salt. Simmer briskly until there is no water left on the surface of the rice. Clamp the lid of the saucepan on tightly, and immediately reduce the heat to the lowest. Leave for about 10 minutes. Turn the heat off, and allow the rice to stand for another 10 minutes before uncovering.

For the chilli and ginger sambal, process or blend the chillies, garlic and ginger to a fine paste, adding the oil and chicken stock (obtained from what was reserved earlier) to facilitate the process. Scrape into a bowl. Stir in salt, sugar and kalamansi juice to taste. Divide into 4 small individual serving saucers.

When ready to serve, chop the chicken Chinese-style into bite-sized pieces with skin and bone intact. Start by halving the chicken with a cut that stretches from head to tail with a Chinese cleaver. The wings are usually cut off and sliced into two or three segments to give you a small drumstick, wing-tip and middle wing section. The drumsticks are also severed at the joint then chopped crosswise into bite-sized pieces. The remaining parts of the two halves are usually halved again (giving you four quarters) and then chopped into bite-sized pieces. Place on a platter over the sliced cucumber. Garnish with the sprigs of coriander. Dish around 1 tablespoon of dark soy sauce into 4 small individual serving saucers. Bring the remaining chicken stock to the boil. Season to taste with salt and ground white pepper. Ladle into 4 small soup bowls and garnish with the sliced spring onions. For each serving, pack a small bowl with rice, then invert the rice onto a plate. Each person gets a plate of aromatic rice, a bowl of shimmering chicken broth and 2 small dishes of dipping sauces – the chilli and ginger sambal, and the dark soy sauce. Everyone helps themselves to the platter of Hainanese chicken placed in the centre of the table.

Serves 4

Cze Cha (Pick 'n' Mix) Stalls

You will recognise these stalls from their beautiful displays of fried rolls, meat and fish balls, stuffed chillies, tofu and other bits and pieces. There is usually a stack of empty bowls or plates placed to one side of the display. At these stalls, diners usually help themselves to a plate and a pair of tongs, and pick the items that they like. Watch to see what the people ahead of you do. Some stallholders prefer to pick up the items themselves as you point to them.

A few different dishes are sold in this fashion. Indian **rojak** (also known as rojak Singapore) consists of pieces of hard-boiled egg, tofu, fried fish cake and other specialities which are often deep fried again after you've picked them out, cut into bite-sized pieces and then served with a spicy-sweet dip. Note that Penang rojak is more of a salad, made of pineapple, turnip and cucumber slices tossed in a sauce consisting of shrimp paste, dried shrimp, dark sauce, chillies and ground peanuts (you don't get to pick the ingredients for this).

Yong tauhu stalls similarly boast a selection of fish balls, tofu cubes stuffed with minced pork, bitter gourd slices and green chillies stuffed with fish paste that you can choose to have in a clear soup, with rice vermicelli and **kangkong** (water convolvulus) if you wish, or served over rice vermicelli and doused in a sweet-and-savoury sauce.

Roadside rojak stall, Kuala Lumpur

Mee (Noodle) Stalls

You learn to tell, by the sweet aroma in the air, what kind of fried noodle stall you're nearing even before you see it. Does it have the smell of caramelised sweet dark sauce and fatty Chinese sausage? That would be **char kway teow**. Or perhaps there's the scent of fatty pork, squid and shrimp plus the bouquet of freshly squeezed **kalamansi** (sour lime)? It's got to be fried **Hokkien mee** (stirfried dish filled with squid and tiny shrimp, pork and vegetables). An eggy spiciness coupled with the smell of cabbage cooking in the air? That's **mee goreng** (spicy fried noodle dish). The rhythmic scraping of a metal spatula against the sides of a wok is a clear indication that you're nearing a fried noodle stall. If the base of the stallholder's pan is flat, they're likely to be selling **chai tau kueh** (stirfried radish cake) or **kway kak** (similar to char kway teow, but using cubes of rice noodle instead of flat rice noodles).

Kway teow at a hawker stall, Penang

But if there's no hot wok action, and all the hawker has is a steaming cauldron of soup, then you are heading towards noodle soup territory, which just means that the noodles are cooked in boiling hot water, much like pasta, and served either in a broth or dry with the broth on the side. Variations abound. **Hokkien mee** consists of yellow, thick egg noodles stirfried with, squid, tiny prawns, pork, vegetables and egg, while **xia mian** is made with the same noodles tossed in a spicy sauce and topped with cooked prawns. **Bak chor mee** is noodles doused with Chinese black vinegar and the hawker's special sauce, then topped with minced pork, fish balls, pickles, freshly chopped spring onions and toasted dried fish. **Wonton mee** or **cha siew mee** is a soup featuring delicate wontons filled with minced pork, Chinese mushrooms, and water chestnuts, thin slices of barbecued pork, egg noodles and chopped spring onions. Can't take the spice? Ask for no chilli, but try the ketchup sauce. You'll be surprised by how well the salty-sour flavour of ketchup works with most local noodle dishes.

Rice Cake & String Hopper Stands

These South Indian specialities can be eaten as snacks or for breakfast. **Idli** are steamed rice-flour and lentil cakes that look like little flying saucers (they are steamed in shallow moulds). They can be eaten with coconut chutney and **sambar** (spicy vegetable and lentil stew), with a mango or onion chutney, or even with just sweetened coconut milk. **Appam** or hoppers are fermented rice cakes. You'll spot a stall selling them by the tiny woks lined up in a row. Each pan is just big enough for one appam – it has a thin, delicate outer ring that's fairly crisp, and a thicker, moist centre. Eaten sprinkled with brown sugar, it makes a scrumptious breakfast or snack. **Idiappam**, otherwise known as string hoppers, look like steamed rice vermicelli. Served as a disc of fine netting, it is either eaten with brown sugar and grated coconut, or with a curry.

Bagging a meal of hoppers, Melaka

Roti (Bread) Stalls

The first thing you'll see in the morning at a **roti paratha** stall is the owner kneading his dough, slapping it onto the counter-top and pinching it into individual portions. Like a pizza chef, he flicks his ball of dough into the air, effortlessly stretching it into a thin disk which he then folds into itself. The resulting flaky flat bread is panfried on a griddle. Traditional versions include the **roti canai** (plain roti paratha) served with curry (or sprinkled with sugar), **roti telur** (with an egg cracked into the middle) and **roti bawang telur** (with egg and chopped onions). **Murtabak** is a heavier version with the roti paratha filled with spiced minced mutton or chicken, somewhat reminiscent of lasagne. Of course, modern variations have been created. These include **roti 'I love you'** (filled with cashew nuts, raisins, butter and milk), **roti pisang** (filled with banana) and **roti Planta** (filled with a layer of butter; Planta is a popular brand of tinned butter).

Murtabak

At the front of the roti stall you'll see a huge griddle. **Dosai** is a paper-thin rice-and-lentil crêpe that is made by ladling the batter onto a lightly greased dosai pan. Plain dosais are served with tomato and onion chutney, coconut chutney and yellow **daal** (cooked lentils). **Vengaya dosai** (onion dosai) has fried onions sprinkled over it. **Masala dosai** is filled with a dry, spicy potato filling, then folded into a triangular package.

Making roti in the morning at a roadside Indian coffeeshop, Kuala Lumpur

Muslim & Malay Stalls

In most parts of Malaysia, you'll find Muslim or Malay street stalls grouped together. Similarly, in hawker centres and food courts in Singapore, most Muslim stalls are situated along the same stretch. Apart from **nasi lemak** (coconut rice with fried fish) and nasi campur, they offer an extensive selection of halal dishes. These include **sop kambing** (mutton soup), **mee rebus** (thick egg noodles in a sweet and spicy sweet sauce served with hard-boiled eggs and freshly cut green chillies), **mee siam** (rice vermicelli in a spicy, tangy sauce), **mee soto** (thick egg noodles in broth with shredded chicken and bean sprouts), **tauhu goreng** (fried tofu topped with blanched bean sprouts, slivers of cucumber and a spicy-sweet peanut sauce) and halal chicken rice (the chicken is usually fried). You'll also find fried chicken wings coated in a deliciously spicy batter, **otak** (spicy fish paste wrapped in banana leaves), **epok epok** (pyramid-shaped pastries filled with spicy vegetable or meat curry), **sardine puffs** (tinned sardines in tomato sauce fried with shallots and chilli, then wrapped in pastry – an odd yet tasty combination) and Malay cakes and sweets (see Dessert Stalls; p 193). Other Muslim or Malay stalls sell only **bubur** (rice porridge served with side dishes).

Grilled Dishes Stalls

Barbecued chicken wings are extremely popular. You'll find stalls just selling chicken wings served with wedges of lime (especially kalamansi) and a dollop of chilli sauce. You will be able to identify these stalls by their rather unique barbecue and skewer contraptions specially designed by the hawkers themselves to be able to maximise the number of chicken wings that can go over the charcoal fire at any given time. Also very popular, is **ikan bakar** (grilled fish). Grilled **pari nyiru** (stingray) slathered in **sambal** (a chilli-based condiment) and served on a banana leaf is a definite must-try.

Other tantalising treats available at such stalls include otak (spicy fish paste wrapped in banana leaves) and satay. Satay can be eaten as a meal on its own. Diners have been known to eat from 50 to 100 sticks in one sitting! Pieces of chicken, beef and mutton are marinated, tenderised and threaded onto bamboo sticks before they are grilled over a charcoal fire. Other more exotic satay options include turkey, chicken feet, cow intestines and duck liver. Chinese also enjoy pork satay, which is easily identifiable by the layers of fat that is left in-between the pork flesh. Satay is sold by the stick (feel free to order any number you'd be comfortable eating) and served with a spicy peanut dip, **ketupat** (pressed rice cooked in a case made from strips of coconut fronds), sliced pineapple and chunks of onion. Once you've eaten the meat from your bamboo skewer, use the skewer to pick up cubes of rice, pineapple or onion.

Dessert Stalls

Malaysians and Singaporeans love desserts and sweet things, a fact proven by the endless varieties available at dessert stalls. Chinese sweets tend to be soupy: **tau suan** (yellow beans in a starchy, sweet soup), **cheng teng** (a sweet syrupy dessert filled with nuts and dried fruit), **ah bo ling** (glutinous rice-flour dumplings filled with black sesame paste, peanut paste, white sesame paste or red bean paste, served in a sweet peanut or ginger soup), **lek tau teng** (sweet green-bean soup), **ang tau teng** (sweet red-bean soup). Most of these desserts are served hot.

You're likely to lose yourself among the pretty and sweet **kueh-kueh** (little teacakes) displayed at Malay and Peranakan stalls. Choose from steamed **kueh lapis** (unlike the baked, Indonesian version, this cake is made of rice flour and consists of layers of different colours), **talam ubi** (double-layered cake with a coconut top layer and a lower, dark-brown tapioca layer), **putri salat** (glutinous rice topped with a green, pandanus leaf-infused custard), **bingke ubi** (brown-coloured baked tapioca slice) and **kueh bakar** (green, heart-shaped cake) among other lovely options. Indian sweets are truly only for the sweet-toothed. From sugary balls of **gulab jamun** (fried coconut-milk balls) and slices of **palgoa** (dessert made of cow's milk, ghee and sugar) to balls of **laddu** (dessert made of yellow lentils, cow's milk and sugar), these beautiful, intensely sugary sweets take a little getting used to.

Laddu

To beat the heat, **ais kacang** (mixture of shaved ice with syrup over red beans, jelly, sweet corn and evaporated milk) is a favourite. Another fast-melting dessert is the **ais ball**. Filled with a mixture of beans, the shaved ice is shaped by hand into a large ball and covered with rose syrup, condensed milk and palm sugar syrup. It's presented to you in a plastic sheet and the challenge is for you to eat it all before the heat reduces it into a mushy slush.

Making an ais ball dessert, Melaka

Ice cream in a sandwich, Singapore

Ice-cream trucks are little fridges on wheels, usually propelled by a bicycle attached to their frame. Listen out for the tinkle of a bell, indicating that the ice-cream truck is in the neighbourhood. Forget chocolate, vanilla and strawberry, the flavours to taste in Malaysia and Singapore are durian, coconut, sweet corn and sour plum. While ice-cream cones are common, the traditional way to eat ice cream is to wedge a slice between two rectangular sheets of wafer, or to tuck scoops of it into a slice of bread.

Enticing ais kacang, Penang

WHERE TO EAT & DRINK

Fruit Stalls

You can't miss them. They have wedges of ready-cut fruit in their display cases – anything from local guavas, jambus and rambutans to watermelons, apples and honeydew melons. Pick what you want, and the stallholder will place them all on a dish for you. Guava is often served with sweet-and-sour-plum powder, and jambu with dark soy sauce and chilli.

But the truly adventurous should look out for durian stalls that set up tables along the street. Choose your durian, have it opened for you, then just sit down and dig right in. It's just the thing for those of you who can't bring the fruit back to your hotel room (many hotels and some public transport have durian bans).

Snacks

Snack stalls are everywhere. You'll find a vast selection of sustenance including: roasted chestnuts, salted or sugared **kacang** (peanuts, peas, beans), **you char quay** (deep-fried dough sticks often served sliced in rojak or porridge and sometimes dipped into soybean milk), **keropok** (deep-fried crackers; street hawkers come around to your table laden with bags of them), **pisang goreng** (bananas deep-fried in a batter), fried tapioca pancakes, **vadai** (deep-fried fritters made of daal), **pong piah** (baked buns filled with yellow-bean paste, a Penang speciality), and even corn-on-the-cob slathered with margarine.

Above: A moveable feast, Penang
Left: You char quay, a crispy accompaniment, Penang

WHERE TO EAT & DRINK

DURIAN VIRGIN

The novelty of watching a foreigner eat out in Asia eventually wears off on locals. But line up to buy a durian, the 'king of fruit', and there will always be a crowd of onlookers. I remember my first time. Kuala Lumpur, height of the season, Little India. Even amidst the blare of Bollywood films and the sizzle-smack of **roti canai** (plain panfried rice dough, usually served with curry) sellers, my senses were engaged when a pick-up truck selling the fruit pulled up. Of course, at first I didn't have a clue. I simply watched the hooting crowd work into the type of excited frenzy that, in my experience, could either be orgiastic or murderous. My reaction was to sit and observe, in the safety of a teahouse, sipping **teh tarik** (local frothy tea). Prickly green pyramids rose from the flatbed of the truck. Men raised their arms with little hatchets. The crowd ebbed and flowed; some approached while others ran off to corners. The runners-off would then squat and soon emerge to reveal mini-stacks of leftover durian skins. And they'd always be smiling, wide and goofy.

Ten minutes later, I decided I wanted to try the curious fruit, and approached the pick-up, now ringed with a constant two-deep skirt of buyers. The big eyes of local Tamils, smiling Malays, baffled Chinese – they all looked at me with 'Are you sure?' gazes. I nodded and watched the ritual grabbing of the thin, snake-like stalk, the banging of the unopened fruit (a full-yet-hollow sound being ideal) and the sectioning, revealing rugby-ball shapes the colour of sunflowers. It was a life-changing moment when, trying to feign composure, I took a section with my right hand and tongue-fumbled my first piece. I tasted burnt caramel, almonds and wild honey. I licked my fingers and sucked the seeds, which are the kind of polished brown I'd want in my living room. This time, with audience eyes widening and fingers pointing, I held the fruit firmer and seized it for a second taste. Salted-sweetness and onion. Fibrous flesh and oozing pulp.

Everything they say about the fruit is true. It is not just prickly in looks, but also in character. Each bite reveals flavours with the capriciousness of a lover. My first durian was shorter and more uniformly round, whereas the second was oval and elegant. It had the kind of ephemeral balance that is hard to conjure in the best of cooking – onion and vanilla in alternating bites.

Feeling triumphant, I gave away the last half of my second durian and scurried off for another. And, as any virgin-turned-addict will tell you, the whole experience made me uncomfortably hot. I had yet to learn that every king, heaty and moody, is to be eaten with a queen, the cooling and calming purple-skinned manggis (mangosteen).

Rob McKeown

WHERE TO EAT & DRINK

Splitting a durian, Penang

Kedai Kopi & Kopi Tiam (Coffeeshops)

The neighbourhood kedai kopi or kopi tiam – both the Malay and Hokkien terms are commonly used, the latter more so in Singapore – serves as a meeting place where neighbours may stop for a **kopi** (coffee) or **teh** (tea), and a meal. They usually occupy the ground-level space of old shop-houses and have tables and chairs that spill out onto the pavement (to maximise their seating capacity). They are usually open throughout the day and much like the hawker centre, you order from individuals stalls that specialise in specific dishes. The variety is similar. You will find the char kway teow vendor, Indian mee goreng stall and nasi lemak counter. Each coffeeshop has its own unique mix of stalls. The best way for you to tell what kind of joint it is, is to take a walk around inside. You're not obliged to stay and have a meal simply because you've taken a look around. The only constant is the drinks stall, which is usually owned by the person who owns the property. At a good number of coffeeshops, you'll discover that the hawkers working in the morning may be serving quite different things to their counterparts at night. They may share the same counter space, but one hawker serves a speciality in the morning, while the other serves the same speciality at night (they split the rent, reducing their running costs). You could conceivably go to the same coffeeshop at different times of the day and have quite different meal choices presented to you.

Don't expect fancy table-side service or air-conditioning. Walk up to the stall you wish to patronise, place your order, indicate which table you're seated at, then return and wait. The stallholder will usually come up to your table to ask you for your drink request. Most brands of soft drinks will be available, in addition to local drinks such as soybean milk, **air cincau** (black-coloured drink filled with black strings of jelly), barley water or sweet chrysanthemum tea. But you won't find the drinks homemade in large vats the way you get them at hawker centres. Some places will also

Coffeeshop on Jalan Selamat, Penang

WHERE TO EAT & DRINK

serve local **bir** (beer) such as Tiger and Anchor. But what locals usually come for is the local thick coffee and tea, sweetened with condensed milk. Weight watchers can opt for kopi-c or teh-c, which contains evaporated milk and sugar (for tips on ordering and more information see p 213). Don't be surprised if some of the older chaps around you pour a portion of their coffee or tea into their saucers and sip out of them! This is a favoured method for quickly cooling down a piping-hot drink.

Apart from coffee and tea, another way for older folk to while away the hours is to sip on **bak kut teh** (pork bone tea; see the recipe). It really contains pork ribs and is a soup. Served at selected coffeeshops that are usually identified by the little charcoal stoves set up next to each table, with a large tea kettle filled with water bubbling away – the peppery pork soup filled with short lengths of pork rib, tender flesh just falling away from the bone, is served to you in bowls. And once you've downed all your soup (which is usually served with a bowl of plain white rice), you are welcome to ask for a top-up at no extra charge. But that's just for the soup, not the meat that comes in it. The pork flesh, while not the focus of the meal, tastes lovely when dipped in soy sauce that has been infused with the spiciness of chopped red chillies. The large kettles of boiling water are for making the Chinese tea that you usually have along with this dish. The teapot and cups are usually doused in hot water (to ensure that they are clean and warm) before the packet of tea leaves is emptied into the pot. Allow the tea to brew for a few minutes (your tea should look fairly weak) – before you pour it out into the Chinese teacups. You may find bak kut teh stalls at some hawker centres as well.

Bak kut teh (pork bone tea) served with meatballs and beancurd

Bak Kut Teh (Pork Bone Tea)

The literal translation of this recipe's name belies its restorative, mouth-watering tastiness. If you can get hold of the dried Chinese roots and barks specified (available at any Chinese herbalist), all the better – they infuse the resulting broth with an irresistible herbal quality. Bak kut teh is usually served with plain white rice and a little saucer of sliced red chillies in light soy sauce.

Ingredients

600g	meaty pork ribs, chopped into 4cm (1½ in) lengths
2	heads of garlic, separated into cloves, skins left intact
5 cups	water
2 tbs	light soy sauce
1 tbs	dark soy sauce
	salt, to taste

Optional herb mixture

5	slices dang gui (angelica root)
5	slices yok chok (Solomon's seal rhizome)
1 tbs	kei chee (boxthorn fruit/berries)

The other coffeeshop experience not to be missed is the classic breakfast that is served in Singapore coffeeshops. **Roti kaya**, bread grilled over a charcoal fire, then slathered with **kaya** (a coconut egg jam), topped with thick slices of ice-cold butter, then covered with yet another slice of toast is one option. Or try **kuay neng** (soft-boiled eggs) cracked into a saucer, top with dark soy sauce and pepper, then mixed by gently breaking up the yolk. You can either slurp this mixture down (it's quite acceptable to drink it from the lip of your saucer) or use it as a dip for your roti kaya. Bizarre indeed, but it's a tasty combination. Of course, you need to wash it all down with a good cup of coffee or tea.

Yet another fabulous gastronomic stop is the coffeeshop that just serves **dian xin** (dim sum). These are the beautiful, old-fashioned precursors to the dim sum restaurants we are now familiar with internationally. You sit at old, chipped marble-topped tables and some places still use the push cart steamers that are brought right to your table. Choose from **siu mai** (minced-pork dumplings); **har kow** (prawn dumplings); **fong zhao** (braised chicken feet), which the Cantonese prefer to call phoenix claws; **pai quat** (steamed pork ribs, usually with salted black beans); and a multitude of other steamed and fried delicacies. Don't expect to get as wide a selection of items as in dim sum restaurants you're accustomed to.

Muslin whole-spice pouch

1	muslin pouch
2	cinnamon sticks
6	cloves
1	star anise
1 tsp	black peppercorns
1 tsp	white peppercorns
1/2 tsp	coriander seeds
1/2 tsp	fennel seeds

Put the pork ribs and unpeeled garlic cloves into a deep saucepan. Insert the whole spices into the muslin pouch and seal. (You may have to make your own pouch from a square of muslin about the size of a napkin tied together with kitchen string.) Place the muslin pouch amid the meat. The optional herb mixture can be placed directly into the pot. Pour the water into the saucepan. Bring slowly to the boil, add the soy sauces and salt accordingly to taste. Reduce the heat to low and simmer until the pork ribs are very tender. Remove and discard the spice pouch. Ladle the liquid into generous soup bowls.

Serves 4

Remember that these are small establishments that often have tiny kitchens. They keep their menus pretty simple, offering just the classic crowd pleasers. Ordering is a simple matter of pointing at what you want. The meals are usually accompanied with cups of Chinese tea. Locals start streaming in for dim sum early in the morning – as early as 6am.

Taking tea and dim sum for breakfast, Melaka

WHERE TO EAT & DRINK

DANNY LEE – Faces of Gastronomy

It's 11pm on a Sunday in Geylang, Singapore's red-light district. The humidity hangs veil-like in the air. Danny Lee, chef and owner of Sin Huat Eating House, is talking about his uncle on Desker Rd who is famed for fish balls.

'You just don't see that anymore,' he says, commenting on the man's one-dish commitment. Danny, whose facial features usually dart about with athletic speed, thoughtfully contemplates his uncle's skills before launching into an explanation of noodle shortcomings.

Welcome to the realm of Singaporean cooking. It's a flavour-mad place where fish balls are talked of in lofty tones and where fluorescent strip-lit storefronts are presided over by cooks who make Michelin-starred superchefs seem lazy. Danny Lee is one example. He took over Sin Huat from his father and, in one decade, has turned the open-air location into a legendary destination. Customers include local families, Goldman Sachs board members, celebs and even government ministers.

Throughout the morning, Danny sells homemade **roti kaya** (flatbread spread with coconut egg jam) and coffee made with beans that have been roasted to specification. From 11am until dusk he rents out space in the shop to a pair of well-regarded vendors who specialise in turtle soup and sambal stewed duck.

Come nightfall, as the strip-lights buzz on, Danny can be found moving at pace in rubber boots, dark shorts, and a white T-shirt. On the menu? Seafood cooked with the kind of purposeful passion that borders on the fanatic. 'Why would anyone want to do anything else to seafood but steam it?' Danny questions. Steaming is the first pillar of his art. Freshness is the second. He goes to Marco Polo-like lengths to ensure this: king crabs are flown in daily by Singapore Airlines; grouper comes from Indonesia; stingrays arrive from reefs near Pulau Tioman. Ask and Danny will show you an old government-issue book on seafood that he first ploughed through years ago in search of the perfect steaming candidate.

The success of Sin Huat, like that of any long-lasting eatery, is in the details. While all seafood is steamed, each is given special treatment: crayfish are black-peppered; frog's legs are doused with chicken bouillon essence; whelks come with a salsa-thick chilli sauce and homemade soy sauce; and king crabs are mingled with rice vermicelli noodles until the whole is stained crab roe orange. Such minimalism allows for maximum expression of both the briny sea and the house ingredient of choice, garlic, whose flowery and bittersweet tones follow all guests home.

Sin Huat Eating House is at 659/661 Geylang Rd, Geylang, Singapore
Rob McKeown

Tze Char Stalls

The local English translation for this category of eatery is 'cooked food stall'. They serve Chinese food. What it really means is that you order your entire meal from a menu, or sometimes based on your knowledge of key dishes that such places serve, and the chef cooks the food for you on the spot. This is the closest you get to a restaurant experience in a hawker context (you order everything from the one place). You'll find tze char stalls in hawker centres and coffeeshops – sometimes occupying entire coffeeshops themselves. The best way to identify them is by the uncooked fish hanging in the prominent chiller display and possibly bunches of fresh vegetables laid out in front.

They serve anything from **yu pian tang** (fish-slice soup) and **chee cheong fun** (rice-flour rolls stuffed with shrimp or pork), to **kangkong sambal belacan** (water convolvulus fried with sambal belacan), **hor fun** (thick rice-based noodles cooked in a thick broth with seafood and pork) and **ou nee** (a yam-paste dessert). Some will even serve steamed, chilli or pepper crab. Chances are, the tze char stall will have a menu, but another strategy is to take a look at what other diners are eating and point out what looks enticing to the person taking your order.

Chee cheong fun served at a tze char stall, Penang

WHERE TO EAT & DRINK

Restoran (Restaurants)

The term restaurant is used to refer to a broad variety of eateries ranging from no-frills joints with no air-conditioning, surly service and decidedly local items on the menu, to swish fine-dining establishments with designer interiors, foreign chefs and sommeliers, and modern French cuisine. But generally, the more contemporary the style of the restaurant, the less likely it will append the term 'restoran' to its name (take note when you are planning a night out). At most, it will use the English equivalent, restaurant.

Kedai Makanan Laut (Seafood Restaurants)

This is a prime example of the casual, no-frills restaurant. Seafood restaurants are often on or near the beach, sometimes with tables in the open (the kitchen is usually a permanent structure, while the seating area might not be). Otherwise, they are housed in airy buildings cooled by huge electric fans. These restaurants are beloved by both locals and tourists for their affordable seafood cooked the local way.

Some restaurants also offer **ikan otak otak** (spiced rectangles of Spanish mackerel – wrapped in banana leaves and grilled over a charcoal fire), rojak and satay. On the menu, you will find the fresh catch of the day – steamed **kerapu** (red grouper), **kerang** (cockles) topped with chilli, deep-fried **ikan merah** (red snapper), **sambal kepah** (clams cooked in a chilli paste), **ketam batu** (mud crab) cooked in a variety of curries, the most popular being simply known as **chilli crab** (see the recipe). Other favourites include **ngoh hiang** (deep-fried liver or prawn rolls), **you char kway** (dough sticks) stuffed with seafood paste and deep-fried, **kangkong sambal belacan** (water convolvulus fried with sambal belacan) and **hor fun** (thick rice-based noodles

Beach Restaurant, Penang

cooked in a thick broth with seafood and pork). The meal is usually eaten communally and a series of dishes are eaten with plain rice. In addition, you may choose to order a noodle dish.

Old-Fashioned, Mid-Priced Restaurants

These feel like, and are likely to be, restaurants built or set up in the '60s and '70s. This is where you're mostly likely to find restaurants serving local cuisine – Peranakan, Malay, Chinese, sometimes Eurasian and Indian. The restaurants are low on ambience (the interior and piped-in music are likely to strike you as being kitschy), but serve good, local food at reasonable prices.

COLONIAL FAVOURITES

The Hainanese inhabit a unique corner of the gastronomic market since many of them once cooked for colonials, and mastered the techniques of western cuisine – meaning lots of English staples such as chicken à la king, oxtail soup and stew, shrimp cocktail and steak with pepper or mushroom sauce. Decades ago, many older Hainanese set up quaint, cosy restaurants, with interiors that resemble old English gentlemen's clubs. The really local kick comes from the somewhat surly service (they seem to be renowned for that) and wacky menu additions such as curry chicken and rice, grilled threadfin stuffed with sambal, and deep-fried chicken marinated in spices (this is often served with Worcestershire sauce as a dip).

To end your meal, treat yourself to glamorous desserts of yore, such as bombe Alaska, cherries jubilee and banana flambé!

Traditional Restaurants

Where do locals take out-of-town guests for a formal night out? In the larger cities, you'll find formal restaurants serving traditional cuisine, usually Chinese, Indian and Malay. These can be fancy joints with expensive menus and increasingly impressive wine lists.

The Chinese restaurants tend to be region-specific, choosing to serve either Cantonese (most common), Teochew or Hokkien specialities. But recently restaurants have also been choosing to specialise in Shanghainese and Hakka foods, among the cuisines of other minority dialect groups. There tend to be more North Indian restaurants than South Indian ones. But the foods of Kerala and Goa are slowly gaining popularity in the restaurant circuit as well. There are few formal Malay restaurants. It seems that Malays prefer home cooking for special or formal occasions. Many of the Malay restaurants that do exist cater, to some extent, to a tourist crowd, featuring cultural shows and other performances as part of the package. But the handful of truly formal Malay eateries are veritable homages to the intricacies of Malay cuisine and culture.

Upmarket Restaurants

Both Kuala Lumpur and Singapore have thriving restaurant scenes that plug into the dining trends that spread from New York and California to London, Paris and Sydney. Take your pick from Italian, French, Japanese, Vietnamese, Californian and Australian. Ingredients from Australia, the USA and Europe are flown in regularly. French restaurants stock truffles when they are in season, pastas are handmade and the concept of a menu degustation is so widely accepted that even forward-thinking Chinese chefs are offering similar menus at their restaurants.

Patrons and decorative screens at Equinox, a complex of five restaurants and bars, on the 70th floor of the Raffles City Complex, designed by IM Pei, Singapore

The two cities foster great creativity in the kitchen, and it is worth seeking out the most talented contemporary chef around. Whether it's modern Chinese cuisine or a subtle fusion of different cuisines (be it Japanese and French, Vietnamese and French or Hawaiian and Californian), the dining experiences open to you are unique, adventurous and of an impressively high quality.

WHERE TO EAT & DRINK

The Coliseum is one of the most famous Chinese western restaurants in Kuala Lumpur

Hotel Restaurants

The best five- or even six-star (as some hotels rate themselves) hotels provide some of the finest dining experiences available in the region. Formal Indian, Chinese or Malay restaurants recreate the pomp and extravagance of traditional food service. Many hotels have coffee-houses that offer a selection of authentic street food, served in impeccable surroundings. (Even locals sometimes choose to have their char kway teow at a hotel and will know which hotel coffeehouse serves the best.) You'll be surprised, too, by the number of distinctive European or western restaurants that thrive in hotels.

Traditional Chinese architecture, Penang

Where to Drink

Roving drink stalls are commonly found on most busy street corners in Malaysia. In Singapore, you'd have to search for them in hawker centres, food courts and shopping malls. But they are easily identified by the large colourful displays of the different kinds of drinks they have on offer for the day. Some stalls offer both homemade drinks and commercial soft drinks and fruit juices. If they do, you'll most likely see a sample of the products they carry lined up at the front of the stall. Other than sweet syrupy drinks, herbal teas (served chilled) and fruit juices are extremely popular. Coffeeshops are another great place to take a seat, get some respite from the heat and grab a drink. Some have liquor licences and serve beer. Locals (excluding Muslims) will sometimes indulge in a beer or two in the evening over a meal. It's particularly popular at seafood restaurants where Tiger Beer girls (the other brands have similar representatives too) assiduously try to convince diners to buy a jug or two of their brew.

A coffeeshop that specialises in desserts, Melaka

Many contemporary western-style restaurants will have a lounge area where you can indulge in an aperitif before you head in for dinner, as do most good hotels. Wine bars are also a growing business in both Kuala Lumpur and Singapore. Getting an alcoholic drink, be it a cocktail, wine or other liquor is not exceptionally difficult – even with your meal. Wine lists are common and they usually offer a selection of New and Old World wines.

A private courtyard garden in one of the city's top boutique hotels, Melaka

Velvet Underground, one of Singapore's stylish nightclubs

To live it up on the pub, lounge and nightlife strips is the preoccupation of a relatively younger set. Enclaves such as Bukit Bintang in Kuala Lumpur and Boat Quay in Singapore have become recognised as party strips, especially for tourists. Here, the regular spirits, mixed drinks and cocktails will be available in addition to beer and most likely wine. For a walk on the wild side, check out a karaoke bar, where patrons take turns to sing at the microphone. Most patrons at these places tend to be a little older and prefer to drink hard liquor or beer.

understanding
the menu

Deciphering menus in Malaysia and Singapore should be a cinch. Most locals speak a little English; at hawker stalls, some basic sign language and polite pointing generally gets your order across; and at restaurants, menus are usually self-explanatory. It's deciding what to order from the vast variety of culinary temptations on offer that's likely to cause you more trouble.

Laksa at a hawker centre, Penang

When attempting to dive headlong into the food culture of Malaysia and Singapore, don't be afraid to ask a fellow diner for his or her help and advice. Food-loving locals are bound to be only too happy to oblige. You'll invariably spot curious (and perhaps a tad greedy) diners indiscreetly peering at their neighbour's table as dish after scrumptious-looking dish is served. It's quite acceptable to peer, point and stare in most outdoor and casual eateries (at formal dining places, try to do it inconspicuously). Just remember to put on your friendliest smile. And if driven to desperation, you can quite easily order yourself a fabulous meal by asking for whatever looks good at the next table.

Restaurants

Most, if not all, restaurants have menus printed in English, which will be offered to you when you are seated. Wine lists are quite common too, especially if it's a contemporary restaurant. Most good Chinese restaurants will also have a selection of wine. If the menu contains names of local dishes in Malay or Chinese, an English description of the dish will usually follow, more often than not.

Menus are offered at most restaurants. In Chinese (and some Malay) restaurants, dishes are often categorised under food groups such as poultry, beef, seafood, vegetables, soups, noodles and rice. As Asian meals are traditionally communal, it would be best to order several dishes to sample and share. Most Chinese and Malay restaurants offer dishes in small, medium and large portions. Be sure to indicate your preference to the serving staff. If you are unsure, they should be able to make recommendations.

As a rough guide, single servings are sufficient as a one-dish meal for one person, when paired with a serving of rice. However, the general rule of thumb for couples is to order no more than three different dishes to share. A word of advice: it's always tempting to order lots when faced with a large menu (as Chinese and Malay menus tend to be – in the chicken section alone you'll find 10 different dishes), but bear in mind that you can always order more later.

A chef rests after a long day, Kuala Lumpur

Hawker Stalls

At hawker centres and food courts, menus are generally displayed on a signboard. These menus often state, quite simply, the names of the dishes, some in English, some not. If you are unsure, ask the vendor or one of the other hungry customers. Most locals speak some English, are proud of their local cuisine and will be happy to provide you with a lowdown on the various dishes. Some stalls also display photographs of their dishes to help you along. Otherwise, simply watch as the chef throws together another diner's order and decide whether you like the look of the dish.

When placing your order, though, be sure to jump right in there and catch the vendor's attention. Get in line if there is a queue. If not, be assertive and go up to the vendor and tell him or her exactly what you want. Feel free to ask for more or less chilli, or request that other elements of the dish to be adjusted to your liking. Some hawker tables are numbered. Remember your number before placing an order, so your food is sent to the right table. At places where tables aren't numbered, point at your table and rest assured the vendor will find you.

Don't feel obliged to order from just one stall. The point of hawker centres is that patrons get to order from many stalls and sample a variety of local fare. Also note there are some self-service stalls that require you to take your own dishes to the table (a sign stating this will be prominently displayed on such a stall). If there are no vacant tables, sharing a table with strangers is not a problem. In fact, it can be the perfect way to strike up a conversation about food. Simply ask, before you sit down, whether the seats are taken. A friendly smile goes a long way, of course.

Hawker-style dining in Penang

Bagging lunch at a mixed rice stall, Kuala Lumpur

Chap Chai Peng (Economy Rice) & Nasi Campur (Mixed Rice)

At some hawker centres, you will find stalls that sell an array of cooked dishes such as curries, fried vegetables, fried chicken wings and **sambals** (chilli-based condiments), all displayed on glass shelves. Chinese know this arrangement of dishes by its Hokkien name, **chap chai peng**, while Malays call their version **nasi campur**, Indonesians **nasi padang** and Indians **nasi kandar**. These stalls charge a standard amount for three dishes (two meats and one vegetable) on a plate of rice and then charge extra for any other dish you might choose to add. Generally, the vegetable dishes are the cheapest while the beef tend to be the most expensive. Feel free to ask about the price of each dish before ordering as these stalls don't usually have a written menu. Instead, simply point at the dishes you want and the vendor will pile your choices onto a plate of rice.

Prices

Prices at hawker stalls and restaurants are fixed and the menus should state the price of your dish. If they don't, then you're likely to be in a tourist trap. If you think you're getting ripped off, ask any of the local diners around you what you should be paying and they should be happy to tell you.

COFFEESHOP LINGO

You will not find caffé lattes (skinny or otherwise), decaf cappuccinos or camomile tea in Malaysia's and Singapore's local coffeeshops. But coffee and tea, served in the local style, are very much part of everyday culture. To get what you want, you must learn the colloquial codes.

Both beverages are most often referred to by their Malay names: **kopi** (coffee) and **teh** (tea).

If you want	Ask for
coffee with sweet condensed milk	**kopi**
tea with sweet condensed milk	**teh**
coffee with sugar but no milk	**kopi-o** or **kopi kosong**
tea with sugar but no milk	**teh-o** or **teh kosong**
coffee with sugar and evaporated milk	**kopi-c**
tea with sugar and evaporated milk	**teh-c**
iced coffee	**kopi peng** or **kopi ais**
iced tea	**teh peng** or **teh ais**

coffee to go	
in a recycled condensed milk tin	**kopi kong**
in a plastic bag or takeaway cup	**kopi bao**

a malaysian &
singaporean
banquet

When dining at a Malaysian or Singaporean home, expect to be fed to excess – no self-respecting host would allow you to leave until you're groaning from the evening's overindulgence. You're likely to have sampled a tasty cultural mix, with a Malay rendang sitting comfortably next to Chinese-style fried rice, Peranakan soup and Indian samosas.

No matter their diverse cultural background, Malaysians and Singaporeans find commonality in the rich language of their food. Together, these cultures have coalesced to create a distinct cuisine that is among the world's most complex, varied and delicious.

There is no mistaking the intent of holding a Malaysian/Singaporean banquet for your friends – to eat. It is an act of gusto, carried out without any pretence. With this basic tenet in mind, invite your guests over to come *makan* (eat). Feel free to be creative in setting the mood. This can be accomplished by well-thought-out table decorations. Tables can be laid with batik runners. For each place setting, you could use mats fashioned from bamboo slats or improvise with rectangles of banana leaf. Provide each guest with a fork and spoon; they then have the option of deciding whether or not they wish to use cutlery with each dish that comes along (it's totally acceptable to reuse the cutlery with each dish). A dramatic centerpiece can be easily created by filling a large punch bowl with water, and floating in it tea candles and fragrant sprigs of jasmine. Alternatively, fill a vase with orchids or lotus blossoms.

As with most Southeast Asian cuisines, everything is served at once at a home-cooked meal. However, don't let that stop you from designing a sumptuous multicourse repast for your friends. Another advantage of serving separate courses is that you allow your guests to fully acquaint themselves with and appreciate each unfamiliar yet wonderful creation, undistracted by other tempting sights and smells.

Many local dishes lend themselves well to being served as starters. **Satay** (spicy grilled meat skewers; see the recipe), **epok epok** (pyramid-shaped pastries filled with spicy vegetable or meat curry), and **ikan otak otak** (spiced fish rectangles wrapped in banana leaves and grilled over a charcoal fire), for instance, are self-contained morsels that do not necessarily have to be served piping hot, and as such are ideal as nibbles to go with aperitifs. A modest portion of a tasty local noodle soup, such as **laksa** (spicy, soupy noodle dish) or **hay mee** (Hokkien prawn noodle soup; see the recipe), is perfect as a first course.

Hands-on dining is traditional in both Malay and Indian cultures

BANQUET

BANQUET

Satay (Spicy Grilled Meat Skewers)

This legendary dish of skewered meat has Malay origins but has been so widely assimilated that you are equally likely to come across a Chinese hawker stall. The aromatic meat is served with a spicy peanut gravy. You'll need about fifty bamboo skewers for this dish.

Ingredients

500g	beef rump steak, cubed into 1½cm pieces

Marinade

1	stalk lemongrass (tender inner stem only), sliced
1 tbs	galangal, chopped
1 tbs	ginger, chopped
2	candlenuts (or substitute macadamia nuts)
5	shallots, peeled and chopped
2	garlic cloves, peeled and chopped
2 tsp	coriander, ground
1 tsp	cumin, ground
1 tsp	turmeric powder
¼ tsp	cinnamon, ground
1 tsp	salt
2 tbs	sugar
2 tbs	vegetable oil

Satay sauce

3 tbs	galangal, chopped
6	shallots, peeled and chopped
3	garlic cloves, peeled and chopped
10	dried red chillies, soaked and de-seeded
½ tbs	**belacan** (fermented shrimp paste)
6 tbs	vegetable oil
1	stalk lemongrass, bruised
2 tbs	tamarind, soaked in 150mL water (strain and reserve the liquid, discarding the tamarind)
2 tbs	sugar, or to taste
½ tbs	salt
300g	peanuts, roasted and coarsely ground
400mL	water

Garnish

1	cucumber, peeled and sliced
1	onion, peeled and cut into chunks

Place all the marinade ingredients in an electric blender and blend until smooth. Marinate the beef in this paste for at least an hour. Soak the bamboo skewers in water for 20 minutes (this prevents them from burning later), then thread the meat onto the skewers. Grill the skewers over a charcoal fire, or on a ridged grill pan. Brush occasionally with oil and cook until the meat is just done (6 to 8 minutes).

For the sauce, blend the galangal, shallots, garlic, chillies and belacan together in a food processor. In a saucepan, heat the vegetable oil and fry the blended paste and stalk of lemongrass until fragrant. Add the tamarind liquid, then bring the mix to the boil. Add the sugar, salt, ground peanuts and water. Lower the heat and simmer the sauce until it thickens. Discard the lemongrass.

Serve the skewers of meat with the cucumber slices, chunks of onion and satay sauce in separate bowls for people to help themselves. To eat, dip the skewers in the sauce.

Serves 8–10

BANQUET

Singapore Laksa (Noodles in Spicy Coconut Broth)

Travelling through Malaysia and Singapore you'll realize that the term **laksa** applies to a number of regional noodle soup dishes. In Singapore, laksa is creamy with coconut milk. There are endless debates as to *the* original version from Katong (a famous food precinct in Singapore that has come to be associated with a number of dishes, the most popular being laksa). In contrast, Penang-style laksa omits coconut milk and has a piquant flavour.

Ingredients

Spice paste

2	stalks lemongrass (tender inner stems only)
5 tbs	galangal, chopped
10	candlenuts (or substitute macadamia nuts)
10	dried red chillies, soaked, drained, de-seeded and chopped
5	garlic cloves, peeled and chopped
10	shallots, peeled and chopped
2 tbs	**belacan** (fermented shrimp paste)
2 tbs	dried prawns, washed and soaked for 15 minutes in warm water, then drained
1 tbs	turmeric powder
2 tbs	coriander, ground

Chilli oil

10	dried red chillies, pounded into fragments
1 cup	vegetable oil

Soup

500g	raw prawns, de-shelled and de-headed (reserve the shells and heads)
5 tbs	chilli oil (ingredients listed above – see below for method)
10 cups	water
2	deep-fried fishcakes, sliced (available ready-fried from any Asian grocer)
3 cups	coconut milk
1 tbs	sugar, or to taste
1 tbs	salt, or to taste

To serve

300g	bean sprouts, blanched and drained
500g	**laksa mee** (laksa rice noodles), parboiled then drained
100g	raw cockles, shelled (optional)
1	cucumber, peeled and shredded
1 handful	**daun kesum** (Vietnamese mint), destalked and finely shredded (or substitute kaffir lime leaf)

Blend all the ingredients for the spice paste together in a food processor, adding a little vegetable oil to facilitate the process.

Make the chilli oil by heating the vegetable oil in a frying pan. When hot, add the pounded chillies. Lower the heat and stirfry until fragrant (do not burn the chillies). Pour into a bowl and let the chilli flakes settle to the bottom. Spoon out 5 tablespoons of the oil (without the chilli flakes) and reserve this for frying the spice paste. Serve the rest in a small saucer at the table for those who want extra heat.

For the soup, heat 1 tablespoon of the reserved chilli oil. Add the prawn shells and heads and stirfry until they turn red. Add the water. Bring to the boil and simmer covered for 1 hour until reduced by a third. Strain the stock, and discard the shells and heads. Reheat the stock and boil the peeled raw prawns till cooked (this will take a couple of minutes. Remove and set aside. Blanch the slices of fishcake. Remove and set the fishcake stock aside. Heat the remaining 4 tablespoons of chilli oil in a deep saucepan, and stirfry the blended spice paste in the oil over a low heat until fragrant. Turn up the heat, pour in the coconut milk and reserved stock and bring to a boil. Add the sugar and salt to taste. Lower the heat and simmer for 15–20 minutes, stirring continuously.

To serve, put a handful of bean sprouts and laksa mee into each soup bowl. Top with the cockles, reserved prawns and fishcake slices. Ladle the boiling broth over the top. Garnish with the cucumber and daun kesum and serve immediately.

Serves 8–10

Chilli Crab

Chilli crab is a messy affair; you may as well embrace the messiness involved. Dispense with the utensils and attack the pieces with fingers just as any self-respecting local would. Designate a large dish on the table for discarded shells and debris, provide a few pairs of crackers to dislodge stubborn pieces of shell, and set out finger bowls filled with tea and lemon slices. Show your guests how to dig into the crevices where the tenderest morsels reside. It is perfectly acceptable to dip this meat into the sauce of the communal platter.

Ingredients

8 tbs	vegetable oil
4	fresh raw crabs, cleaned and quartered

Spice paste

1 tbs	ginger, chopped
2	garlic cloves, peeled and chopped
4	fresh red chillies

Sauce

2 tbs	sugar	2 tbs	ketchup
1 tbs	salt	2	eggs, beaten

Blend all the ingredients for the spice paste in a food processor, adding a little vegetable oil to facilitate the process. Mix together the sugar, salt and ketchup for the sauce. Heat a wok until smoking hot. Add the oil. Stirfry the pieces of crab until the shells change colour (about 2 minutes). Remove and set aside, turning the wok heat down to medium. Stirfry the blended spice paste for 2 minutes. Add the sauce mixture to the wok and stir well. Return the crab to the wok, and simmer for 3 minutes, adding a sprinkle of water now and then if the sauce reduces too much. Finally, stir in the eggs and cook until they set into soft strands dispersed throughout the gravy. Serve immediately.
    Serves 8

For mains, it is hard to beat a generous communal tureen of **babi pong teh** (stewed pork), **ayam masak merah** (chicken in thick red curry), **feng** (pork curry, best eaten a day old) or some other gravy-rich dish. Each of your guests can then ladle as much as they wish onto their plates, smothering their serve of rice with the wonderful gravies and sauces redolent with exotic spices and herbs. Steamed white rice is a great canvas against which to showcase Malaysia and Singapore's distinctive flavours. However, you may prefer the more jewelled appearance of a flavoured rice such as **nasi kuning** (yellow rice; see the recipe).

Chilli crab at Roland Seafood Restaurant, Singapore

Whether you decide upon **kari ayam** (curry chicken), **rendang** (beef in a thick coconut-milk curry sauce; see the recipe), **chilli crab** (spicy chilli and tomato-based stirfry dish; see the recipe) or any other gravy-laden local dish as your *pièce de résistance,* don't shy away from offering a basket of sliced white bread. As inauthentic as it may appear, this is a prevalent, bona fide local practice. A visit to any hawker centre will reveal locals tucking into a bowl of steaming curry accompanied by a plate of sliced French loaf (a localised and fluffier version of the baguette) to sop up the juices. In serving a dish as sensually messy as chilli crab, you are demonstrating your level of familiarity and comfort with your guests. Bonding over food couldn't get more hands-on than this. Chilli crab is so revered by Singaporeans that you can order extra portions of the gravy alone in seafood restaurants just so you have more in which to dunk your bread.

As Malaysian and Singaporean dishes tend to be spicy, iced water will be a welcome addition to the table (but plain rice is the best spice extinguisher). Other refreshing options include chilled soybean milk or lime juice. An icy cold lager (Tiger or Anchor) is also good for washing the meal down. Chinese tea is also good for cleansing the palate.

BANQUET

Mango Pudding

A dessert to be found on the menu of any dim sum restaurant, mango pudding is sweet without being cloying – the perfect end to an indulgent meal.

Ingredients

2	envelopes gelatine powder (14g)
200g	sugar
250mL	hot water
750mL	fresh mango purée
750mL	fresh pouring cream

To serve
Fresh mango slices
Fresh pouring cream

Dissolve the gelatine and sugar in the hot water. In a large mixing bowl, stir together the mango purée and cream. Pour in the gelatine mixture and stir. Pour the mixture into 8 individual dessert moulds. Chill until set. To serve, dip the mould briefly into hot water and invert the dessert out onto a plate. Serve with fresh mango slices and leave a jug of the fresh cream on the table for people to help themselves.

Serves 8

Mango pudding

To end, you may decide to skip making a dessert in favour of serving sliced fresh fruit. Tropical thirst-quenchers such as watermelon, star fruit, lychee, longan, rambutan and mango, prepared and attractively displayed on a large serving platter atop a bed of crushed ice, is a no-fuss but delicious alternative to making a sweet from scratch. But don't dismiss the region's many sweet dishes, including the delectable **mango pudding** or **sago gula Melaka** (sago pudding; see the recipes).

fit & healthy

The worst heath risk you could expose yourself to while eating and drinking in Malaysia or Singapore is to partake to excess. Otherwise, for the most part, the food and water are safe to consume. Read on for some tips that ensure you'll never have to call upon your travel insurer.

Hygiene

The level of hygiene at most Malaysian and Singaporean eateries is fairly good. In Singapore, all eateries are legally required to display their hygiene rating (issued by a governing body) in a prominent spot so that visitors can decide whether or not they want to dine there. An A denotes the highest grading, while C denotes the lowest. If an eatery is given a D rating it gets shut down. Most hawker centres and roadside stalls are safe too, but go with your gut feeling. If the food looks suspicious or the atmosphere feels a tad dubious, it's probably not worth the risk. One sure way to tell is by the number of local patrons dining there.

Water

Tap water in both Singapore and Malaysia is treated and safe to drink in major towns and cities, but be sure to have your water boiled if you're out in a *kampung* (village) or undeveloped area. If you're not convinced of the cleanliness of tap water in the city or you feel your body is unaccustomed to the local water, bottled mineral water is widely and cheaply available. As temperatures can soar during the day, you should carry a bottle of water with you, sipping often to keep yourself hydrated. If you have space in your daypack, carry a water bottle with you on your explorations as you're meant to drink a couple of litres of water a day. A 500mL bottle of water should cost you around RM1.50 or S$1, while a 1L bottle will set you back about RM3 or S$2.

Heat

For those unaccustomed to tropical weather, the daily heat and humidity can be overwhelming. To beat the temperatures, opt to dine in air-conditioned comfort during the day and save alfresco meals for the evenings. When traipsing around attractions during the day, remember to wear sunscreen and drink plenty of water.

If you are suffering from any of the following symptoms, it's possible you have a case of heat exhaustion: headache, dizziness, nausea, feeling weak and exhausted, muscle aches or cramps, and passing small quantities of dark urine. Resting in a cool environment and drinking lots of fluids, such as water, oral rehydration salts or diluted fruit juice, should help you cool down and retain fluids. If you don't treat these early symptoms, heat exhaustion can progress to heat stroke, which is characterised by the symptoms for heat exhaustion in addition to confusion, a lack of sweating and a flushed and red appearance. Heat stroke can be fatal, so you should use the above remedies for heat exhaustion, as well as seeking urgent medical help and trying to cool down further with the use of ice packs, or spraying with cold water.

Hanging out in Kuala Lumpur

BEATING THE HEAT THE CHINESE WAY

The Chinese believe in the concepts of 'heatiness' and 'coolness' as the body's primary forces. In line with the concepts of yin and yang, the idea is to maintain a balance between the two. When you hear someone saying that they are feeling heaty, chances are they're experiencing the onset of a dry sore throat and have been overindulging in heaty foods such as chilli, durian or fried fish. Cooling foods can include green tea, cucumber and barley water. The trick is to consume more cooling foods if you are feeling heaty, or conversely increase your consumption of heaty foods if your body is too cool.

Kicking back in Penang

You'll notice that herbal tea stalls are fairly common across the region, catering to people's health needs. Ask the stall-holder for advice. He or she should be able to recommend a tea to suit your needs. Otherwise drinks such as barley water, chrysanthemum tea, coconut water and **air cincau** (grass jelly drink) are considered cooling. Red date and longan teas are heaty. Beware of over-consumption, though. If your body is already cool, too much cooling tea in addition to cooling foods can give you the runs. Similarly, too much heaty food coupled with heaty teas can give you constipation.

Diarrhoea & Constipation

Simple things like a change of water, food or climate can all cause a mild bout of diarrhoea, but a few rushed toilet trips with no other symptoms is not indicative of a major problem. However, if diarrhoea is only one symptom and, for example, you're also suffering a high fever or passing blood, consult a doctor immediately.

Dehydration is the main danger with any diarrhoea. Under all circumstances fluid replacement (at least equal to the volume being lost) is the most important thing to remember. Check your urine to assess how much liquid replenishment you need: small amounts of dark urine means you should increase your intake by drinking small amounts regularly. Good sources of fluid are water and carbonated drinks left to go flat and mixed with an equal amount of clean water. If diarrhoea is hefty you may need extra help with replacing minerals and salts. There are a range of oral rehydration salts available. For DIY rehydration, take one litre of water and mix into it half a teaspoon of salt and six teaspoons of sugar.

> ### Food on the Runs
> You can ease diarrhoea symptoms by eating plain rice, bread, noodles, dry biscuits (salty or not too sweet) and bananas.
>
> Avoid eating fruit and vegetables (except bananas), spicy foods, greasy foods and dairy products (including yogurt).

For another remedy, head to any neighbourhood Chinese medicinal hall and ask for a bottle of Po Chai pills. This Chinese diarrhoea medication comes in the form of minuscule, rust-coloured pearls packaged in a plastic bottle. Having cured stomachs reeling from dodgy foods for centuries, Po Chai has been the medication of choice for generations of Chinese. According to the information on the side of its tiny, red, cardboard case, 'this medicine is good for fever, diarrhoea, vomiting, overeating, over-intoxicating and gastrointestinal disease'.

For loose bowels, the Portuguese-Eurasian community turns to strong, hot tea. These folks swear by the two-teabags-in-half-a-teacup-of-water remedy when having 'the runs' – which doesn't refer to a 100m dash (except, perhaps, to the toilet). If your problem is with flatulence, then get yourself a cup of **teh halia** (milky ginger tea) at an Indian drinks stall. It's bound to rid you of the problem.

Be aware that anti-diarrhoeal drugs don't actually cure the problem, they just slow the plumbing down so you don't have to visit the loo so often. These drugs can be helpful if you're ill and have to make a long journey, otherwise let things run their course.

On the flip side, if you find your belly hoarding your daily food intake, head to a fresh fruit stall and load up on papayas. The bright orange flesh of papaya contains papain enzyme, an agent that once made the fruit useful for tenderising meat. It also serves as a superb natural substitute for chemist-bought laxatives. Alternatively, a pack of prunes or a bottle of prune juice should help things along.

Allergies & Food Poisoning

You'll usually be able to see what goes into your food, but there are a few things to be aware of. Most dishes will contain a healthy dose of garlic and onions. Many local desserts contain red beans and soybeans, while some sauces like **satay sos** (satay sauce) and the dressing in **rojak** (salad with shrimp paste-based dressing) contain nuts.

Avoid uncooked fish, shellfish and meat. You may also want to avoid uncooked vegetables (especially salads), and pre-peeled fruit. In many instances, food poisoning occurs due to unsanitary food preparation, so avoid anything that is likely to have been exposed to flies – look out for proper food storage and display cases. Most cases of food poisoning result in diarrhoea. Be sure to rehydrate if you've been struck by the runs and avoid oily, greasy and spicy food. Steer clear of dairy products as well. Stick to rice, plain noodle soups and plain bread. If you start vomiting, it would be advisable for you to go see a medical practitioner.

Seafood

Seafood can bring out allergies in many people, but the range of seafood in Malaysia and Singapore may often be too tempting to pass up. If you are allergic to seafood, avoid it and watch out for cockles, which go in to some noodle dishes like **laksa** (spicy, soupy noodle dish) and **char kway teow** (broad, flat rice-flour noodles stirfried with Chinese sausage and egg in a sweet, dark soy sauce). Fish and shellfish are often very fresh, so as long as they're cooked properly, you shouldn't have problems. But avoid uncooked fish. When indulging in a steamboat meal, be sure to use one set of utensils to handle the raw food and another set to bring the food to your mouth.

Healthy Eating

It's terribly difficult to eat healthily when dining out in Malaysia and Singapore, as most foods are fried (some in pork lard). There are a lot of hidden sugars and fat in many dishes and coconut milk tends to feature strongly in many curries and desserts. If you are watching your diet, be sure to ask about eliminating salt, sugar or oil when placing your order. In some eateries like dim sum restaurants, food is prepared beforehand, so the cooks may not be able to alter dishes to suit your requirements. Try to choose vegetable options that are not curries (curries tend to contain coconut milk) at **nasi kandar**, **nasi campur** and **nasi lemak** stalls. Also ask for plain steamed rice instead of coconut rice. At economy rice stalls, there will probably be stirfried vegetable dishes available. These are relatively lower in fat. You are unlikely to find steamed vegetables (a more western convention than you imagine). But most hawker dishes do come with a small helping of vegetables. If you come across crunchy deep-fried bits that look

Serving up preserved fruit in Penang

like croutons (but taste a little oilier) in your Chinese noodle dishes, don't eat them. They're likely to be cubes of deep-fried pork lard thrown in for additional flavour. For dessert, have fruit or protein-rich **tauhuay** (sweet soybean). Bear in mind that many Asian eateries also use monosodium glutamate (MSG) in their food. You can request for your meals to come without MSG, but not all eateries will be able to meet that request, especially hawker stalls since parts of the dishes they serve are usually pre-prepared.

MSG RELIEF

Ten minutes after a scrummy meal, you suddenly suffer from an insatiable thirst, your lips feel like they're swollen and dry, your mouth tastes yucky and you're kind of sleepy. You may have the beginnings of a migraine. If this happens to you, you're probably having an adverse reaction to monosodium glutamate (MSG). How to get some quick, if only temporary, relief? Down an ice-cold sugary, carbonated drink like cola or lemonade, or try a good dose of freshly squeezed orange juice.

Diabetics

Malaysians and Singaporeans like their sweets. Whether it's brightly coloured **ais kacang** (Malaysian ice dessert) and Malay **kueh-kueh** (little teacakes), or Indian **kulfi** (ice cream made with reduced milk and flavoured with a variation of nuts, fruits and berries) and Peranakan **pulut hitam** (sweet, sticky black-rice pudding), there's always a dessert stall offering sugary local delights at any hawker centre. These desserts are practically impossible to resist, but do note (particularly if you're diabetic) that they have an immensely high sugar content and possibly a high fat content, as most desserts contain coconut milk.

FIT & HEALTHY

eat your words
language guide

Pronunciation Guide

Malay, an Austronesian language, is also known as Bahasa Melayu (language of the Malays) or Bahasa Malaysia. Other languages of the region include Chinese dialects like Cantonese, Hakka and Hokkien. The majority of the region's Indians speak Tamil, although there are also groups who speak Malayalam, Hindi or other Indian languages. Many different dialects are spoken by the Dayak peoples of Sabah and Sarawak in Malaysian Borneo.

One peculiarity of written Malay is its endlessly evolving spelling. On Peninsular Malaysia, for example, you will find the word for 'new' spelled at least three different ways: bharu (as in Kota Bharu), bahru (as in Johor Bahru) and baharu (as in Wakaf Baharu). For this reason, if you see a word spelled differently from the way it appears in this book, you can usually assume that it refers to the same thing.

The four official languages of Singapore are Mandarin, Malay, Tamil and English. Malay is the national language. It was adopted when Singapore was part of Malaysia, but its use is mostly restricted to the Malay community. Mandarin is becoming something of a lingua franca as it is now part of the national school curriculum. Other Chinese dialects are still spoken, especially among older Chinese. The most common dialects are Hokkien, Teochew, Cantonese, Hainanese and Hakka. Tamil is the main Indian language; others include Malayalam and Hindi. English is widely understood across Singapore, but less so in Malaysia.

Malaysian Pronunciation

Most letters are pronounced as in English, with the exception of the following

Consonants

b	at the end of a word, as the 'p' in 'up', elsewhere, as the 'b' in 'better'
k	at the end of a word, a glottal stop (the sound made between the syllables in 'uh-oh') elsewhere, as the 'k' in 'king'
g	as the 'g' in 'goat', never as the 'g' in 'gentle'
'	glottal stop; the sound made between the syllables in 'uh-oh'
h	stressed a little more strongly than in English, as if you were sighing – particularly when the 'h' appears between two identical vowels
c	as the 'ch' in 'chair', never as the 'c' in 'cable' or the 'c' in 'cedar'
j	as the 'j' in 'joke'
ng	as the 'ng' in 'sing' (but when followed by another 'g', as the 'ng' in 'anger')
ny	as the 'ny' in 'canyon'
r	always trilled clearly and distinctly
sy	as the sound 'sh'

Vowels

a	as the 'a' in *The Sound of Music's* 'do-re-me-*fa*' (the 'a' as in 'bat' is not found in Malay)
e	when stressed, as the 'e' in 'bet' when not stressed, as the 'a' in 'about'
i	as the 'i' in 'unique'
o	at the end of a syllable, as the 'o' in 'hot', elsewhere, as the the 'o' in 'for'
u	as the 'oo' in 'book'

Diphthongs
Malay has three vowel combinations:

ai	as the 'y' in 'fly', but longer
au	as the 'ow' in 'cow', but longer
ua	as the 'wa' in swan
oi	as the 'oy' in toy

Stress
Stress falls on the second-last syllable of a word. Therefore the first syllable is stressed in two-syllable words.

Enak!	*en-ahk!*	Delicious

Mandarin Pronunciation
In this guide we have used the Pinyin system for writing Mandarin. This system replaces Chinese characters with the Roman alphabet making it easier for non-Mandarin speaker to communicate at the local level. Most letters are pronounced as in English, with the exception of the following:

Consonants

c	as the 'ts' in 'bits'
ch	as in 'chop', but with the tongue curled back
h	as in 'hay', but articulated from farther back in the throat
q	as the 'ch' in 'cheese'
r	as the 's' in 'pleasure'
sh	as in 'ship', but with the tongue curled back
x	as in 'ship'
z	as the 'ds' in 'suds'
zh	as the 'j' in 'judge' but with the tongue curled back

The only consonants that occur at the end of a syllable are n, ng and r.

Vowels

a	as in 'father'
e	as the 'u' in 'fur'
i	as the 'ee' in 'meet' (or like the 'oo' in 'book' after c, ch, r, s, sh, z or zh)
u	as in 'flute'
o	as in 'or'

Diphthongs
Mandarin has nine vowel combinations:

ai	as the 'i' in 'high'
ao	as the 'ow' in 'cow'
ei	as the 'ei' in 'weigh'
ian	as in 'yen'
ie	as the English word 'yeah'
ou	as the 'oa' in 'boat'

ui	as in the word 'way'
uo	like a 'w' followed by 'o'
yu	as in the German 'ü' – pucker your lips and try saying 'ee'

Tones

Chinese is a language with a large number of words with the same pronunciation but a different meaning; what distinguishes these 'homophones' is their 'tonal' quality – the raising and lowering of pitch on certain syllables. Mandarin has four tones: high, rising, falling-rising and falling, plus a fifth 'neutral' tone which you can all but ignore. To illustrate, look at the word 'ma' which has four different meanings according to tone:

high	*mā*	mother
rising	*má*	hemp/numb
falling-rising	*mǎ*	horse
falling	*mà*	scold/swear

Mastering tones is tricky for newcomers to Mandarin, but with a little practice it can be done. The main thing is to have a go – any attempt to use the local language in Malaysia and Singapore will be well received.

Useful Phrases

	Malay	**Mandarin**
Do you speak English?	*Adakah anda berbahasa Inggeris?*	*Nǐ huì jiǎng yīng yǔ ma?*
Are you hungry?	*Anda lapar?*	*Nǐ è ma?*
I am hungry.	*Saya lapar.*	*Wǒ è le.*
Have you eaten yet?	*Sudah makan, belum?*	*Nǐ chī bǎo le ma?*
I've already eaten.	*Saya sudah makan.*	*Wǒ chī bǎo le.*

Eating Out

... restaurant	*restoran ...*	*... fàn guǎn*
Cantonese	*Cina*	*Guǎng dōng*
Malay	*Melayu*	*Mǎ lái*
Indian	*India*	*Yìn dù*
Peranakan	*Baba*	*Baba*
Japanese	*Jepun*	*Rì běn*
French	*Perancis*	*Fǎ guó*
Italian	*Itali*	*Yì dà lì*
Where's a ...?	*... di mana?*	*Nǎ li yǒu ...?*
cheap restaurant	*Kedai makan murah*	*pián yi de cān guǎn*
restaurant	*Kedai makan*	*cān guǎn*
hawker centre	*Pusat penjaja*	*xiǎo fàn zhōng xīn*
Table for ..., please.	*Ada meja untuk ..., orang.*	*... wèi, xiè xie.*
Please join me.	*Jemput makan.*	*Wǒ mén yì qǐ zuò.*
Do you accept credit cards?	*Sentuju dengan kad kredit?*	*Shōu xìn yòng kǎ ma?*

	Malay	Mandarin

Just Try It!

What's that/this?	*Apa itu/ini?*	*Zhè shì shén me?*
What's the speciality here?	*Apa keistimewaan di sini?*	*Zhè lǐ yǒu shén mé tè bié de cài?*
What do you recommend?	*Anda menyaran apa?*	*Zhè lǐ yǒu shén me hǎo jiè shào?*
What are they eating?	*Mereka makan apa?*	*Tā mén zài chī shén me?*

The Menu

Can I see the menu?	*Minta senarai makanan?*	*Qǐng gěi wǒ kàn kan cài dān?*
Do you have a menu in English?	*Ada senarai makanan dalam Inggris?*	*Nǐ mén yǒu yīng wén cài dān mā?*
What are today's specials?	*Apa istimewa hari ini?*	*Jīn tiān yǒu shén me tè bié de cài?*
I'd like ...	*Saya mau ...*	*Wǒ xiǎng yào ...*

Throughout the Meal

What's in this dish?	*Ini termasuk apa?*	*Zhè dào cài lǐ miàn yǒu shén me?*
Do you have sauce?	*Ada kecap?*	*Yǒu jiàng mā?*
Not too spicy, please.	*Kurang pedas.*	*Qǐng bù yào tài là.*
Is that dish spicy?	*Apakah makanan itu pedas?*	*Nà dào cài huì là mā?*
I like it hot and spicy!	*Saya suka pedas lagi!*	*Wǒ xǐ huān bǐ jiào là yī diǎn de!*
It's not hot. (temperature)	*Ini tak panas.*	*Zhè bù huì tàng.*
It's not hot. (spicy)	*Ini tak pedas.*	*Zhè bù huì là.*
I didn't order this.	*Saya tak persanan ini.*	*Wǒ méi yǒu diǎn zhè dào cài.*
I'd like something to drink.	*Saya mau minum.*	*Wǒ xiǎng lái bēi hē de.*
Can I have a (beer), please?	*Minta (bir), terimah kasih?*	*Qǐng gěi wǒ yī bēi pí jiǔ?*
It's taking a long time, please hurry up.	*Sudah lama, tolong lebih cepat.*	*Wǒ děng tài jiǔ le, qǐng kuài yī diǎn.*
The bill/check, please	*Minta bon.*	*Qǐng jié zhàng.*
This food is ...	*Makanan ini ...*	*Zhè dào cài ...*
cold	*sejuk*	*lěng le*
hot temperature/spicy	*panas/pedas*	*hěn tàng/là*
delicious	*sedap*	*hěn hǎo chī*
spoiled/stale	*basi*	*fā chòu le*
undercooked	*mentah*	*hái méi yǒu shú*
very oily	*berminyak*	*tài yóu le*

	Malay	**Mandarin**
Thank you, that was delicious.	*Sedap sekali, terima kasih.*	*Tài hǎo chī le, xìe xìe nǐ.*
Please bring me ...	*Minta ...*	*Qǐng ná ... gěi wǒ.*
an ashtray	*tempat abu rokok*	*yī gè yān huī gāng*
some/more bread	*roti lagi*	*yī diǎn miàn bāo*
a cup	*cawan*	*yī gè bēi zi*
a fork	*garpu*	*yī zhī chā*
a glass	*gelas*	*yī gè bō li bēi*
a knife	*pisau*	*yī bǎ dāo*
a napkin	*tisu*	*yī xiē zhǐ jīn*
a plate	*piring*	*yī gè dié zi*
a spoon	*camca*	*yī zhī tāng chí*
a toothpick	*pencungkil gigi*	*yá qiān*
rice	*nasi*	*yī wǎn fàn*
salt	*garam*	*yī diǎn yán*
pepper	*lada*	*yī diǎn hú jiāo*
soy sauce	*kecap*	*yī diǎn jiàng yóu*
water	*air minum*	*yī bēi shuǐ*

You May Hear

Anything else?	*Ada lagi?*	*Hái yǒu shén me?*
We have no ... today.	*Hari ini tak ada ...*	*Jīn tiān méi yǒu ...*
Enjoy your meal!	*Selamat makan!*	*Hǎo hǎo chī ba!*
What would you like to drink?	*Minum apa?*	*Nǐ yào hē xiē shěn me?*

Family Meals

Let me help you.	*Saya bisa menolong.*	*Ràng wǒ lái bāng nǐ.*
Can I watch you make this?	*Saya boleh pemerhatian anda membuat ini?*	*Wǒ kě yǐ kàn nǐ zěn me zuò mā?*
You're a great cook!	*Anda tukang masak yang baik!*	*Nǐ shì yī míng hǎo chú shī!*
This is brilliant!	*Sedap lagi!*	*Tài bàng le!*
Do you have the recipe for this?	*Anda ada resipi untuk makanan ini?*	*Nǐ yǒu zhè dào cài de shí pǔ mā?*
Is this a family recipe?	*Ini resipi makanan keluarga?*	*Zhè shì jiā chuán mì fāng mā?*
Are the ingredients local?	*Ini bahannya dari daerah ini?*	*Cái liào shì běn dì de mā?*
I've never had a meal like this before.	*Saya belum pernah makan makanan ini.*	*Wǒ cóng méi chī guò zhè yàng de cài.*
Is this a vegetable?	*Ini adakah sayur?*	*Zhè shì shū cài mā?*
Is this a fruit?	*Ini adakah buah?*	*Zhè shì shuǐ guǒ mā?*
Could you pass the (salt)?	*Minta (garam).*	*Qǐng bǎ (yán) chuán guò lái.*

English	Malay	Mandarin
If you ever come to (Australia) I'll cook you a local dish.	Kalau nada ke (Australia) saya masak makanan (Australia).	Nǐ lái (ào zhōu) wǒ huì zhǔ yī dào běn dì jiā yáo ràng nǐ cháng cháng.
One is enough, thank you.	Satu cukup, terima kasih.	Xiè xiè nǐ, yī gè jiù gòu le.
Do you use ... in this?	Ada ... dalam ini?	Nǐ yǒu yòng dào ... mā?
No thank you, I'm full.	Terima kasih, sudah kenyang.	Wǒ yǐ bǎo le, xiè xiè.
Thanks very much for the meal.	Terima kasih banyak atas makanan.	Xiè xiè nǐ zhè dùn fàn.
I really appreciate it.	Saya sangat menghargai.	Wǒ fēi cháng gǎn ji.

Vegetarian & Special Needs

English	Malay	Mandarin
I'm a vegetarian.	Saya hanya makan sayuran.	Wǒ shì chī sù de.
I'm a vegan; I don't eat meat or dairy products.	Saya tidak makan daging dan susu.	Wǒ bù chī ròu huò rǔ zhī pǐn.
Is it cooked with pork lard or chicken stock?	Ini ada masak babi atau ayam?	Zhè yǒu yòng zhū yóu huò shāng tāng mā?
I don't want any meat at all.	Saya tak mau daging.	Wǒ shěn me ròu dōu bù yào.
Don't add egg.	Jangan pakai telur.	Qǐng bù yào jiā dàn.
I don't eat ...	Saya tak makan ...	Wǒ bù chī ...
chicken/poultry	ayam	jī ròu
meat	daging	ròu
fish	ikan	yú
pork	daging babi	zhū ròu
seafood	makanan laut	hǎi xiān
eggs	telur	dàn
Do you have any vegetarian dishes?	Ada makanan nabati?	Nǐ yǒu sù shí mā?
Can you recommend a vegetarian dish?	Dapatkan anda mengusulkan suatu makanan nabati apa?	Nǐ yǒu shěn me sù shí jiè shào mā?
Does this dish have meat?	Makanan ini ada dagingnya?	Zhè dào cài yǒu ròu mā?
Can I get this without the meat?	Boleh tak masak tanpa daging?	Kě yǐ bù jiā ròu mā?
Is the sauce meat-based?	Adakah kecap ini dari daging?	Zhè shì ròu jiàng mā?
Does it contain eggs/ dairy products?	Makanan ini ada telur/ susu tak?	Zhè lǐ yǒu dàn/rǔ zhī pǐn mā?
I'm allergic to ...	Saya tak boleh tahan makan ...	Wǒ duì ... mǐn/gǎn.

	Malay	**Mandarin**

Children

Are children allowed?	*Anak-anak boleh masuk?*	*Xiăo hái néng jìn mā?*
Is there a children's menu?	*Ada senarai untuk bayi?*	*Zhè lĭ yŏu ér tóng cài dān mā?*
Do you have a highchair for the baby?	*Ada kerusi untuk bayi?*	*Yŏu yīng ér yĭ mā?*

At the Market/Self-Catering

Where's the nearest (market)?	*Di mana (pasar) terdekat?*	*Zuì kào jìn de (shì chăng) zài nă lĭ?*
Where can I find (sugar)?	*(Gula) di mana?*	*(Táng) fàng zài nă li?*
Can I have a ...	*Minta ...*	*Qĭng gĕi wŏ ...*
bottle	*botol*	*píng zĭ*
box	*kotak*	*xiāng zĭ*
can/tin	*tin*	*guàn zĭ*
packet/sachet	*paket*	*yī bāo*
How much (cost)?	*Berapa harga?*	*Duō shăo qián?*
How much is (a kilo of cheese)?	*Berapa harga (satu kilo kaju)?*	*(Yī gōng jìn de rŭ lào) duō shăo qián?*
How much (for) ...?	*Berapa harga (untuk) ...?*	*... duō shăo qián?*
both	*keduanya*	*liăng gè*
per fruit	*satu buah*	*yī lì*
per piece	*satu bahagian*	*yī kuài*
this	*ini*	*zhè gè*
Do you have anything cheaper?	*Adalah yang lebih murah?*	*Yŏu méi yŏu gèng pián yi de?*
Give me (half) a kilo, please.	*Minta (setengah) kilo.*	*Qĭng gĕi wŏ (bàn) gōng jīn.*
I'd like (six) ...	*Saya mau (enam) ...*	*Wŏ xiăng yào (liù gè).*
I'm just looking.	*Saya lihat lihat saja.*	*Wŏ kàn kan bà le.*
No!	*Tidak!*	*Bù!*
Where can I buy ...?	*Saya bisa membeli ... di mana?*	*Nă li kĕ yĭ măi dào ...?*
Can I taste it?	*Boleh cicip?*	*Wŏ kĕ yĭ cháng cháng kàn mā?*
Best before ...	*Makan sebelum ...*	*Zài ... zhī qián shĭ yòng.*
Is this the best you have?	*Apakah ini yang terbaik?*	*Zhè shì zuì hăo de mā?*
Do you have anything better?	*Adalah yang lebih baik?*	*Yŏu méi yŏu gèng hăo de?*
What's the local speciality?	*Makanan khas daerah ini apa?*	*Bĕn dì de tè chăn shì shén me?*
Can you give me a discount?	*Boleh potongan harga?*	*Kĕ yĭ dă gè zhé kòu mā?*

	Malay	**Mandarin**
I'd like to buy ...	*Saya mau membeli ...*	*Wǒ xiǎng mǎi ...*
bread	*roti*	*miàn bāo*
butter	*mentega*	*níu yóu*
cheese	*keju*	*rǔ lào*
eggs	*telur*	*jī dàn*
flour	*tepung*	*miàn fěn*
fruit and vegetables	*buah dan sayur*	*shuǐ guǒ hé shū cài*
honey	*manisan*	*mì táng*
margarine	*mentega*	*cài yóu*
milk	*susu*	*níu nǎi*
oil	*minyak*	*yóu*
pepper	*lada*	*hú jiāo*
rice (uncooked)	*beras*	*mǐ*
salt	*garam*	*yán*
sugar	*gula*	*táng*
I am looking for ...	*Saya mencari ...*	*Wǒ zài zhǎo ...*

At the Bar

Shall we go for a drink?	*Mau pergi minum?*	*Wǒ mén qù hē diàn dōng xi hǎo mā?*
I'll buy you a drink.	*Saya membelikan anda minuman.*	*Ràng wǒ qǐng nǐ hē yī bēi.*
Thanks, but I don't feel like it.	*Terima kasih, tidak.*	*Xiè xiè, wǒ bù xiǎng hē.*
I don't drink (alcohol).	*Saya tidak minum (minuman keras).*	*Wǒ bù hē (jiǔ) de.*
What would you like?	*Anda mau minum apa?*	*Nǐ xiǎng hē shén me?*
You can get the next one.	*Anda boleh bayar yang berikut.*	*Xià yī bēi nǐ qǐng ba.*
It's on me.	*Saya bayar.*	*Wǒ qǐng kè.*
It's my round.	*Saya bayar kali ini.*	*Dào wǒ qǐng le.*
OK.	*Baik.*	*Hǎo.*
Can I buy you a coffee?	*Saya membeli kopi untuk anda ya?*	*Wǒ qǐng nǐ hē bēi kā fēi hǎo mā?*
I'm next.	*Saya yang berikut.*	*Xià yī gè dào wǒ le.*
Excuse me.	*Permisi.*	*Duì bu qǐ.*
I was here before this person.	*Saya menunggu lebih dulu daripada dia.*	*Wǒ xiān lái de.*
I'll have (a) ...	*Saya mau minum ...*	*Wǒ xiǎng hē yī bēi ...*
beer	*bir*	*pí jiǔ*
wine	*wain*	*pú tao jiǔ*
Cheers!	*Selamat!*	*Gān bēi!*
No ice.	*Tidak air batu.*	*Wǒ bù yào bīng.*

English	**Malay**	**Mandarin**
Can I have ice, please?	*Minta air batu.*	*Gěi wǒ yī diàn bīng, xiè xiè.*
Same again, please.	*Yang sama, terima kasih.*	*Zài lái yī yàng de.*
Is food available here?	*Adalah makanan di sini?*	*Zhè lǐ yǒu chī de mā?*
I'm a bit tired. I'd better get home.	*Saya penat. Pergi rumah dulu.*	*Wǒ lèi le. Xiǎng huí jiā.*
I've drunk too much.	*Saya minum terlalu banyak.*	*Wǒ hē tài duō le.*
I'm drunk.	*Saya mabuk.*	*Wǒ hē zuì le.*
I feel ill.	*Saya mual.*	*Wǒ bù shū fu.*
I want to throw up.	*Saya mau muntah.*	*Wǒ xiǎng tù.*
She/he's passed out.	*Dia pingsan.*	*Tā yūn le.*
I'm hung over.	*Saya kepala sakit.*	*Wǒ de tóu hěn tòng.*
So, do you come here often?	*Anda sering ke sini?*	*Nǐ cháng lái mā?*
I really, really love you.	*Saya benar-benar cinta kamu.*	*Wǒ hěn ài nǐ.*
What did I do last night?	*Saya buat apa tadi malam?*	*Wǒ zuó wǎn zuò le shén me?*

Wine

English	**Malay**	**Mandarin**
May I see the wine list, please?	*Minta senarai wain?*	*Qǐng ná jiǔ dān gěi wǒ.*
What is a good year?	*Apalah tahun baik?*	*Nǎ yī nián hǎo?*
Can you recommend a good wine?	*Andalah boleh menyaran wain yang baik?*	*Nǐ néng jiè shào yī xià mā?*
May I taste it?	*Say boleh rasa ini?*	*Wǒ néng cháng yī cháng mā?*
Please bring me another bottle.	*Satu botol lagi, terima kasih.*	*Zài lái yī píng, xiè xiè.*
I'd like a glass/bottle of ... wine	*Saya mau satu glas/botol ... wain.*	*Wǒ yào yī bēi/píng ... pú tao jiǔ.*

English–Malay–Mandarin Glossary

The following notation is used throughout the Eat Your Words section:

/ forward slash indicates when single words on either side of the slash are interchangeable. It also separates two (or more) alternatives where they consist of *one* word only. These could be synonyms or different forms of the same word.

A	Malay	Mandarin
abalone	kerang laut	bào yú
allergic	alergik	mǐn gǎn
almond	buah badam	xìng rén
anchovy	ikan bilis	jiang yú zǎi
aperitif	minuman alkohol	kāi wèi jiǔ
appetiser	pembuka selera	kāi wèi cài
apple	buah epal	píng guǒ
apricot	buah aprikot	xìng
asparagus	asparagus	lú sǔn
aubergine (eggplant)	terung	qié zi
avocado	apokat	è lí

B		
bacon	babi panggang	yān ròu
to bake	membakar	hōng
bakery	kedai roti	miàn bāo diàn
baking soda	soda penaik	sū dá fěn
bamboo	bambu	zhù
–shoot	bambu redang	zhù sǔn
banana	pisang	xiāng jiāo
–leaf	daun pisang	xiāng jiāo yè
to barbecue	daging panggang	shāo kǎo
barley	barli	yì mǐ
batter	adunan telur	miàn hú
bean	kacang	dòu
black	kacang hitam	hēi dòu
broad	kacang lepar	cán dòu
green	kacang hijau	lù dòu
long	kacang panjang	cháng dòu
red	kacang merah	hóng dòu
–sprout	taugeh	dòu yá
beancurd (*see* tofu)	tauhu	dòu fu
beef	daging lembu	niú ròu
beer	bir	pí jiǔ
stout	stout	hēi pí jiǔ
berry	beri	jiāng guǒ
beverage	minuman	yǐn liào

	Malay	**Mandarin**
bill	bon	zhàng dān
bird	burung	niǎo
bird's nest	sarang burung	yàn wō
biscuit	biskut	bǐng gān
bitter	pahit	kǔ
bitter gourd	perai	kǔ guā
blackberry	beri hitam	hēi méi
blender	alat pengisar	jiǎo bàn ji
to boil	rebus	zhǔ fèi
bok choy	sayur putih	bái cài
bottle	botol	píng
−opener	pembuka botol	kāi píng qì
bowl	mangkuk	wǎn
bran	sekam	kāng
bread	roti	miàn bāo
breakfast	sarapan pagi	zǎo cān
breast	dada	xiōng
broccoli	bunga kubis	xi jiè lān huā
broth	bubur	shàng tāng
Brussels sprouts	kol mini	qíu yá gān lán
buffet	pukulan	zì zhù cān
burnt	bakar	shāo jiāo
butter	mentega	niù yóu

C

cabbage	sayur kubis	bāo cài
café	restoran	kā fēi guǎn
cake	kuah	dàn gāo
can (tin)	tin	guàn tóu
−opener	pembuka tin	kāi guàn qì
cantaloupe	rockmelon	mì guā
caramel	gula hangus	jiāo táng
capsicum (pepper)	lada	dēng lóng jiāo
green	lada hijau	qīng lóng jiāo
red	lada merah	dēng lóng jiāo
carrot	lobak merah	hóng luó bo
cashew	biji gajus	yāo dòu
cauliflower	bunga kubis	huā yē cài
caviar	telur ikan	yú zǐ jiàng
cayenne	ladar emas	hú jiāo fěn
celery	sayur saderi	qín cài
champagne	air anggur	xiāng bīn
cheap	murah	pián yi
cheese	keju	rǔ láo
chef	juru masak	chú shi
cherry	buah ceri	yīng táo
chestnut	buah berangan	mǎ tí

English	Malay	Mandarin
chicken	ayam	jī
–feet	lihat ayam	jī jiǎo
–liver	hati ayam	jī gān
spring	anak ayam	tóng zǐ jī
–wing	kepak ayam	jī chì pǎng
chilli	cili	là jiāo
–sauce	sos cili	là jiāo jiàng
chives	kucai	jiǔ huáng cài
chocolate	coklat	qiǎo kè lì
chopsticks	sepit	kuài zi
cider (apple)	air epal	píng guǒ zhī
cilantro	ketumbur	xiāng cài
cinnamon	kulit kayu manis	guì pí
citrus	jenis limau	gān jí
clam	kepah	gé
to clean	membersihkan	qīng lǐ
closed	tutup	guān le
clove	bunga cengkih	dīng xiāng
cockle	kerang	niǎo gě
cocoa	buah koko	kě kě
coconut	kelapa	yē zi
–flesh	isi kelapa	yē ròu
–milk	santan	yē jiāng
–water	air kelapa	yē zi shuǐ
cod	ikan kod	xuě yú
coffee (see p 218)	kopi	kā fēi
–black	kopi kosong	kā fēi wū
–grinder	alat pengisar	jiáo bǎn qì
–with milk	kopi susu	kā fēi
–without sugar	kopi tanpa gula	kā fēi wū
cold	sejuk	lěng
condiments	rempah	tiáo wèi pǐn
confectionery	kilang roti	táng guǒ
congee (rice porridge)	bubur	zhōu
consomme	kaldu	qīng dùn tāng
cookbook	masak buku	shí pǔ
coriander	ketumbur	xiāng cài
corn	jagung	yū mǐ
cornflakes	emping jagung	yū mǐ piàn
courgette (zucchini)	hijau terung	yì dà lì qīng guā
crab	ketam	páng xiè
crackers, prawn	keropok udang	xiā bǐng
crayfish	udang kerang	xiā pó
cress	selada	shuǐ qín
cucumber	timun	huáng guā
cup	cawan	bēi zi
curd	dadih	níng rǔ

GLOSSARY

	Malay	**Mandarin**
currant	buah kimis	jiā lùn zi
curry	kari	gā lí
–paste	perekat kari	gā lí jiāng
–powder	serbuk kari	gā lí fěn
to cut	potong	qiē
cutlery	alat pemotong	cān jù
cutlet	sayaran	ròu piàn

D

dates, red	kurma	hōng zǎo
to deep fry	goreng	yóu zhá
dessert	pencuci mulut	tián pǐn
to dice	memotong	qiē chéng xiǎo kuài
dinner	makan malam	wǎn fàn
dirty	kotor	zāng
dried	kering	gān
to drink, drink	minum, minuman	hē, yǐn liào
duck	itek	yā
dumpling	bakso	shuǐ jiǎo

E

eel	belut	màn yú
egg	telur	dàn
chicken	telur ayam	jī dàn
century	telur abad	pí dàn
duck	telur itek	yā dàn
fried	telur goreng	jian dàn
quail	telur puyuh	ān chún dàn
eggplant (aubergine)	terung	qié zi
entrée	berhak masak	qián cài

F

fig	buah ara	wú huā guǒ
fillet	pengikat rambut	liǔ ròu
fish	ikan	yú
anchovy	ikan bilis	jiang yú zǎi
–cake	kueh ikan	yú bǐng
halibut	halibut	bǐ mù yú
–maw	perut binatang	yú biào
roe	telur ikan	yú luǎn
salmon	ikan salmon	sān wén yú
sardine	sardin	shā dīng yú
–sauce	sos ikan	yú lù
flavour	perasa	wèi
flour	tepung	miàn fěn
corn	tepung jagung	shú fěn

English	Malay	Mandarin
food	makanan	shí wù
food processor	pemprosesan makanan	jiǎo bàn jī
food stall	gerai/warung	shú shí tān
fork	garpu	chā zi
free (of cost)	membeku	miǎn fèi
french fries	keropok	suì piàn
fresh	baharu	xīn xiān
frog	kodok	qīng wā
–legs	kaki kodok	qīng wā jiǎo
fruit	buah-buahan	shǔi guǒ
–juice	jus buah-buahan	gǔo zhī
dried	buah-buahan kering	shǔi gǔo gān
to fry	menggoreng	jiān
full (content)	kenyang	mǎn

G

garlic	bawang putih	suàn tóu
gelatin	agar agar	dòng wù jiāo
ghee	minyak sapi	cài yóu
gherkin	timun kecil	xiǎo huáng guā
giblets	jeroan	nèi zàng
ginger	semangat	jiāng
pickled	acar halia	suān jiāng
ginseng	ginseng	rén shēng
glutinous rice	nasi lekit lekit	nuò mǐ fàn
goat	kambing	shān yáng
goose	angsa	ē
grapefruit	limau bali	pú táo yòu
grapes	buah anggur	pú táo
to grate	memarut	mó suì
gravy	kuah	ròu zhī
grease	gris	yóu zhì
greens	sayur	lú yè shū cài
to grill	tempat salai	kǎo
guava	jambu batu	fān shí líu

H

halibut	halibut	bǐ mù yú
ham	daging babi	huǒ tuǐ
hamburger	hamburger	hàn bǎo bāo
hare	terwelu	yě tù
heart	jantung	xīn zàng
honey	madu	fēng mì
horseradish	lobak	là gēn
hot (spicy)	pedas	là
hot (temperature)	panas	rè
hungry	lapar	è

	Malay	Mandarin
I		
ice	ais	bīng
−cream	ais krim	bīng qí lín
icing	aising	táng shuāng
ingredient	bahan	cái liào
J		
jam	jem	guǒ jiàng
jelly	agar agar	guǒ dòng
juice	joos	zhī
K		
kebab	kebab	kǎo roù chuàn
kettle	cerek	shǔi hú
kidney	buah pinggang	yāo
kitchen	dapur	chú fáng
kiwi fruit	kiwi	qí yǐ guǒ
knife	pisau	dāo
L		
ladle	senduk	tāng sháo
lamb	anak kambing	yáng ròu
lard	lemak babi	zhū yóu
leek	bawang perai	suàn
leg	kaki	jiǎo
legume	kacang	dòu lèi shū cài
lemon	limau	níng méng
lemonade	air limau	níng méng zhī
lentil	pokok kacang	xiǎo biǎn dòu
lime	asam	suān gān
liqueur	likur	tián liè jǐu
liquorice	likurois	gān cǎo
liver	hati	gān
lobster	udang galah	lóng xiā
loin	pinggang	tuǐ ròu
longan	lengkeng	lóng yǎn
lotus	teratai	lián
−leaf	bunga teratai	lián yè
−nuts	kacang teratai	lián zǐ
lunch	makan tengahari	wǔ cān
lychees	laici	lì zhī
M		
main course	masakan terutama	zǔ cài
mandarin	sejenis limau	gān
mangetout pea	kacang kampri	nén wān dòu
mango	mangga	máng guǒ
margarine	mentega	cài yóu

English	Malay	Mandarin
to marinate	memerapkan	yān zhì
market	pasar	shì chǎng
night	pasar malam	yè shì chǎng
marmalade	jem limau	jú zi jiàng
mayonnaise	krim minyak	dàn huáng jiàng
meat	daging	ròu
–ball	daging bola	ròu wán
melon	buah tembikai	guā
–seeds	benih tembikai	guā zǐ
menu	senari makanan	cài dān
milk	susu	niú nǎi
condensed	susu kental	liàn nǎi
powdered	tepung susu	níu nǎi fěn
soy	air soya	dòu jiāng
millet	sekoi	xiǎo mǐ
to mince	kisar	qiē suì
mineral water	air mineral	kuàng quán shuǐ
mint	mint	bò he
to mix	mencampurkan	jiǎo bàn
money	duit/wang	qián
MSG	MSG	wèi jīng
mushroom	cendawan	gū lèi
abalone		bāo yú gū
black		dōng gū
button		mó gū
straw		cǎo gū
oyster		háo gū
shiitake		rì běn xiāng gū
mussels	kupang	dàn cài
mustard	sawi	jiè mò
mutton	daging kambing	yáng ròu

N

English	Malay	Mandarin
napkin	lampin	cān jīn
neck	tengkuk	bó zi
noodles	mee	miàn
egg	mee telur	jī dàn miàn
rice	mee	hé fěn
udon	udon	wū dōng miàn
wonton	wan tan mi	yún tūn miàn
nut	kekeras	dòu
nutmeg	buah pala	dòu kòu

O

English	Malay	Mandarin
octopus	sotong kurita	zhāng yú
oil	minyak	yóu
olive	minyak zaitun	gǎn lǎn yóu
peanut	minyak kacang	huā shēng yóu
sesame	minyak bijan	má yóu
vegetable	minyak sayur	cài yóu

English	Malay	Mandarin
olive	buah zaitun	gǎn lǎn
black	buah zaitun hitam	hēi gǎn lǎn
omelette	telur dadar	jiān dàn bǐng
onion	bawang	yáng cōng
open	buka	kāi
organic	organic	yǒu jī
oven	ketunar	kǎo lú
oxtail	ekor lembu	niú wěi
oyster	tiram	háo
–sauce	sos tiram	háo yóu

P

English	Malay	Mandarin
papaya	betik	mù guā
paprika	paparika	hóng là jiāo
parsley	pasli	yán suī
parsnip	parsnip	ōu zhōu fáng fēng
pasta	pasta	miàn shí
paste	kuah	jiàng
pastry	campuran tepung	gāo diǎn
peach	persik	táo zi
peanut	kacang tanah	huā shēng
–sauce	kuah kacang	shā diē jiàng
pear	buah pear	lí
to peel	kulit	xiāo
pepper	lada	hú jiāo
green	lada hijau	qīng lóng jīao
red	lada merah	dēng lóng jiāo
peppermint	peppermin	bò he táng
persimmon	buah kesemak	shì zi
pheasant	burung kuang	yě jī
pickle	acar	pào cài
pickled	menjeruk	yān pào
picnic	perkelahan	yě cān
pie	pai	xiàn bǐng
pig	babi	zhū
pigeon	burung merpati	gē zi
pine nut	pokok pain	sōng zi
pineapple	nanas	fèng lí
pistachio	buah kekeras	kāi xīn guà
plate	piring	pán
plum	plum	méi
–sauce	sos plum	méi jiàng
to poach	merebus	shuǐ zhǔ
pomegranate	buah delima	shí liu shù
pomelo	limau bali	yòu zi
popcorn	bertih jagung	bào mǐ huā
pork	daging babi	zhū ròu
–chop	chop babi	zhū pá

English	**Malay**	**Mandarin**
–belly	perut babi	zhū nán ròu
–roast	babi panggang	shāo zhū
porridge, rice	bubur	zhōu
potato	kentang	mǎ líng shǔ
baked	kentang panggang	kǎo mǎ líng shǔ
chips/crisps	kentang keropok	shǔ piàn
mashed	kentang campuran	shǔ ní
fried	kentang keropok	shǔ piàn
poultry	ayam itik	jiā qín
prawn	udang	xiā
–crackers	udang keropok	xiā bǐng
pressure cooker	pengukus tekanan	gāo yā guō
price	harga	jià qián
pulses (legumes)	kacang	dòu lèi shū cài
pumpkin	labu	nán guā
puree	sup sayur sayuran	guǒ ní

Q

| quail | burung puyuh | ān chún |
| –eggs | telur puyuh | ān chún dàn |

R

rabbit	arnab	tù zi
radish	lobak	bái luó bo
raisin	kimis	pú táo gān
raspberry	rasperi	mù méi
raw	mentah	shēng de
receipt	resit	shōu jù
recipe	resipi	shí pǔ
reservation	tempahan	yù dìng
restaurant	restoran	fàn guǎn
ribs	tulang rusuk	pái gǔ
rice		
cooked	nasi	fàn
glutinous	lekit-lekit	nuò mǐ fàn
–pudding	nasi pudding	dà mǐ bù dīng
fried	nasi goreng	chǎo fàn
–flour	tepung beras	mǐ fěn
uncooked	beras	mǐ
–vinegar, black	padi wain, hitam	hēi cù
–vinegar, red	padi wain, merah	hóng cù
–vinegar, white	padi wain, putih	bái cù
–wine	tuak	mǐ jiǔ
–wine, yellow	kuning padi wain	huā diāo jiǔ
ripe	masak	shóu
to roast	panggang	kǎo

GLOSSARY

GLOSSARY

English	Malay	Mandarin
roast	panggang	shāo
–chicken	ayam panggang	shāo jī
–duck	itik panggang	shāo yā
–pork	babi panggang	shāo ròu
rock sugar	gula batu	bīng táng
roe	telur ikan	yú luǎn
rosemary	rosemary	mí dié xiāng

S

English	Malay	Mandarin
sago	sagu	xī mǐ
salad	salad	shā lā
salmon	ikan salmon	sān wén yú
salt	garam	yán
salty	asin	xián
sardine	sardin	shā dīng yú
satay	satay	shā diē
–sauce	sos satay	shā diē jiàng
sauce	sos	jiàng
chilli	sos cili	là jiāo jiàng
fish	sos ikan	yú lù
oyster	sos tiram	háo yóu
plum	sos plum	méi jiàng
sweet and sour	kecap manis	suān tián jiàng
soy	kecap	jiàng yóu
sausage	sosej	xiāng cháng
scallop	tiram	dài zi
scissors	gunting	jiǎn dāo
seafood	makanan laut	hǎi xiān
sea cucumber	trepang	hǎi shēn
seasoning	bahan perasa	tiáo wèi pǐn
seaweed	lumut laut	hǎi cǎi
seaweed, dried	rumpai laut	zǐ cài
sesame seed	bijan	zhī má
shallot	bawang merah	xiǎo cōng tóu
shark	ikan jerung	shā yú
shrimp	menangkap udang	xiā rén
dried	udang kering	xiā mì
–paste	belacan	xiā jiàng
to shop	membeli-belah	gòu wù
sifter	penapis	guò lù qì
to simmer	mendidih perlahan lahan	mèn
to skin	kulit	qù pí
to slice	memotong	qiē piàn
slice	sepotong	piàn
to smoke (cook), smoke	mengasap, asap	yān
snack	makanan ringan	xiǎo chī/diǎn xīn
soft drink	air soda	qì shuǐ
soup	sop	tāng
soy sauce	kecap	jiàng yóu

English	Malay	Mandarin
soybean	kacang soya	huáng dòu
–curd	soya dadih	dòu huā
–milk	soya susu	dòu nǎi
sparerib	tulang iga	pái gǔ
spinach	bayam	bō cài
spoon	camca	tāng chí
spring onions	daun bawang	cōng
spring roll	spring roll	chūn juǎn
squid	sotong	mò yú
starfruit (carambola)	belimbing	yáng táo
to steam	stim	qīng zhēng
steam basket	stim bakul	zhēng lóng
stew	rebusan	mèn
stirfry	menggoreng	chǎo
stock	air daging	shàng tāng
strawberry	strawberi	cǎo méi
sugar	gula	táng
–cane	tebu	gān zhē
caster	castor gula	zhē táng
icing	menambah gula	táng shuāng
palm	gula Melaka	huáng táng
supermarket	pasaraya	chāo jí shì chǎng
supper	makan malam	xiāo yè
sweet	manis	tián
sweet potato	erom	fān shǔ
syrup	air gula	táng jiāng

T

English	Malay	Mandarin
table	meja	zhuō zi
tablecloth	alas meja	zhuō bù
tap water	air	zì lái shuǐ
tangerine	limau manis	jú zi
tea (see p 218)	teh	chá
Chinese	teh cina	zhōng guó chá
green	teh hijau	lǜ chá
herbal	teh herba	liáng chá
lemon	teh limau	níng méng chá
–with milk	teh susu	nǎi chá
teaspoon	camca	chá chí
tip (gratuity)	tip	xiǎo fèi
to toast (cooking)	membakar	hōng
toast (cheers!)	bersorak	gān bēi
tofu	tauhu	dòu fu
–skin	tauhu kulit	dòu fu pí
deep-fried	tauhu goreng	zhà dòu fu
tomato	tomato	fān qié
trotter	kaki binatang	zhū jiǎo

GLOSSARY

	Malay	Mandarin
tuna	ikan tongkol	jīn qiāng yú
turkey	ayam belanda	huǒ jī
turmeric	kunyit	huáng jiāng
turtle	penyu	shān ruí

V

vanilla	vanila	xiāng cǎo
veal	daging anak lembu	xiǎo niú ròu
vegetable	sayur-sayuran	shū cài
–oil	minyak sayur	cài yóu
salted	menggarami sayur	xián cài
vegetarian (person)	nabati/vegetarian	chī sù de
venison	daging rusa	lù ròu
vinegar	caka	cù

W

waiter	pelayan	fú wù yuán
walnut	walnut	hú táo
to wash	mencuci	xǐ
water	air	shuǐ
boiled	air masak	kāi shuǐ
bottled	air botol	shuǐ píng
mineral	air mineral	kuàng quán shuǐ
tap	air	zì lái shuǐ
water chestnut	sengkuang cina	mǎ tí
watercress	selada air	zī yáng cài
watermelon	tembikai	xī guā
well done (cooked)	bakit	shóu
wheat	gandum	xiǎo mài
wine	wain	pú tao jiǔ
–bar	wain bar	jiǔ bā
red	merah wain	hóng jiǔ
rice	tuak	mǐ jiǔ
white	wain putih	bái jiǔ
wok	kuali	guō
wonton	wonton	hún tún
–noodles	wonton mi	hún tún miàn

Y

yam	keladi	yū tóu
yellow	kuning	huáng sè
yolk	kuning telur	dàn huáng
yogurt	dadih	rǔ suān jūn

Z

zucchini (courgette)	hijau terung	yì dà lì qīng guā

Malaysia & Singapore Culinary Dictionary

The following notation is used throughout the Eat Your Words section:

/ forward slash indicates when single words on either side of the slash are interchangeable. It also separates two (or more) alternatives where they consist of *one* word only. These could be synonyms or different forms of the same word.

; semicolon separates two (or more) alternatives where one (or more) consists of *more* than one word

bolded words within the English definition denote that the word has its own entry within the dictionary

italicised words denote origin of culinary term

A

achar *Malay* preserved mixed vegetables

agar-agar *Malay* gelatine-like substance obtained from seaweed, commonly used as a condiment in desserts

ah bo ling *Hokkien* glutinous rice-flour dumplings filled with black sesame paste, peanut paste, white sesame paste or red-bean paste served in sweet peanut or ginger soup

air asam *Malay* tamarind juice

air barli *Malay* barley water; barley boiled to create a murky, white liquid. Its primary flavouring comes from the rock sugar dissolved in it as it boils.

air kelapa *Malay* coconut water/juice

air mata kuching *Malay* longan water; longan tea

air soya *Malay* soy milk; see the recipe

ais ball *Malay* shaved ice shaped into a large ball and covered with rose syrup, condensed milk and palm sugar syrup, and filled with a mixture of beans

ais kacang *Malay* shaved ice with red and brown syrup over red beans, jelly, sweet corn and evaporated milk

ak *Hokkien* duck

ang cho *Hokkien* red dates

ang ku kueh *Hokkien* peanut paste wrapped in sweetened glutinous dough

ang mo dang *Hokkien see* **rambutan**

ang tau teng *Hokkien* red-bean soup

anis *Malay* nutmeg

appam *Malay* fermented rice cakes; also called **hoppers** (Kuala Lumpur)

asam *Malay* tamarind; sour

asam gelugor *Malay* dried tamarind slices

asam jawa *Malay* pulp obtained from the tamarind pod

asam laksa *Malay* **laksa** with flaked fish, wild ginger buds, Vietnamese mint, **belacan** and shredded pineapple garnish (Penang)

ayam *Malay* chicken

ayam buah keluak *Malay* sour and spicy chicken dish with **buah keluak**

ayam dada *Malay* chicken breast

ayam masak merah *Malay* chicken in thick red curry

ayam rendang *Malay* chicken in thick curry sauce

ayam siyow *Malay/Cantonese* chicken in tamarind sauce

ayam soto *Malay* chicken soup

B

babi *Malay* pork

babi pong teh *Peranakan* stewed pork

bah kut teh *Hokkien* pork rib soup

bai chu *Mandarin* white vinegar

bai guo *Mandarin* ginkgo nut

bai mu er *Mandarin* white fungus

bak chang *Hokkien* dumplings stuffed with meat, chestnuts and mushrooms

bak chor mee *Hokkien* noodles doused with black vinegar sauce then topped with minced pork, fish balls, pickles, chopped spring onions and dried fish

bak choy *Cantonese* cabbage

bak kuah *Hokkien* barbecued sweetened pork slice

bak kut teh *Hokkien* pork rib soup; see the recipe

bakwang kepiting *Peranakan* crabmeat ball soup

bambu *Malay* spices

ban mian *Mandarin* noodle soup with minced meat and vegetables

bandung *Malay* milky pink drink made from rose syrup (product consisting of rose-water, sugar syrup and pink colouring) and condensed milk

bao *Cantonese* steamed bun

bao yu *Cantonese* abalone

batu giling *Malay* grinding stone

batu lesong *Malay* mortar and pestle

bawal puteh *Malay* pomfret steamed with salted vegetables, pickled sour plums and tomato wedges

bawang *Malay* onions

bawang besar *Malay* Bombay onion

bawang merah *Malay* shallots

bawang putih *Malay* garlic

beehoon *Hokkien* rice vermicelli

beehoon goreng *Hokkien/Malay* stirfried spicy vermicelli

beijing yah *Mandarin see* **Peking duck**

belacan *Malay* fermented shrimp paste

belimbing manis *Malay* star fruit

betel leaf small, deep green, heart-shaped leaf, with a slightly bitter taste, chewed together with betel nut. It is also soaked in sugared water and used as a wrapping for food.

betel nut fruit of the betel plant crushed and chewed to give a numbing effect

bhindi *Hindi* okra; ladies' fingers

bihun *Malay see* **beehoon**

biji nangka *Malay* jackfruit seeds

bingke ubi *Malay* brown-coloured baked tapioca slice

bir *Malay* beer

biryani *Hindi* dish of steamed rice oven-baked with meat, vegetables and spices

biryani dam *Hindi* Indian and Arabic speciality where rice and meat is laid out layer upon layer

black pepper crab stirfried crab with sweet pepper-based sauce

blangah *Hindi* earthenware vessels for slow-cooked curries

bobo chacha *Malay* yam dessert soup

bok choy *Cantonese* Chinese white cabbage

buah keluak *Malay* black hard-shell nut originally from Brazil, grown in Indonesia

buah keras *Malay* candlenuts; also called **kemiri**

buah pala *Malay* nutmeg

buah pelaga *Malay* cardamom; also called **kapulaga** and **krawan**

bubur *Malay* plain rice porridge; *see also* **chok** *and* **muay**

bubur hitam *Malay* sweet porridge made of black glutinous rice served with coconut milk

bubur lambuk *Malay* savoury rice porridge flavoured with ginger, cinnamon, star anise, coconut, coarsely chopped beef, diced chicken and diced prawns

bunga cengkih *Malay* cloves

bunga lawang *Malay* star anise; small, aromatic star-shaped fruit. Imparts a slightly tingly taste to food.

bunga siantan *Malay* torch ginger buds

bunga telang *Malay* butterfly or blue tea flower, provides the natural blue colouring for desserts and rice dishes

C

cai xim *Hokkien see* **choi sum**

cao fan *Cantonese* fried rice

cendol *Malay* drink/dessert of coconut milk and palm sugar syrup with fine, short strings of green-bean flour dough, all topped with shaved ice

cha *Mandarin* tea

cha kueh teow *Hokkien* fried noodles with black sauce

cha siew *Cantonese* barbecued sweet roast pork

cha siew bao *Cantonese* steamed bun with **cha siew**

cha siew mee *Cantonese* egg noodles served in soup; fine, yellow noodles served with minced pork dumplings. Also called **wonton mee**.

chai peng *Hokkien* economy rice, similar to **nasi campur**

chai poh *Hokkien* preserved vegetable diced and served as a condiment

chai tau kueh *Hokkien* stirfried radish cake

chao *Mandarin* stirfried

chao gu *Hokkien* straw mushroom

chap chai *Hokkien* mixed vegetable dish

chap chai peng *Hokkien* Chinese version of **nasi campur**

chapati *Hindi* griddle-fried breads

char dan *Mandarin* braised eggs in tea

char kway teow *Hokkien* stirfried broad, flat rice-flour noodles tossed with cockles, slivers of Chinese sausage and egg in a sweet, dark soy sauce

chee cheong fun *Hokkien* rice-flour rolls stuffed with either shrimp or pork

cheng teng *Hokkien* 'clear soup', sweet dessert containing sweet potato, white fungus, sago seeds and longan. May be served hot or cold.

chilli crab stirfried crab with chilli and tomato sauce; see the recipe (Singapore)

chin chow *Malay* Chinese cabbage leaf, used in **air cincau**

choi sum *Cantonese* Chinese vegetable that gets its name from the yellow flowers at the heart of its stem. Crisp and mild in taste, used in soups or stirfries.

chok *Cantonese* Cantonese version of **bubur**, rice porridge with the rice grains broken down to a pasty consistency, with such ingredients as century egg and meat

chu shi *Mandarin* chef

chwee kueh *Hokkien* steamed rice cakes served with **chai poh**, commonly eaten as a snack or for breakfast

ciku *Malay* oval fruit with a dull, pale rusty brown skin, with pinky-brown flesh that tastes lightly sweet

cili padi *Malay* bird's eye chilli

cincaluk *Malay* fermented shrimps

codial floris sapatu *Malay* hibiscus tea or cordial with lime, sugar and ginger

coubes gulung *Eurasian* stewed cabbage rolls

curry debal *Eurasian* 'devil's curry', spicy Eurasian meat curry. Can include ham, luncheon meat or sausages; cooked with a racy blend of spices and flavoured with vinegar; see the recipe.

curry leaf small, tear-shaped leaves used in Indian curries for their strong and aromatic flavour

cze cha *Hokkien* 'pick 'n' mix', eatery where diners choose their meal from a display of fried rolls, meat and fish balls, stuffed chillies and beancurd

D

daal *Tamil* generic term for cooked and uncooked lentils or pulses

daging asam *Malay* tamarind beef

daging bakar *Malay* grilled beef

daging kambing *Malay* mutton

daging lembu *Malay* beef

daging masak kecap *Malay* beef cooked in soy sauce

dao *Hokkien* soybeans; also called **tau**

dau gok *Cantonese* long beans

daun bawang *Malay* spring onions; scallions, widely used in Chinese cooking, with the green tops often finely chopped, or cut into slivers, and used as a garnish

daun cajus *Malay* young cashew leaves

daun kadok *Malay see* **betel leaf**

daun kaduk *Malay* wild pepper leaf, used in North Malaysian rice dishes

daun kari *Malay* curry leaf

daun kesum *Malay* Vietnamese mint, used as a garnish in **asam laksa**

daun ketumbar *Malay* coriander; also called **xiang cai** and **wang swee**

daun kunyit *Malay* turmeric, used in Malay dishes such as **rendang**. Often shredded as a garnish.

daun limau purut *Malay* kaffir lime leaves used to enhance flavour

daun pandan *Malay* pandanus leaves; also called screwpine leaves, used to flavour and colour cakes, drinks, rice and desserts

diam mee *Malay/Hokkien* egg noodles and hard-boiled eggs (some use quail eggs) in a sweet, sugary soup

dian xin *Mandarin see* **dim sum**

dim sum *Cantonese* lightly steamed Chinese delicacies, often consumed as a snack or as part of a main meal

doldol durian *Malay* black, chewy sweet formed by stewing **durian**

dong gu *Cantonese see* **xiang gu**

dong gua *Mandarin* wintermelon, used in the preparation of soup

dong gua tang *Mandarin* candied wintermelon

dosai *Tamil* paper-thin rice-and-lentil crêpes served with coconut chutney and curry

dou fu *Mandarin* beancurd

dou fu shui *Mandarin* soybean milk

dun *Mandarin* stew; double boil

durian *Malay* large thorny fruit with pale yellow flesh that has a creamy, custard-like texture and a strange, sweet taste. Many find its odour unpleasant.

durian kueh *Malay* porridge-like sweet made by cooking **durian** pulp, coconut cream and palm sugar

durian pengat *Malay* **durian** puréed into a dessert with a custard-like consistency

E

eng chai *Hokkien see* **kangkong**

epok epok *Malay* deep-fried, pyramid-shaped pastry filled with vegetable or meat curry. Malay version of the Indian **samosa**.

F

fen si *Mandarin* mung-bean noodles, very popular noodle served in soup

feng *Mandarin* diced lean pork from the pig's hind leg in a curry with **feng curry powder**; may also contain liver, tongue, lungs, heart and sometimes blood (Eurasian dish)

feng curry powder curry powder with coriander, cumin and fennel

fennel seeds seeds that have a sweet taste and an aromatic quality, essential for Malay cuisine

floss meat cooked until dry and flaky; it breaks down into a coarse, thread-like consistency

fong zhao *Cantonese* braised chicken feet

fujian mian *Mandarin see* **Hokkien mee**

G

gai lan *Cantonese* Chinese broccoli; kale

galangal *Malay* spicy aromatic rhizome that is pinkish-yellow in colour and has a faint camphor flavour; also called blue ginger

gan bei *Mandarin* dried scallop commonly used in Chinese soups

garam masala *Malay* aromatic blend of spices, including black pepper, cumin seeds, cinnamon, cardamom, cloves, coriander seeds, bay leaves and nutmeg

gau choi *Cantonese* Chinese chives

geragau *Malay* tiny shrimp found in the seas off the Strait of Melaka

ghee *Hindi* clarified butter

gon yu chu *Cantonese see* **gan bei**

gong gong *Hokkien/Malay* whelk, steamed and served with chilli dip

gu lu rou *Mandarin* sweet and sour pork

guai bee *Hokkien* lime juice served with dried sour plums that have been soaked in a sugar solution. It is sweet, sour and just a little salty.

gula jamun *Malay* fried coconut-milk balls

gula Melaka *Malay* palm sugar; sweet dessert drink with coconut as its base gulai daging *Malay* beef curry

guo tie *Mandarin* Chinese dumpling

H

haam daan *Cantonese* salted eggs, most often duck; also called **kiam neng** and **xian dan**

hai shen *Mandarin* sea cucumber

Hainanese chicken chicken lightly cooked in water with onion, ginger and garlic, chopped up and covered with sesame oil, soy sauce, coriander and spring onions

Hainanese chicken rice **Hainanese chicken** and rice with chilli-ginger sauce; see the recipe

halia *Malay* ginger

hao you *Mandarin* oyster sauce

har cheong kai *Cantonese* chicken deep fried in a prawn-paste batter

har kow *Cantonese* prawns wrapped in glutinous rice skin, a **dim sum** item

hay bee *Hokkien* dried shrimp

hay koh *Hokkien* shrimp paste

hay mee *Hokkien* prawn noodle soup; see the recipe

hei chu *Mandarin* black vinegar

hei hu jiao pang xie *Mandarin* black pepper crab

hei jiang you *Mandarin* dark soy sauce

hei mu er *Mandarin* black fungus

her *Hokkien* see **yu**

her peow *Hokkien* fish maw

hinava *Malay* fish marinated with lime juice and herbs (Sabah)

hinava tongii *Malay* Spanish mackerel, chilli, ginger and shallots drenched in lime juice (Sabah)

hoisin sauce thick, red-brown Chinese sauce that is both sweet and spicy. Made from fermented black beans, soybeans, garlic and spices.

Hokkien mee *Hokkien* yellow, thick, egg noodles; a stirfry dish with egg noodles, squid, shrimp, pork, vegetables and an egg that is cracked into the noodles to attain a sauce-like texture. Can also be made as a soup with seafood broth. Also called **fujian mian**.

hong chu *Mandarin* red vinegar

hong dao *Cantonese* red bean

hong mao dan *Mandarin* see **rambutan**

hoppers see **appam**

hor fun *Cantonese* thick rice noodles cooked in a thick broth with seafood and pork

hor lan dao *Cantonese* see **kacang kampri**

hua diao jiu *Mandarin* glutinous rice wine; commonly used for flavouring in Chinese cuisine

hua sheng *Mandarin* peanut

huat kueh *Hokkien* 'a cake that grows', auspicious food item usually found during the new year. Chinese custom dictates that great fortune will follow should the cake start to turn mouldy.

hum chim bang *Cantonese* deep-fried salted rice dough

hun tun *Mandarin* see **wonton**

hun tun mian *Mandarin* see **wonton mee**

huo guo *Mandarin* steamboat

I

idiappam *Tamil* string hoppers, thin rice-flour noodles served as a disc of fine netting, eaten either with brown sugar or a curry

idli *Hindi* spongy fermented rice-flour and lentil cakes that are steamed

ikan *Malay* fish

ikan bakar *Malay* grilled fish

ikan bilis *Malay* dried anchovies

ikan kasam *Malay* fermented preserved fish with black beans

ikan kembung *Malay* mackerel

ikan kurau *Malay* threadfin

ikan merah *Malay* red snapper

ikan otak otak *Malay* spiced rectangles of Spanish mackerel wrapped in banana leaves and grilled

ikan parang *Malay* wolf herring

ikan tenggiri *Malay* Spanish mackerel

ikan tenggiri masak nangka *Malay* braised mackerel fillet with coconut milk and jackfruit inche kabin *Malay* Hainanese-style fried chicken served with Worcestershire sauce (Kuala Lumpur)

Indian rojak *Malay* deep-fried vegetables and seafood served with chilli sauce, cucumber, tomato and onion

Ipoh curry laksa *Malay* curry **laksa** with Chinese barbecued roast pork and stock made with curry leaves (Perak)

Ipoh kway teow *Hokkien* rice noodles topped with sauce, shredded chicken and mushroom (Perak)

itek *Malay* duck

itek sio *Malay* stewed duck in coriander

itek tim *Malay* duck and vegetable soup

J

jambu *Malay* rose apple, bell-shaped fruit that is bright pink with a waxy skin. Its flesh is watery and sweet. Locals enjoy it sliced and dipped in a mix of soy sauce and sliced chillies.

jew her *Hokkien* dried squid

ji *Mandarin* chicken

ji dan mian *Mandarin* egg noodles

ji gan *Mandarin* chicken liver

jian *Mandarin* pan fry

jiang qing *Mandarin* light soy sauce

jiang you *Mandarin* soy sauce

jiang yu zai *Mandarin* dried anchovies

jin zhen gu *Mandarin* golden mushroom

jintan manis *Malay* fennel seeds

jintan puteh *Malay* cumin seeds

jiu cai *Mandarin* Chinese chives

jiu hoo char *Hokkien* stirfried shredded cuttlefish with yam bean

K

ka li yu tou *Mandarin* fish-head curry

kacang *Malay* peanuts, peas, beans

kacang bendi *Malay* okra

kacang kampri *Malay* mangetout pea; both the pod and peas are eaten

kacang panjang *Malay* long beans

kai fan *Cantonese see* **Hainanese chicken rice**

kai yik *Cantonese* chicken wing

kailan *Cantonese* vegetable with slender stems, loose leaves and tiny white or yellow flowers; Chinese broccoli

kalamansi tiny, dark, sour lime

kambing *Malay* lamb/mutton

kampung *Malay* village

kangkong *Malay* water convolvulus

kangkong sambal belacan *Malay* water convolvulus stirfried in **sambal belacan**

kanji Kedah *Malay* porridge filled with chicken, beef or prawns, with ginger, lemongrass and fenugreek (Kedah)

kao *Mandarin* grill

kapitan *Malay* curry dish Eurasians serve on special occasions

kapulaga *Malay* cardamom; also called **buah pelaga** and **krawan**

kari ayam *Malay* chicken curry

karipincha *Malay see* **curry leaf**

katong laksa *Malay* noodles in a spicy coconut gravy, served with prawns, clams, fish cake, cockles, bean sprouts and beancurd (Katong, Singapore)

kaya *Malay* coconut egg jam

kayu manis *Malay* cinnamon

kecap manis *Malay* thick, sweet soy sauce, sweetened with palm sugar

kelongtong *Malay* fruit

kemiri *Malay* candlenuts; also called **buah keras**

kepah *Malay* Manila clams

kerabu *Malay* salads

kerabu nangka *Malay* boiled jackfruit, sliced and tossed in a spicy salad

kerabu tau geh *Malay* bean sprout salad

kerang *Malay* shellfish

keraup *Malay* red grouper

keropok *Malay* crackers, made with prawn, vegetable or fish

keropok lekor *Malay* crackers made from fish and sago flour (Kelantan & Terengganu)

ketam *Malay* crab

ketam batu *Malay* mud crab

ketam renjong *Malay* blue crab

ketumbar *Malay* coriander seed powder

ketupat *Malay* pressed rice made out of regular rice, shaped by a case made from strips of coconut fronds

ketupat pulut *Malay* glutinous rice half-cooked in coconut milk before being rolled into thick logs wrapped in banana leaves. The logs are then steamed before they are unwrapped and served in cylindrical slices with **serunding daging**. (Kedah)

keuh lapis *Malay* a multi-layered sweet dessert cake

kiam chai *Hokkien* preserved vegetable; salted mustard cabbage

kiam her *Hokkien* salted fish

kiam neng *Hokkien* salted duck eggs; also called **haam daan** and **xian dan**

kong bak pau *Hokkien* belly pork braised in a dark stock (often consisting of dark and light soy sauce, caramelised sugar, Chinese cooking wine, star anise and cassia bark), with the pork then sliced into portions and slipped into flat bun pockets

kong bao *Mandarin* dried chilli

koo chai pau *Hokkien* chive dumplings

kopi *Malay* local coffee sweetened with condensed milk

kopi-o *Malay* black coffee with sugar

kopi peng *Malay* iced coffee served with condensed milk

korma *Hindi* rich, thick, mild curry of chicken, mutton or vegetables. The meat is tenderised by marinating it in curds and spices before cooking.

krawan *Malay* cardamom; also called **buah pelaga** and **kapulaga**

ku gua *Mandarin* bitter gourd

kuali *Malay* wok

kuay neng *Hokkien* soft-boiled eggs

kueh *Hokkien/Malay* cake

kueh bakar *Peranakan* green, heart-shaped cake

kueh belanda *Peranakan* Dutch cake

kueh chap *Hokkien* 'fruit juice', but has surprisingly nothing to do with fruit. You may choose from a variety of pork

items (intestines, brisket etc) that have been braised in a light soy-based soup. Served with rice noodles.

kueh heng bak *Hokkien* chicken breast

kueh lapis *Peranakan* rice-flour cake consisting of layers of different colours

kueh pie ti *Peranakan* Peranakan snack served in a deep-fried flour cup and filled with steamed turnip, prawn and sweet chilli sauce

kueh sit *Hokkien* chicken wing

kueh-kueh *Malay* little Malay and Peranakan teacakes

kulfi *Hindi* ice cream with reduced milk, pistachios and rose-water

kunyit *Malay* turmeric

kupang *Malay* mussels

kurma *Malay* red dates

kway chap *Hokkien* meal of braised pig's innards, pork, hard-boiled eggs, braised beancurd and sheets of rice noodle

kway kak *Hokkien* similar to **char kway teow** but using rice cubes instead of flat rice noodles

kway teow *Hokkien* medium-width white noodle

kway teow kerang *Hokkien* halal version of **char kway teow**

L

la jiao pang xie *Mandarin* chilli crab

la mian *Mandarin* wheat-flour noodles

lada *Malay* peppercorns

lada hitam *Malay* black peppercorns

lada kering *Malay* dried chillies

lada puteh *Malay* white peppercorns

laddu *Hindi* a dessert made of yellow lentils, milk and sugar

lah lah *Hokkien* clams

laksa *Peranakan* spicy, soupy noodle dish that blends ingredients of Malay, Chinese and Indian influences. Variations abound.

laksa Johor *Malay* rich, coconut-based, fish-based **laksa**. Includes cumin, coriander seeds and turmeric, fried shredded coconut meat, cucumber, bean sprouts and Vietnamese mint. The boldest inclusion may be the use of spaghetti as noodles. (Johor)

laksa Kedah *Malay* **laksa** with tamarind, without coconut as its broth (Kedah)

laksa lemak *Malay* **laksa** with coconut milk, curried chicken, bean sprouts and deep-fried beancurd. Prawns are sometimes included.

laksa mee *Malay* white, rice noodles used specifically for **laksa**

laksa Pahang *Malay* fish-based **laksa** served with rice vermicelli

laksang *Malay* **laksa** with rolled up and sliced sheets of steamed rice flour. The gravy consists of fish, coconut, garlic and shallots. (Kelantan & Terengganu)

lap cheong *Cantonese* Chinese preserved sausage; wax is used to hold the meat (pork or duck) together after it has been soaked in oil. The sausage has a distinctly sweet flavour.

lassi *Hindi* curd drinks, often flavoured with salt or sugar, and rose-water

lau leen *Cantonese* durian

leen ngau *Cantonese* lotus root

leen yong *Cantonese* lotus seed paste

lek tau teng *Hokkien* green-bean soup

lemang *Malay* glutinous rice flavoured with coconut milk and cooked over an open fire in bamboo poles lined with young banana leaves

lengkuas *Malay see* **galangal**

li zhi *Mandarin* lychee

lian ow *Mandarin* lotus root

lian rong *Mandarin* lotus seed

lian rong *Mandarin* lotus seed paste

limau kesturi *Malay* small limes

linut *Malay* thick translucent sago paste, eaten hot with **sambal** (Sarawak)

liu lian *Mandarin* durian

long xia *Mandarin* lobster

long yan *Mandarin see* **longan**

longan *Peranakan* small, sweet and juicy tropical fruit. Eaten fresh or dried.

lor ak *Hokkien* braised duck

lor bak *Cantonese* white radish; *Hokkien* pork braised in soy sauce and spices

lor mai kai *Cantonese* steamed glutinous rice with chicken

lor mee *Hokkien* noodles with braised pork-loin and fish slices, in thick sauce

lor neng *Hokkien* braised egg

lou ark *Teochew* braised duck

lui char fan *Hakka* 'thunder tea rice', Hakka version of **bubur**. Ingredients such as peanuts, sesame seeds, peppercorns, Chinese tea leaves, mint leaves and sweet potato leaves are ground, then steeped in hot water, brought to boil and poured over cooked rice.

M

ma tai *Cantonese* water chestnut

ma ti *Mandarin* water chestnut

ma you *Mandarin* sesame seed oil

macher tarkari *Bengali* fish curry

Maggi mee goreng *Malay* noodles (Maggi brand) softened in boiling water before being fried and topped with a fried egg (Kuala Lumpur)

main xian *Mandarin* dried wheat-flour noodles

mang guo *Mandarin* mango

mang hik *Hokkien see* **san ju**

manggis *Malay* mangosteen

masala *Tamil* spice blend

masala dosai *Tamil* **dosai** filled with a dry, spicy potato filling and folded into a triangular package

mata kuching *Malay see* **longan**

mee fen *Mandarin* rice-flour noodles

mee goreng *Malay* spicy fried noodles coloured with tomato sauce and red food colouring, filled with cubes of potato, cabbage and occasionally minced meat (most likely mutton)

mee hun kueh *Hokkien see* **ban mian**

mee pok *Hokkien* flat yellow egg noodles

mee rebus *Malay* thick egg noodles in a viscous, sweet and spicy sauce, served with hard-boiled eggs and green chillies

mee siam *Malay* rice vermicelli in a spicy, tangy sauce

mee soto *Malay* thick egg noodles in broth, served with shredded chicken and bean sprouts

mee suah *Hokkien see* **mian sian**

mee suah tow *Hokkien* stirfry with prawn, chicken and mushrooms; also called birthday noodles

mian jing *Mandarin* gluten

mian sian *Mandarin* rice noodles; also called longevity noodles

mu gua *Mandarin* papaya

mua chee *Hokkien* cooked rice dough shaped into strips and cut into bite-sized pieces then tossed in a chopped peanut and sugar mixture

muay *Teochew* variation of **bubur**, rice porridge with the grains remaining whole, so that the porridge looks like rice in soup. Served with pickles, omelette, braised and stewed meat dishes, fish and beancurd.

murg makhanwala *Tamil* butter chicken

murtabak *Tamil* pan-fried rice dough with minced or diced chicken, beef, mutton, or vegetables

muruku *Tamil* deep-fried noodle-like snack made from rice and **daal** flours

N

naan *Hindi* bread made from plain flour and cooked in a **tandoor**

nangka *Malay* jackfruit

nasi ayam *Malay see* **kai fan**

nasi ayam percik *Malay* barbecued chicken marinated with spicy coconut gravy (Kelantan)

nasi biryani *Malay* rich, aromatic rice casserole often layered with meat (most often chicken or mutton) then steamed

nasi bubur *Peranakan* similar to **muay**, but served with accompaniments such as fried stingray, fried quail, pickled garlic, and cuttlefish with honey

nasi campur *Malay* 'mixed rice', plate of white rice topped with whatever meat, fish and vegetable dishes are available

nasi dagang *Malay* red or brown glutinous rice served with coconut milk,

flaked fish, desiccated coconut and a variety of herbs and sauces (Kelantan)

nasi goreng *Malay* steamed rice fried with other ingredients

nasi kandar *Malay* Indian version of **nasi campur**

nasi kerabu *Malay* rice dish tinted blue using the petals of a flower called bunga telang (Kelantan)

nasi kuning *Malay* yellow rice; see the recipe

nasi lemak *Malay* coconut rice with fried fish. Lightly salted rice is cooked with coconut milk, topped with **sambal ikan bilis** and a few slices of cucumber, and wrapped up in a banana leaf.

nasi minyak *Malay* rice dish cooked with **ghee** and spices

nasi padang *Malay* Indonesian version of **nasi campur**

nasi tomato *Malay* tomato-flavoured rice

nga choi *Cantonese* bean sprouts

ngau pa *Cantonese* steak

ngor hiang *Hokkien* deep-fried mixture of pork, prawn, water chestnut and chives wrapped in beancurd skin

niang toufu *Mandarin* fish paste stuffed in various food items like bitter gourd, **taupok**, chilli or mushroom; also called **yong taufu**

niu nan mien *Mandarin* beef-brisket noodles

niu pai *Mandarin* steak

nona rostu bremeilu *Malay* 'maiden's blush'; sweet red wine mixed with lemonade and fresh rose petals. Served in goblets with rose petals on top.

O

or luah *Hokkien* 'fried oyster', oysters fried with egg, tapioca flour and chives (Singapore)

otak *Peranakan* spicy fish paste wrapped in banana leaves

otak udang *Malay* prawn sauce (Kedah)

ou nee *Teochew* yam-paste dessert

oyster omelette *see* **or luah**

P

pada *Malay* salt-fish pickle

pai kuat wong *Cantonese* sweet and sour spare ribs

pai quat *Cantonese* steamed pork ribs, usually with salted black beans

pak chiok har *Cantonese* steamed prawns

palgoa *Tamil* dessert made of cow's milk, **ghee** and sugar

pandanus leaf *Malay* screwpine leaf, used to flavour and colour rice and desserts

papadam *Hindi* deep-fried crackers with garlic spices (Indian)

paratha *Tamil* fried flatbread

pari nyiru *Malay* grilled stingray

parut *Malay* coconut grater

pasembur *Peranakan* salad of cucumber, yam bean, bean sprouts, beancurd, cut-tlefish and prawn fritters topped with sweet, sour and spicy gravy (Penang)

pau *Mandarin* bun

pei daan *Cantonese* century egg

pei dan zhok *Cantonese* century-egg por-ridge

pek kueh *Hokkien see* **bai guo**

pek mak zhi *Hokkien* white fungus

Peking duck duck immersed in condi-ments and roasted over flames until red, shining with oil, but with crisp skin and tender meat. The meat is sliced, each having a piece of skin, and served with thin pancakes, Chinese onions and sweet, five-spice sauce.

pembasuk tangan *Malay* finger bowls used for washing

Penang asam laksa *Malay* rice noodles topped with a spicy and sour fish gravy, flakes of mackerel and garnished with fresh pineapple, cucumber, chilli, mint, finely shredded torch ginger flower and a dollop of shrimp paste (Penang)

peria *Malay* bittergourd

perut ikan *Malay* fish innards cooked in coconut curry with mint, served on sliced beans and pineapple (Penang)

petai *Malay* stink beans

pisang goreng *Malay* deep-fried bananas

pohpiah *Hokkien* 'thin biscuit', Peranakan spring rolls that are not deep fried; fillings can include turnip, carrot, lettuce, prawn, mashed egg, bean sprouts and sweet sauce; see the recipe

pong piah *Hokkien* flaky puff pastry filled with white molasses (Penang)

por choy *Cantonese* Chinese spinach

pulut hitam *Malay* sweet, sticky black-rice pudding

putri salat *Malay* double-layered dessert consisting of a glutinous rice base cov-ered with a thick, green, custard-like topping. Usually made in big sheets, then sliced into rectangular tiles of green and white.

putu mayam *Tamil* string hoppers, or rice noodles

Q

qing chao *Mandarin* grass jelly

qing chong *Mandarin* spring onion

quai su mian *Mandarin* instant noodles

R

rambutan lychee-like fruit with sweet, succulent, semi-translucent flesh and a red hairy skin

rempah *Malay* spice paste

rendang *Malay* Indonesian-style thick coconut-milk curry, usually made with beef; see the recipe

rendang tok *Malay* beef left to marinate with coconut flesh and coconut milk, then simmered (Perak)

rojak *Malay* salad consisting of such ingredients as cucumber, pineapple, turnip, deep-fried rice dough and bean sprouts, with dressing that may contain **belacan**, chillies and peanuts. See also **Indian rojak**.

roti *Hindi* bread

roti bawang telur *Malay* **roti paratha** with an egg and onion

roti kaya *Malay* grilled bread slathered with coconut egg jam, topped with thick slices of ice-cold butter, then covered with another slice of toast

roti paratha *Hindi* unleavened flaky fried flat bread

roti paratha canai *Tamil* plain **roti paratha** served with curry or sugar

roti pisang *Malay* **roti paratha** with banana

roti Planta *Malay* **roti paratha** with a layer of butter

roti telur *Malay* **roti paratha** with an egg cracked into the middle

S

sa po taufu *Cantonese* claypot beancurd

sago gula Melaka *Malay* dessert of palm sugar and coconut milk sauce poured over sago pudding; see the recipe

sambal *Malay* chilli-based condiment. Variations abound.

sambal belacan *Malay* spicy chilli paste containing chillies, **belacan** and salt; see the recipe

sambal cili taucheo *Malay* onions, chilli and preserved soybeans

sambal goreng *Malay* prawns, meat and soybean cake cooked in chilli and coconut milk

sambal ikan bilis *Malay* dried anchovies fried and mixed with a spicy **sambal**

sambal kangkong *Malay* stirfried water convolvulus and chilli paste

sambal kepah *Malay* clams cooked in a chilli paste

sambal olek/ulek *Malay* simple **sambal** of mixed chilli, vinegar and salt

sambar *Tamil* spicy vegetable and lentil stew

sambar idli *Tamil* spongy fermented rice-flour and lentil cakes steamed and served with **sambar**

samosa *Hindi* deep-fried triangular pastries filled with spiced vegetables (mostly peas and potato) and meat

san ju *Mandarin* mangosteen

sanggang *Malay* sour fish soup made with lemongrass, galangal, chilli and a

light tamarind juice (Kelantan & Terengganu)

santan kental *Malay* coconut milk

santan pekat *Malay* coconut cream

Sarawak laksa dark-coloured chicken **laksa** with toasted rice, coconut, and lime (Sarawak)

sardine puffs sardines in tomato sauce fried with shallots and chilli, then wrapped in pastry

satar *Malay* fish, tamarind water, grated coconut, chilli, **belacan**, onion and sugar. The ingredients are blended, then wrapped in cones of banana leaves and grilled. (Kelantan & Terengganu)

satay *Malay* spicy grilled meat skewers

satay celup *Malay* meat, seafood, vegetables, fish balls and boiled quail eggs skewered and cooked in a boiling stock and eaten with peanut sauce (Melaka)

satay Johor *Malay* **satay** basted with coconut milk and oil, brushed on with a lemongrass stalk (Johor)

sayur *Malay* vegetables

sek bak *Hokkien* pork belly in spicy black sauce

sek mee *Hokkien* thick yellow noodle

sengkuang *Malay* yam bean

serai *Malay see* lemongrass

serbuk halia *Malay* ginger powder

serbuk kunyit *Malay* turmeric powder

serbuk lima rempah *Malay* Chinese mixed spice usually containing star anise, cassia bark, cloves, Sichuan pepper and fennel seeds. Sometimes also includes cardamom, coriander seeds, dried orange peel and ginger powder.

serunding *Malay* desiccated coconut fried with chilli

serunding daging *Malay* spicy beef **floss**

sha bou fan *Cantonese* claypot rice; rice is cooked over a slow fire with chicken, **lap cheong**, salted fish and soy sauce

shao shing jiu *Mandarin* Chinese cooking wine

shao tao *Cantonese* longevity peach buns, shaped like peaches and filled with red-bean or lotus-seed paste shu fen *Mandarin* tapioca flour

si guah *Mandarin* watermelon

siat *Malay* sago grubs stirfried with shallots and ginger (Sarawak)

siew mai *Cantonese* mince pork wrapped with wonton skin

silken tofu soft beancurd; also called **tauhu** and **toufu**

Singapore laksa *Malay* rich, sour **laksa** with **ikan bilis**, coconut milk, **belacan** and fish cakes (Singapore)

siput *Malay* razor clams

sireh *Malay see* **betel nut**

siu mai *Hokkien* pork dumplings

siu yoke *Cantonese* crispy pork belly

soldadu chocolat *Portuguese* 'chocolate soldier', milk, chocolate, black coffee, brown sugar, rum, almond slivers and a trace of nutmeg or cinnamon. Served hot in mugs.

sop ekor lembu *Malay* oxtail soup

sop kambing *Malay* mutton soup

sos cili *Malay* chilli sauce

sos satay *Malay* satay sauce

sotong *Malay* squid

soursop large, dark green fruit covered with soft prickles and with pulp that has a slightly acidic flavour

suan rong *Mandarin* minced deep-fried garlic

sugee kueh *Malay* moist sweet sponge cake

sun kueh *Hokkien* braised julienne turnip wrapped in rice flour, steamed and served with sweet sauce

sze chuan cai *Mandarin* spicy preserved vegetables

sze gua *Cantonese* Chinese okra

T

talam ubi *Malay* double-layered cake with a coconut top layer and dark brown tapioca bottom layer

tambun piah *Hokkien* **pong piah** filled with yellow-lentil paste (Penang)

tandoor *Tamil* clay oven

tandoori *Tamil* meat cooked in a **tandoor** after being marinated with spices

tang *Mandarin* blanch

tapai *Malay* Malay dessert often served at weddings, made from sticky rice and **gula Melaka**, touched with powdered yeast and left to its own ageing devices

tau *Hokkien* soybeans

tau sar piah *Hokkien* **pong piah** filled with red-bean paste (Penang)

tau sha *Hokkien* red-bean paste

taucheo *Hokkien* salted soybeans, used sparingly in Chinese, Eurasian and Peranakan cooking. They add a distinct texture and saltiness to the taste. Also crushed and mixed into food.

taugeh *Hokkien* bean sprouts

taugua pok *Hokkien* deep-fried beancurd

tauhu *Hokkien* soft beancurd; also called **silken tofu** and **toufu**

tauhu goreng *Hokkien* fried beancurd topped with blanched bean sprouts, slivers of cucumber and a spicy-sweet peanut sauce

tauhu ru *Hokkien* fermented beancurd

tauhuay *Hokkien* sweet beancurd; extremely delicate curd made from soybean milk drizzled with a sweet syrup; see the recipe

tauhuay chwee *Hokkien* sweet soybean milk

taukee *Hokkien* beancurd sheets, the skin that forms on the surface when beancurd is made. The skin is removed, dried and folded into sheets. These need to be soaked in water before use.

taukua *Hokkien* firm beancurd

taukua pau *Hokkien* **taukua** split open to form a pocket and stuffed with vegetables and pieces of braised duck

taupok *Hokkien* beancurd deep fried until its insides are transformed into a spongy hollow

tawa *Tamil* hotplate or iron griddle, used in homes to make bread

teh *Malay* tea

teh halia *Malay* milky ginger tea

teh tarik *Malay* pulled tea, prepared by using outstretched hands to pour the tea from one container into another. The higher the 'pull', the thicker the froth. Also called **teh terbang**.

teh terbang *Malay* 'flying tea'; *see* **teh tarik**

teh-cino *Malay* tea served with a bottom-half layer of milky tea, and a top half that is frothy and milky white

tempeh *Malay* fermented soybean cake

tempoyak *Malay* fermented and near-alcoholic durian pulp (Perak)

terung *Malay* eggplant/aubergine

terung sambal *Malay* eggplant/aubergine with chilli paste; see the recipe

tian ji *Mandarin* frog, only the hind legs are served

tian jiang *Mandarin see* **kecap manis**

timun *Malay* cucumber

tiram *Malay* tiny oysters

toddy *Tamil* palm-sap wine; alcoholic drink made from fermented sap of the coconut flower

tofu fresh beancurd

toktok mee *Malay* noodles served dry and tossed in a sauce usually consisting of soy sauce, sesame oil and chilli sauce or ketchup, topped with **cha siew**, wonton and greens

tong xin fen *Mandarin* macaroni

tong zi ji *Mandarin* spring chicken

tongkat ali *Malay* root found deep in tropical rainforests. Considered to be the herb of 100 healing qualities, and also thought to have aphrodisiac qualities. Commonly found at hawker or coffeeshop stalls served as a drink.

toufu *Mandarin see* **tauhu**

trepang *Malay* sea cucumber/slug used in Chinese cooking

tua suan *Hokkien* yellow beans in a starchy, sweet soup

tua tau *Hokkien* mussel

tuak *Malay* rice wine; milky liquid that tastes like a sweet, fruity white wine

tung fen *Mandarin* mung-bean noodles

tung hoon *Hokkien* dried mung-bean noodles

tze char *Hokkien* 'cooked food stall', used to define Chinese hawker-style dining

U

udang *Malay* prawns

umai *Malay* slivers of raw fish marinated with shallots, chilli, salt and tamarind liquid or lime juice (Sarawak)

V

vadai *Tamil* deep-fried lentil fritters

vengaya dosai *Malay* **dosai** with garnish of fried onions

W

wain *Malay* wine

wang sui *Hokkien see* **xiang cai**

wang swee *Hokkien* coriander/cilantro; also called **daun ketumbar**, **xiang cai**

wonton *Cantonese* dumplings filled with meat, seafood or vegetables; can be fried, steamed or added to soup

wonton mee *Hokkien* egg noodles served in soup; fine, yellow noodles served with minced pork dumplings. Also called **cha siew mee**.

wu tau *Cantonese* yam

X

xia mi *Mandarin* dried shrimp

xia mian *Mandarin* thick egg noodles tossed in a spicy sauce and topped with cooked prawns

xian cai *Mandarin* preserved vegetable

xian dan *Mandarin* salted duck egg; also called **kiam neng** and **haam daan**

xian ya dan huang *Mandarin* salted duck egg yolks

xiang cai *Mandarin* coriander/cilantro; also called **daun ketumbar**, **wang swee**

xiang gu *Mandarin* Chinese mushroom

xing ren *Mandarin* almond

xue yan *Mandarin* a very high grade **yan wo**; the bird's nest is tinged with the blood of the swallow thereby giving it its red colour

DICTIONARY

Y

ya *Mandarin* duck

ya jiao *Mandarin* duck feet

yan wo *Mandarin* bird's nest; part of this Chinese delicacy is derived from the vomit of the swallow

yang rou tang *Mandarin* mutton soup

yong tauhu *Cantonese* variation of **yong tauhu** with minced meat instead of fish paste. Fish paste stuffed in various food items like **taupok**, chilli or mushroom; also called **niang tauhu**

you char kway *Hokkien* deep-fried dough stick

you yu *Mandarin* dried squid

yu *Mandarin* fish

yu chi tang *Mandarin* shark's fin soup

yu du *Mandarin* fish maw

yu lu *Mandarin* fish sauce

yu mi xin *Mandarin* baby corn

yu pian tang *Mandarin* fish-slice soup

yu sheng *Mandarin* raw fish; salad of raw fish, grated vegetables, candied melon and lime, red and white pickled ginger, pomelo sacs, sesame seeds, jellyfish and peanuts tossed in dressing

yu tow *Mandarin* yam

yu yuan mian *Mandarin* fish-ball soup

yue bing *Mandarin* little mooncakes, eaten during the mid-autumn festival

yulian gao *Malay* durian cake sold in cylindrical 20cm sticks

Z

zha *Mandarin* deep fry

zhejiang mian *Mandarin* one-dish meal with minced pork sauce

zhen *Mandarin* steam (cooking method)

zhi ma bai *Mandarin* white sesame seed

zhi ma hei *Mandarin* black sesame seed

zhong qiu jie *Mandarin* mid-autumn festival, celebrated on the 15th day of the eighth lunar month as a celebration of autumn harvests; also called mooncake festival

zhu gan *Mandarin* pork liver

zhu sun *Mandarin* bamboo shoots

zi cha *Hokkien* Chinese style of cooking; denotes foodstalls that serve family style cooked food

Recommended Reading

Andaya, Barbara Watson *A History of Malaysia,* Palgrave (2001)

Gomes, Mary *The Eurasian Cookbook,* Horizon Books (2001)

Lee, Chin Koon *Mrs Lee's Cookbook: Nonya Recipes and Other Favourite Recipes,* Eurasia Press (1974)

Marbeck, Celine J *Cuzinhia Cristang,* Tropical Press (1998)

Sanmugam, Devagi *South Indian Cookbook,* Pen International (2001)

Yvonne, Tan *Penang Food Odyssey* (2000)

Photo Credits

Glenn Beanland	p122, p123 right, p157, p175 top right, p175 bottom, p208, p212.
Anders Blomqvist	p129.
John Borthwick	p146, p147.
Tom Cockrem	p121.
Mark Daffey	p156.
Ryan Fox	p139.
Paul David Hellander	p115 top right.
Clem Lindenmayer	p135.
Christine Niven	p115 bottom left, p116, p117, p118.
Chris Rowthorn	p153.
Susan Storm	p119.

INDEX

INDEX

From the Publisher

This first edition of *World Food Malaysia & Singapore* was commissioned by Lyndal Hall, edited by Joanne Newell, Kyla Gillzan and Patrick Witton, and designed by Brendan Dempsey. Natasha Velleley mapped, Patrick Witton proofed and indexed, Martin Heng and Bridget Blair oversaw the book's production, while Peter D'Onghia, manager, dealt with big picture issues. Thanks to Lonely Planet Images for coordinating the supply of photographs, and for captioning, cataloguing and pre-press work. A big thank you to Andrew Tudor and Mark Germanchis in the Melbourne office for production advice and Shahara Ahmed and Rebecca Hobbs for editorial assistance.